Lean Office Demystified II

Using the Power of the Toyota Production System in Your Administrative, Desktop and Networking Environments

Don Tapping
Anne Dunn
Doug Fertuck
Vlado Baban

ISBN 978-0-9825004-9-1

07 06 05 04 03   5 4 3 2 1

MCS Media, Inc.
888 Ridge Road
Chelsea, MI 48118
United States of America
Telephone 734-475-4301
E-mail: info@theleanstore.com

Cover concept and art direction: Douglas Eklund
Page design: Douglas Eklund
Content edit: Eric Dudek and Chris Tapping

Library of Congress Cataloging-in-Publication Data

This publication is designed to provide the most up-to-date, accurate and authoritative information for the improvement of administrative processes and practices. It is sold with the understanding that neither the authors, editors, nor the publisher are engaged in providing legal, accounting, or other professional service. If legal advice or other expert assistance is required, the services of a competent professional consultant should be sought.

All MCS Media, Inc. books are available at special quantity discounts to use as sales promotions, corporate training programs, and/or any other avenue conveying information to the continuous improvement of administrative areas.

Acknowledgements

To all the readers who found value in Lean Office Demystified and provided ideas for this version. Without their invaluable input, Lean Office Demystified II could not have been written.

Table of Contents

Part One. Get Everyone Aligned and Started in the Right Direction

1. A History of Lean - Brief

2. Five Enablers for the Implementation of Lean

3. Seeing the Challenge

Publisher's Message

After much success with *Lean Office Demystified - Using the Power of the Toyota Production System in Your Administrative Areas,* we have collaborated with two additional authors, as well as received input from numerous readers over the years and therefore, have published *Lean Office Demystified II - Using the Power of the Toyota Production System in Your Administrative, Desktop and Networking Environments. Lean Office Demystified II* now demonstrates through the Global Winds case study how Lean concepts and practices can be leveraged with the Microsoft Office business applications (i.e., Excel, Access, Outlook, Explorer, etc.) to dramatically improve an organization's flow of information (paper-based and/or electronic). It demonstrates how information is organized, analyzed, controlled, shared, communicated (emailed), and the speed and quality (error-free) with which it is done, that will separate Lean organizations from Lean enterprises. It is the Lean enterprise that has adopted Lean principles in *all* their business operations.

It has become apparent that nearly all improvements today must have a Desktop application (IT or networking) component. Email, document control, file management and manipulation, data mining, etc. have importance in today's organization that could not have been anticipated 20, or even 10 years ago. Each of these must be scrutinized in regards to its efficiencies of being value-added or non value-added (waste) to the flow of data and information. *Lean Office Demystified II* will assist organizations on how Lean can be applied in the Desktop and networking environment through understanding the Global Winds case study included at the conclusion of each chapter.

Lean Office Demystified II is an implementation guide for the identification and elimination of process waste (physical and electronic) thru Total Employment Involvement (TEI). This book should serve as your compass, pointing you north towards a Leaner, more productive office. It is no mystery. And, as we continually work to share best practices in applying Lean to all types of office environments, please notify us of *your* progress.

Good luck in your 'total' Lean journey!

Don Tapping

Who Is It For?

This book is designed for organizations that struggle with how to improve their administrative processes, both physical documents and how information flows electronically. This book will assist training managers, Lean facilitators, continuous improvement coordinators, managers, and front-line employees to improve work flow by increasing office productivity and improving the bottom-line.

The business leaders who are guiding organizations to new markets with growth opportunities are struggling with how to streamline current business processes to be more competitive. *Lean Office Demystified II* will assist in this struggle. With the increasing global pressures on many economies, it is more important now than ever to find more efficient means to conduct business.

Reading this book will provide an insight into the challenges faced day-in and day-out by all employees. It will provide the reasoning of why continuous improvement must be a way of life. This book was formatted with chapter summaries, worksheets, actual work-related examples and case studies to assist you to improve the flow of all types of information.

Finally, managers in healthcare, financial services, retail, construction, and manufacturing industries who desire to remain in business in the 21st century will use this book as the basis for business improvement.

What Is Inside?

Lean Office Demystified II is a comprehensive set of detailed instructions on how to implement a Lean Office. It will provide the solid foundation upon which all the Lean tools can be applied. Office employees (i.e., the front-line workers) are continually processing daily requests and must know what to do, where to turn, and who to listen to. This book will guide you down the path of continuous improvement. *Lean Office Demystified II* will provide insights into using many of the Microsoft Office tools (applications) in this Lean endeavor.

This book has been arranged in three separate and distinct parts. It is recommended that a good understanding, along with a good portion of implementation, be done in one part prior to moving on to the next part.

The three parts are:

Part One. Get Everyone Aligned and Started in the Right Direction which will provide the foundation upon which the Lean Office is built. Through explaining the basic tools and concepts of Lean, understanding how behavior and change must occur, and implementing some very useful and productive tools for both the physical and well as electronic documents, you will be well on your way to achieving a Lean Office.

Part Two. Create the Structures Allowing Work Flow to Emerge which will create the necessary support systems for process improvements to occur. This will entail obtaining detailed analysis of current processes, making all types of work visible, creating standard file and folder systems, and balancing work loads evenly to ensure work flows effortlessly and without delay (waste). This is the heart of the Lean Office and will take the most time to implement.

Part Three. Sustain the Gains to World Class which will create the visual controls, mistake proofing devices, and measurement systems for the Lean Office to continually improve. Benchmarks will have been established, roles will have been clearly defined for the new organization, leadership roles taken, processes running error-free, and *then* a new culture will have emerged.

Feel free to utilize this book as a supplement to any current continuous improvement materials you may already have. Though this book is comprehensive and should have everything you require, it should be noted that each organization is its own entity and must adapt the information appropriately. No single book can be the end-all or cure-all for an organization. We do sincerely feel our efforts in writing this book and documenting the Desktop examples will provide you with many answers you may not previously have had in your administrative improvement efforts.

How to Get the Most Out of this Book

By utilizing the concepts and tools within this book, you will be able to create a system to gain process control and improve those processes (eliminate non value-added activities) as part of a Lean enterprise.

What this Book is Based On

This book is not only about understanding basic Lean principles and how they apply to the various types of administrative processes, but also about creating a realistic plan to ensure results are sustained. There are many Desktop tools that can be used to monitor process changes in the workplace. The Lean applications utilized in this book are a compilation of years working within various types of administrative offices in a wide variety of industries, some of them are:

Construction
Processes such as project bids, project planning, and on-site scheduling use metrics of project lead time reduction, man-hour efficiency, and profit to ensure competitive bids and support the infrastructure.

Financial Services
Processes such as mortgage applications, insurance claims, and investment options use metrics of customer retention, profitability, and value-added service opportunity to ensure these services are not outsourced.

Healthcare
Processes such as surgical services, outpatient services, clinical exams, insurance submittals, etc., use metrics of patient-in/patient-out, throughput times, nursing time efficiency, quality of care, patient and staff satisfaction, and hospital system gain efficiency to control costs, and continue to provide premium patient care.

Manufacturing
Processes such as customer service order entry, product development, and quoting use metrics of order entry accuracy, quoted-to-order efficiency, and internal defect to keep work (and jobs) from being outsourced.

National Defense, Federal, and Local Government Agencies
Processes such as logistics, procurement, program management, system acquisition, engineering, and research and development all have large office work structures which can utilize the Lean tools to improve the organizational process and flow, thus creating savings that can be better spent on serving the taxpayer more efficiently.

The format of this book was designed to assist your office in creating an administrative system of continuous improvement that will allow a new culture to emerge.

Become Familiar with the Book as a Whole

There are a few things you can do to make it easier to absorb the content contained in this book. Spend as much time as you need to gain familiarity with all the material. To get a "Big Picture" view of the book:

1. Scan the Table of Contents to get a feel of the topics in each chapter.

2. Read the rest of this "How to Get the Most Out of this Book" for an overview of the book's content.

3. Flip through various sections of the book to get a feel for its style, format, layout, design, and readability. Notice the illustrations (i.e. forms, worksheets, and templates) that accompany each main idea.

4. Read the Lean Look-Ahead on pages 14 - 16 to gain an understanding on how all the Lean tools inter-relate in the Global Winds case study.

Become Familiar with Each Chapter

After you have "Become Familiar with the Book as a Whole," it is time to prepare yourself to learn the content of a single chapter, phase, or section. Follow the steps listed below to get the most out of the readings:

1. Read the Chapter Overview that comprises each chapter.

2. Flip through the chapter, noticing the way it is laid out, specifically the bold headings and the key points identified in the margins.

3. Read the chapter. The time required to read will depend on how familiar you are with the content. Even though you may have some understanding of a particular topic or think it is something you know fairly well, continue to spend the time to read it. This book is based on successful practices from a wide range of experiences.

4. Read the Chapter Summary at the end of the chapter to reinforce what you have learned. If there is something in the Summary you do not understand, go back to that section and review it.

5. Read Observations from the Lean Office at the end of the chapter. If you are the only one reading the book, jot down some ideas to further discuss with your team. If a team will be reviewing the book, then use the observations as discussion items and determine the relevancy and adaptability to your office environment.

6. Read the Application Case Study at the end of the chapter. This will assist you in understanding how the concepts explained in the chapter relate to an actual business case.

How a Reading Strategy Works

When reading a technical book, the best way is to not start with the first word and read it straight through until the end. The steps listed previously will allow your reading to be easier, more fun, and much more effective.

Reading strategy is based on two simple concepts:

1. The first concept deals with pre-conditioning your brain. It is difficult to retain information from the book (i.e., the content) if there exists no structure in your brain in which to place the information. An analogy may be: a house is not built without a blueprint. The preparation or blueprint is similar to reading a book, first reading the overview of the chapter, headings, and key points before reading it word for word. Once the "structure" is in place, then the content has an area to reside in your brain.

2. The second concept is to take the information from the book (i.e., the content) one layer at a time. You do not want to attempt to absorb it all at once. Take the information and build upon what was previously learned.

This book was developed with these two concepts in mind. The format and layout were designed for you to retain as much of the information as possible while providing practical implementation steps.

What is New In this Version

This new version, *Lean Office Demystified II*, demonstrates the application of Lean tools and concepts discussed in the original book, *Lean Office Demystified*, into how they can be applied in an actual business case study. The business case study that will be referenced throughout this book is Global Winds, and particularly one of its subsidiaries, Northwind Traders. The case study will allow you to:

- Understand how Lean tools and concepts can be utilized (or leveraged) with MS Office, networking, and Open Source applications
- Realize the profound impact Lean can have in regards to improving information and data flow of all types
- Look at information and data flow differently, now with a set of "Lean Desktop eyes"
- Identify wastes as applied to all processes within an organization
- Convey to colleagues through these examples on how In-process supermarkets, FIFO lanes, leveling, visual controls, etc. all have relevancy in the Desktop and networking environment
- Create a new generation of front-line Lean "power-users" to readily apply Lean concepts to daily work duties

The Global Winds case study is one example on how Lean tools and concepts can be applied. The overall intent of this case study is to bring awareness that Lean can be done in the Desktop and networking environment. And, by having this example, it may spur others into applying similar type Lean Desktop solutions.

Acknowledgements

This book is an example of teaming, collaborating, and learning-by-doing from a select group of individuals who contributed greatly to getting this in a readable form.

This book was over 5 years in the making, countless iterations of topics, contents, and now is brought to you for your benefit. In 2009-2010, additional contributors allowed for *Lean Office Demystified II* to be published addressing the Desktop and networking environments with the application of Lean.

Many thanks to the following individuals who added valuable input and direction to the writing of this book:

Tom J. Casassa, CQE/SSBB/PM, Head Quality Engineering Lean Office, Naval Surface Warfare Center, Panama City, Florida

Tom Fabrizio, Consultant and Author, Lean Tooling (SME, 2003), 5S for the Office (Productivity Press, 2006)

Eric Gonderson, Director, Information Systems, PDR International, Inc.

Rob Ptacek, Consultant and Author

Susan Richards, Information Systems Analysis, Tricor Corporation

Stu Tubbs, PhD., Darrell H. Cooper Professor of Leadership, Eastern Michigan University (Small Group Discussion, McGraw-Hill, Inc. 1993)

Curtis Walker, President, GDC Consulting

Gregg Knapp, ACT! Certification Consultant, Aspen Tech Consulting Group

Thanks to you the reader, our customers, for your time and effort in advancing Lean practices into administrative areas. We know it is not always an easy journey and sincerely worked for *Lean Office Demystified II* to *further* assist you in these endeavors. Please feel free to contact us regarding your successes and difficulties by emailing us at info@theleanstore.com. We would appreciate hearing from you!

Lean Office Demystified II

Part One.
Get Everyone Aligned and Started in the Right Direction

A History of Lean - Brief

A New Way to Look at Things

Chapter Overview

The Toyota Production System, waste elimination, and process/continuous improvement are all used synonymously with Lean throughout the world. This chapter will briefly explain the overriding theme or philosophical approach upon which Lean is based.

What is Lean?

The purpose of Lean is to eliminate all waste or non value-added activities from a process. The continued focus on the elimination of waste should be a daily, hourly, or minute-by-minute review. Lean is not meant to eliminate people, but to use them wisely. With that thought in mind, work elements or job duties may need to be modified to accommodate a waste-free or Lean environment. This will allow companies to remain globally competitive, develop a cross-trained workforce, and establish a safe workplace.

Lean tools are used to:

- Identify and eliminate waste quickly and efficiently
- Increase communication at all levels of the organization

- Reduce costs, improve quality, and meet the delivery obligations of a product or service in a safe environment
- Initiate improvement activities and empower employees to make improvements themselves

Lean is truly a compilation of world-class practices.

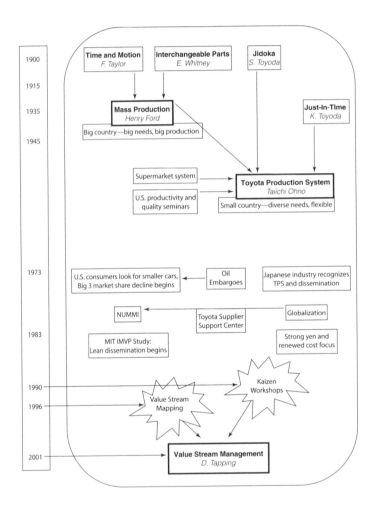

From this illustration note the following key points:

- Henry Ford's conveyor system in the 1930s, in conjunction with the Japanese market, and economic and industrial circumstances, forced the Toyota Corporation to develop original ways of implementing Ford's ideas (kaizen was born). Toyota could not mass produce on a level to compete with the United States, so it had to develop large production efficiencies with small volumes of production (it being a small country with diverse products).
- Taiichi Ohno traveled to America in the 1950s and toured its automobile plants. While there, he was most amazed with the grocery stores and their system of replenishment. He came away with the supermarket concept (customers in a grocery store expect to have what they need, when they need it, and a kanban card was used to signal for replenishment). He later transformed this into the *supermarket pull system* to support the *Just-In-Time* philosophy.
- Market-driven demand for manufacturing improvements brought these concepts and tools to the United States and Europe in the form of the Lean tools of kaizen and value stream mapping. The next logical step was the development of an overall Lean plan of value stream management (Value Stream Management for the Lean Office, Productivity Press 2003).

The important point to remember regarding this brief overview of Lean is that its birth, growth, and continued success are now a world-wide phenomenon. The successes in the manufacturing world are now being achieved in all types of industries with all types of administrative areas.

Keep in mind, as has been stated by the management and employees of the Toyota Motor Corporation, they have been at Lean for over 60 years…
- and they are still improving!

Why Lean?

Lean is based on continually meeting customer requirements efficiently and effectively. In late 1980s, early 1990s, and to this day customers were and are demanding price reductions. The Traditional Thinking model had been when an organization continually increased prices to its customers (Cost + Profit = Price). As raw material prices for manufacturing goods were increasing correspondingly with healthcare cost and employee wages, the only way to satisfy the customer's demand for price reductions and sustain their business was to lower costs internally (the Cost part of the Lean Thinking formula). Toyota also developed this cost-reduction or Lean Thinking philosophy. Market conditions (the constant in the equation) set the selling price. Focusing on internal costs where Price - Cost = Profit, becomes a philosophical (Lean) approach and leads the drive to improvement initiatives. This "new" customer will not pay for waste in the processes and is very astute in determining what they are willing to pay for a product or service.

The following illustration demonstrates the Traditional and Lean Thinking models:

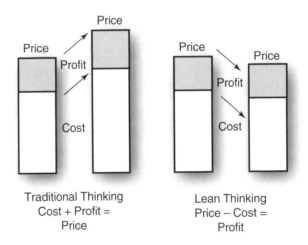

Traditional Thinking
Cost + Profit =
Price

Lean Thinking
Price – Cost =
Profit

Why Lean Office?

With the concepts of the previous figure, managers have realized the need to reduce costs in all facets of their businesses. Lean improvements were first introduced in manufacturing by the Toyota Motor Corporation. Typically, more than sixty percent of the cost of a product or service is attributable to administrative processes. As a result, Lean principles are being applied with great success in customer service, finance, billing, accounting, quoting, and IT departments in all types of industries. Lean is not *just* for the manufacturing industry!

For example, widget manufacturing costs are not different from the following administrative costs of:

- Entering a customer order
- Generating an invoice
- Creating an engineering drawing
- Filling out a medical insurance form
- Filing an insurance claim
- Generating a quote
- Ordering an item via the Internet
- Applying for a mortgage
- Depositing a check at your local bank
- Opening a savings account

These transactions represent how we interact within society to ensure products and services are provided for, profit is obtained, and the customer is delighted. As the economy expands, global competition is there to provide similar products and services. Therefore, it is imperative that costs are maintained or reduced with the same level of service. This can be attained through the application of Lean Office principles.

Successes in the global manufacturing world are now being achieved using the same Lean tools in all types of industries; healthcare, financial services, construction, armed services, etc. with great success.

Regardless of the nature of the business, there are individual tasks or processes that can and need to be standardized, streamlined, and made as efficient as possible. Lean provides excellent tools and concepts to eliminate process variations that can cause waste. For example:

- A customer order entry that takes 4 minutes to enter can be entered in seconds once Lean is adopted
- An invoice that requires two people for approvals (and takes days) can can be done by one person in minutes once Lean is adopted
- An engineering drawing that usually takes two weeks to be approved and moved to the next step can approved within hours (or a day at most) once Lean is adopted
- A patient being moved into or out of a surgical procedure which may take up to an hour can improved to less than thirty minutes once Lean is adopted
- An insurance claim that takes two-three days for settlement can be completed in just a few hours once Lean is adopted
- A mortgage application that takes five days to process can be processed in less than eight hours once Lean is adopted

The most important point to understand about Lean is that it has proven to be effective in every business application. We have compiled these tools and practices from years of research, on-the-job experiences, and examples related to the Desktop and networking environment so that you too can also begin to improve your processes immediately and achieve significant results.

Using Information Technology to Apply Lean

The principles of Lean were developed prior to this age of digital technology (i.e., the office environment of Desktop applications). Lean can be used just as effectively in this environment to:

- Increase the speed and accuracy of data and information flow
- Improve office communications and productivity
- Facilitate common access of information
- Enable ready documentation and sharing of standardized methods and documents
- Permit the efficient scheduling of meetings and events
- Enable the authoring of documents and presentations by multiple contributors

The streamlining and standardizing of analyzing data, formatting reports, and emailing information to colleagues can be easily achieved through the application of the Lean tools and concepts contained in this book.

However, these powerful Desktop and networking tools (i.e., applications) can also cause more clutter and confusion into the office environment by tempting employees to waste time by over-analyzing, over-reporting, and over-emailing data. Therefore, Lean Office concepts must be leveraged with common business sense to keep all types of work moving efficiently and effectively (without any type of waste).

Throughout this book, we will provide best practices from organizations that shared their Lean Desktop successes, as well as some of the pitfalls to avoid.

Chapter Summary

This brief history was meant to create a general understanding of Lean. Once the foundation for eliminating waste is understood throughout an organization, it will be easier to introduce the tools of Lean to your organization.

Observations from the Lean Office

These observations may assist in understanding how to apply the concepts and tools contained in this chapter:

- Communicate to employees the simple concept of waste elimination for both the physical movement of paperwork as well as the electronic movement of work
- Continue to read and learn about Lean from other sources (books, Webinars, conferences, blogs, benchmarking, etc.)
- Keep communication lines open regarding Lean and its purpose
- Lean *complements* other programs such as TQM, Six Sigma, etc.
- Lean tools and practices are from all over the world
- Attempt small improvements first and gain success
- Build an environment which embraces learning; Lean is a learned behavior
- Lean is being applied in all types of industries
- Continue to engage the employees on how Lean should be used to make their work easier and reduce stress

Application Case Study

Throughout this book, we will track the implementation of Lean Office practices at Northwind Traders in Seattle, Washington. Northwind Traders is headed by Andrew Cencini, VP of Sales, and is a subsidiary of a large trading company, Global Winds, Inc. Andrew's Sales Manager is Stephen Thorpe. Andrew reports to Kirk Keating, Executive VP of Sales and Marketing of Global Winds, who feels strongly that Andrew has the leadership skills, personal commitment, and discipline to improve overall office productivity and effectiveness promised by the Lean Office system. The three of them recently attended a Lean Administration workshop at the local university. The workshop introduced them to all the Lean tools and concepts with examples of how it also applied to the flow of electronic information and data. Following the workshop it was determined that the Northwind office would be the first in the company to fully apply the set of Lean Office principles. When successful, the practices developed at Northwind will become the benchmark for the other trading subsidiaries at Global Winds.

Northwind had not been meeting its targets for the year and were as follows:

Operating Margin: Current 6.5% - Target 7.0%
On-Time-Delivery performance: Current 90% - Target 97%
Opportunity Success Rate: Current 10% - Target 15%
Closure of service problems (hrs): Current 6 hours - Target 4 hours
(Also conveyed on their Goal Card, page 315)

The Lean Office initiative was expected to improve these measurements at least to their target levels.

The corporate IT department provides each subsidiary with standard hardware and software, including Microsoft Office, as well as provide access to the company's common financial, communications, technical, and logistics systems. Global Winds sets quarterly goals for all sales managers as well as annual sales targets and operating budgets. Kirk Keating is a stickler for reviewing these results quarterly. The goals (i.e., targets) are tough but attainable. Andrew, as well as all the other VP of Sales from the other groups within Global Winds, are expected to meet or exceed these targets, or provide detailed plans on corrective actions being taken.

Prior to the establishment of the Lean Office initiative, Andrew had set up an Excel-based system for gathering the sales data from his team. The following screen shot shows the first six months sales for Anne, one of the sales representatives.

Excel Spreadsheet of Anne Hellung-Larsen's Six Month Sales

Andrew would compile each of the sales rep's Excel spreadsheet reports from an email attachment and cut and paste each report sorted by order date into a master spreadsheet for all the sales reps in the office as shown below.

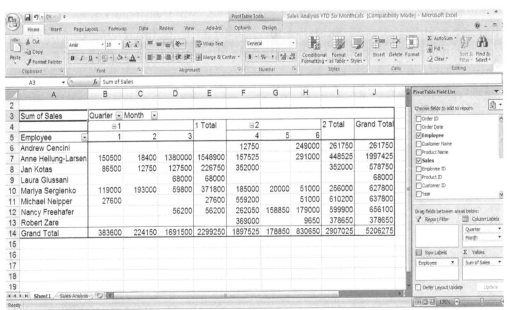

Excel Spreadsheet of Year-To-Date Total Sales for the First Six Months

Andrew then created reports in Excel for his monthly reviews with Kirk, in this case a Pivot Table showing sales by month and quarter by employee.

Pivot Table Report of Sales Representatives by Quarter and Month

"I use Excel all day long, and I'm very comfortable using Pivot Tables, forms, creating reports, and other activities in the program," Andrew says. He continues, "It's a very familiar tool for me. I have access to the information in the server database that stores our information. I can pull up items by department or margin, by sales, and other kinds of criteria for each of our sales representatives. It requires a lot of cutting and pasting with further manipulation of data to put everything in a master worksheet – not a very Lean process. This data also is not easily shared across the team, some of whom are located at various sites throughout North America." Andrew had to keep following up to get the latest data, and the aggregation and reporting of the data took considerable manipulation.

Andrew knew his department could run even more smoothly and efficiently, and thus become more profitable. He knew that budgets and costs are an output and everyone should seek to understand the demand on the system, and, if you do that with the whole system in mind, everyone can then work together to make work flow smoother and reduce unnecessary stress (and waste). Andrew believed that using budgets and costs as a main driver is using the tail to wag the dog. Andrew wanted to focus on Lean measurements (i.e., performance metrics) to motivate and direct the team through Total Employee Involvement. However, Total Employee Involvement is a story for future chapters. Applying the principles of Lean is a continual process. As any business evolves and changes, and as information of the modern business environment increases, as it always seems to do, there will be an increasing need for applying the Lean Office principles to the Desktop and networking environment. For the Northwind Traders and Global Winds sales reporting process, it is expected that a better and more efficient method (i.e., this Lean Office initiative) would provide a more proactive approach to addressing performance issues and get the office back on meeting their targets.

The following Lean Look-Ahead is an overview of the Business Issue, Waste, Lean Tool Application, and Business Resolution relative to the chapters and case study. Now that you have read the first part of the case study it may be of value to see the "big picture" on how all the Lean tools will inter-relate in the case study.

Note: Step-by-step instructions for creating a basic Pivot Table in Excel can be found in Appendix D beginning on page 366.

Chapter Reference	Business Issue	Waste	Lean Tool Application	Business Resolution
1	Sales reports completed using inefficient cutting and pasting of individual spreadsheets	Overprocessing, Waiting	Commitment to initiate a comprehensive Lean Office project and **Communicating** that commitment to all involved	Leadership commitment to support the project with time and resources
2	Poor tracking of new sales prospects	Waiting, Defects, People's Time	Understanding the **Seven Areas of Waste** and eliminating overprocessing and many defects by entering all prospect data only once into a master database	Setting up a Customer Relationship Management (CRM) database in Access
2	Lack of awareness regarding sources of waste in office operations	All forms	**Desktop Waste Audit**	Initial list of potential waste sources on which to gather data, analyze and set priorities to address
3	Organizational Information Technology (IT) was, in some areas, out-of-date and for some team members lacking essential applications	Overprocessing, Defects, Overproduction, Inventory	**Standardization** of IT tools and methods IT support through having a **tech rep** on the team	Common training, usage and sharing of IT Common documents, collaboration, capability, data access
3	Sales force not located geographically close Difficult to conduct effective meetings	Waiting, Overproduction, Defects	Using MS Enterprise Groove for collaboration (effective **Teaming** with clear **Leadership** (and accountability) **Effective Meetings** An overall plan or the **Lean Office Roadmap**	Effective virtual meetings and successful, collaborative problem solving and process documentation
4	Difficulty establishing performance goals due to multiple undocumented office processes	All forms	**Work Flow Analysis** in Excel, also using Pivot Tables to track cycle times	Cycle times of various processes defined, process ownership assigned Basis provided for sharing opportunities for improvement
4	Interruptions of unexpected and unplanned emails	Defects	Creating a common folder organization in Outlook, a form of **Interruption and Random Arrival Log** for capturing and responding quickly to interrupting emails	Improved customer satisfaction resulting from rapid responses to problem reports Data readily collected to identify and fix for all, common cause interruptions.
4	All work allocated to capacity and not to customer demand	All forms	Creating a **Value Stream Map** for the current process in Visio	Baseline established for waste reductions and process improvement and standardization
4	Variation and lack of understanding in how prospects get their work done	Defects, Waiting, Overproduction, Motion, Transport	Creating Visio **Flowcharts** to understand the flow of information required by prospects	Understanding the common information requirements of prospects to permit quick focus on special needs
4	Lack of understanding of why prospects do not return phone calls	Overprocessing, Waiting, Motion	Using Visio's **Cause and Effect or Fishbone Diagram** to identify root causes of problems	Targeted research to learn techniques to deal with the various causes of unreturned phone calls
4	Too much raw data that can be difficult to digest and analyze	Defects, Transport, Motion, Overprocessing, Overproduction	Applying **Data Analysis Techniques** available in Excel such as: Histograms, Pareto Charts, Scatter Diagrams to support rigorous **Problem Solving**	Data visualized in different ways to enable insights and see trends more readily
4	Jumping to conclusions when identifying alternative actions to address a problem	Defects	Using Visio's **Brainstorming** tool to capture free flowing ideas	Better resolutions on all issues Root cause(s) eliminated

Chapter Reference	Business Issue	Waste	Lean Tool Application	Business Resolution
5	Sales reps spending excessive time searching for files; wrong versions of files often noted by the customers	Defects, Waiting, Motion, Transport	**5S** techniques used to organize files and folders on everyone's Desktop	All team members implemented a common folder and file naming conventions to enable easy sharing of information and common filing schemes
5	Email files and folders not organized; many times emails had to be resent	Inventory, Waiting, Motion, Transport	**5S** techniques used to organize files and folders on shared drive as well as Outlook files and folders	All Outlook and shared files adhere to standard naming convention Files easier to locate
5	Preparing and attending trade shows caused significant need for buffer resources	Motion, Waiting, Overproduction	Demonstrating **Safety Resources**	Resulted in better planning for shows, involving more of the office staff to share and level workload, thus decreasing need for added contract resources
5	No consistent overall assessment conducted on all office functions to enable informed priority setting for improvements	Overproduction, Overprocessing, Defects, Wait (Time) Queue, Transport, Defects	Documenting the **Lean Office Assessment** in an Excel radar chart to ensure everyone is on the same page throughout the Lean Office project using **Visual Metrics**, both **Baseline** and **Target**.	Provides the common basis for defining individual and work group plans for short and long term improvements
6	No centralized place or standard system to house documents shared with and transmitted to customers Much frequent and confusing email traffic with customers that is difficult to track and control	Defects, Transport, Motion, Overprocessing, Overproduction	Using internet-based Google Docs to house key communications and **Standard Work** processes and documents with customers, enabling the latest identical **Visible Information** to be available at anytime	Common file sharing standards reduce need for wasteful and potentially confusing email follow-ups resulting in improved customer relations Documents always up-to-date
7	Multiple overlapping and uncoordinated documents recording and tracking prospects	Overprocessing, Defects, Transport, Motion,	Using MS Enterprise Groove to house and control one master prospect document providing **Visual Control** and a single source for **Data Collection** for documents and performance	Common file sharing for prospects and other documents; managers can see most current data being entered by everyone
7	Employees had no direct shared system of feedback regarding their performance for prospecting	Defects, Overproduction, Motion, Waiting	Applying MS Excel Pivot Tables to provide a quick picture, **Visual Information**, of call status	Data aggregated for prospecting available real-time to management and the team as necessary for backing up
7	Lack of focus on those prospecting opportunities that require ongoing attention	Inventory, Motion, Waiting	Using Excel Pivot Tables and filters to identify those prospects for special follow-up and locate in an **In-process supermarket**	Resources focused on key open opportunities and taken off those leads of least promise
8	No standard filing system and controls for business documents	Waiting, Motion, Defects, Overproduction	Setting up all process and system documentation in Groove in a **Lean File System** so that all have instant access to the latest master files using **Standard Work**	No revision issues, no waste seeking documents, clear accountability for the control of process and system documentation

Chapter Reference	Business Issue	Waste	Lean Tool Application	Business Resolution
8	Significant programming effort would be required to build the database and reporting capabilities in Access	Overprocessing, Motion, Transport, Waiting, Defects, Overproduction	Introducing off-the-shelf commercial database software, in this case ACT!, to manage customer and prospect relations thus supporting **Standard Work**, a **Lean File System**, and the tracking and control of **Employee Balance**	Performance readily monitored with many standards and a few tailored reports out of ACT! based on a current and complete customer and prospect database Management decision-making supported with more complete customer and prospect information
8	Concern that going to off-the-shelf CRM software will cause loss of needed reports and data analysis	Defects, Transport, Motion, Overprocessing	Integrating ACT! comes with the ability to an export data to Excel which in turn easily allows designed and produced special reports Pivot Tables and **Data Analysis** tools allows for targeted information analysis resulting in more effective decision-making	Permits production of needed reports and analysis Additional real-time reporting allows for addressing problems earlier and finding root cause of unknown issues
9	Work load was not leveled with consistency and discipline resulting in daily office work that tended to be haphazard and turned easily upside down with "unexpected" service and other calls	Motion, Transport, Waiting, Defects	**Leveling** of the internally generated sales calls with the externally demanded service calls by applying careful measuring and tracking of **Takt Time** and **Pitch**	Work for all sales representatives became leveled in a known daily rhythm that kept the team focused and made it easy to identify unusual special circumstances so that quick reallocation of resources could be applied
10	Andrew Cencini's burning drive for results caused him at times to be too emotional and to jump to conclusions without good and accurate data	Motion, Overproduction, Overprocessing	Using the ACT! database to generate consistent reports and clear graphs to provide Andrew daily accounting of sales status and projections thus tempering his **Leadership Style** with solid **Data Analysis**	Management, and all team members, are always current and informed on progress towards sales targets -- by making results visible
11	The goals of the corporation and of the division were not clearly documented and made available to all so that overall direction was always known and understood	Motion, Overprocessing	Publishing a **Goal Card** laying out all critical goals and strategies in both easy-to-carry hardcopy formats and in readily available digital formats	The organization's reason for being, its fundamental strategies, and the specific measurable goals for all are always understood and visible thus guiding the day-to-day decisions and actions
12	Visual displays of important and driving sales results and activity were not available on a continuous basis Data entry errors at times due to not knowing fields and required data	Overprocessing, Overproduction, Defects	Using the Dashboard as **Visual Office** tool in ACT! Use drop-down menus as **Mistake Proofing** devices for any areas where there are quesitons or concerns about what type of data is required	All team members are informed at least daily of the status of key performance indicators Reduction in data entry errors

Chapter 2

Five Enablers for the Implementation of Lean

People Are Your Greatest Asset

Chapter Overview

There are five enablers to successfully implement the Lean Office. These enablers affect everything you do. They must always be present and understood wherever you are on the Lean journey. You will not succeed without them. Each enabler will involve understanding, educating, and involving your people. They provide the foundation on which all will rest.

The five enablers are:

Enabler #1: Understanding the Behavior - Attitude - Culture Model

This enabler minimizes the resistance to change. The introduction and initial implementation of Lean must change behavior first if a continuous improvement culture is to emerge. The sequencing of Lean outlined in this book will begin to establish the groundwork for change (continuous improvement through Total Employee Involvement). But change cannot be accomplished overnight. Employees must understand that positive change (i.e., Lean) will contribute to the organization's long term success.

Enabler #2: Understanding the Business Case for Lean

This enabler helps employees understand why current ways of doing business may not be good enough. As companies grow and take on more work, waste reduction must become prevalent in all aspects of the organization. Employees must recognize that every type of administrative task has a cost associated to it. This segment will explain how to communicate this need for change.

Enabler #3: The Ten Areas of Waste

Lean tools and concepts assist employees in identifying and eliminating the ten types of waste. The old adage of "you can't manage what you can't see" is similar to "you can't improve what you don't understand." It is critical that employees have a fundamental knowledge and understanding of waste.

Enabler #4: Applying the Power of Information Technology

Almost every office environment now uses computer technology (i.e., IT or Desktop and networking applications) to manage the information that inundates everyone in today's office environment. The Lean tools and concepts apply to all forms of information management, whether paper or digital. Employees must understand how to use today's technology to eliminate waste and to increase work efficiency.

Enabler #5: Management Commitment

Lean implementation must be driven from the top down. Top management must make a 100% commitment to positive change and must be 100% convinced that a Lean enterprise represents the best opportunity for continued or newfound success. A partnership led by top management, and developed and implemented by a motivated work force, will ensure Lean initiatives are not only implemented, but sustained.

Enabler #1: Understanding the Behavior - Attitude - Culture Model

Understanding human behaviors and attitudes within an office or administrative area are critical to achieving success in any improvement initiative.

In the 1990s, the United States was introduced to teaming, self-directed work teams, employee involvement, empowerment teams, etc. Those employee-led teams were charged to change organizational cultures from one of strong managerial style to one of employee participation and involvement. The concept was right, but the approach lacked the specific tools to obtain the results expected.

With the adoption of team leaders, teaming, and self-directed work teams, in the 1990s there became a void of "how" or "what specifically" would an employee need to do differently. Just empowering employees, without specific tools, did not allow for the successes expected. There was some success, but it was not reinforced, and therefore, not sustained.

The Non-Lean Approach figure indicates that U.S. managers attempted to change the culture first, expecting that attitudes would change, and the desired behavior would result. Upon closer examination of Lean and the Toyota Production System models, researchers discovered a drastically different approach. They discovered that as Lean tools are introduced and used, people's behavior changed to one of identifying and eliminating waste. Once employees felt in control of their jobs through eliminating waste and making their jobs easier, their behavior changed to one of continuous improvement. As each employee

changes his or her behavior, the culture of the entire organization begins to change radically from "catching mistakes" to "preventing mistakes" or simply, the Lean Approach.

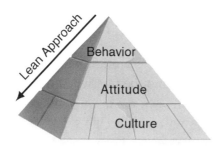

The overall Lean Approach model is simple. It requires a diligent and focused effort from both managers and employees. Established work habits are difficult to break. Discipline, determination, and dedication are required to move the organization forward. Small successes will foster the momentum to move from the simple behavior and attitude change to an organizational Lean culture.

Knowledge Ownership

Another important point regarding behavior in a traditional office or non-Lean environment is that employees typically retain 80% of the process knowledge. This process knowledge that resides with the employee can cause problems when the employee is ill, on vacation or leave, terminated, or has left for another job assignment, in that the work cannot be completed. This specialization and containment of the knowledge by one, or a few individuals, can be an organizational stumbling block.

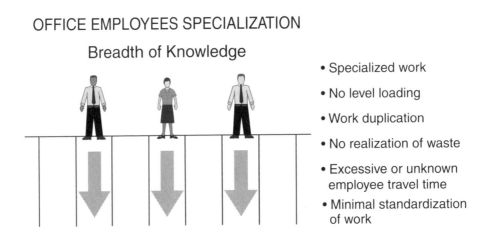

OFFICE EMPLOYEES SPECIALIZATION

Breadth of Knowledge

- Specialized work
- No level loading
- Work duplication
- No realization of waste
- Excessive or unknown employee travel time
- Minimal standardization of work

Since managers can only assist in such instances when they do not have the process or organizational knowledge (due to their lack of knowledge of the process), the organization's efficiency and effectiveness are in jeopardy for the following reasons:

1. When an employee is absent, his or her work cannot be completed as required.
   This is a huge concern in all organizations. Incomplete work contributes to customer dissatisfaction. Customer expectations cannot be met when work is sitting on a desk waiting for someone to return from vacation or for some other reason. Management anticipates that coworkers will pick up the slack; however, this is not always the case. Even if a co-worker has been cross-trained, the training may have been months ago, and there may be fear or avoidance present in the individual being called upon to perform the work.

2. Employee turnover has a major impact on workflow.
   The time involved with a learning curve will impact customer satisfaction. The learning curve for new employees in many organizations is weeks, if not months. It will cost the company money in overtime and customer dissatisfaction when process knowledge requires extra time to be transferred to another individual because the organizational knowledge was not well-documented.

3. The work flow cannot be improved because the work process is not known by others.
   Work process documentation is an asset when workflow and work process knowledge are required at "a moment's notice."

4. The goal should be ensuring that the work process knowledge remains in the organization.
   When a single person retains all process knowledge and it is not shared (or is minimally shared), there is a real risk of losing the information if the person leaves the company unexpectedly or is reassigned. Work process documentation is a key to organizational success.

5. Waste must be recognized as an unnecessary expense.
   Waste appears in many forms. A person who gets up from his or her desk and uses the fax machine ten times a day at different intervals may not see those duplicated efforts as waste. Faxing twice a day, once in the morning and once in the afternoon, makes sense and would save the employees time to do something else.

6. Standardizing processes eliminates work variation.
   Customers expect a consistent (standard) product or service from a process and expect that same service no matter who is providing it. The documentation of all processes is the foundation upon which to improve processes and services to customers. If there are three people responsible for doing similar tasks, it is likely that each has a different approach or method to completing it. Variations like this are a cost to an organization. It is important to use the correct Lean tools, create the standard process, and then improve upon it.

The Lean Office would include, but not be limited to, the following:

1. Process-centered focus rather than employee-centered focus
2. Organizational knowledge that is transferred easily to others
3. Work processes that are understood equate to greater process control and are a basis for continuous improvement
4. Process knowledge that is standardized to ensure minimal work variation
5. Waste that is promptly identified and eliminated as it happens (daily, hourly, or minute-by-minute)

These five qualities will allow an employee to have a broader understanding of not only their work, but that of other employees they work with. This shared process information allows the organization a breadth of knowledge that is distributed among the group.

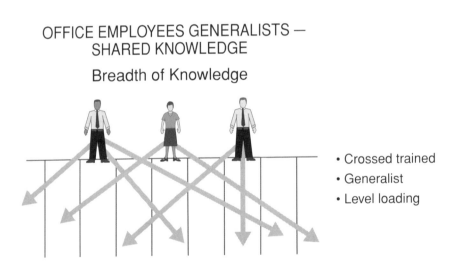

OFFICE EMPLOYEES GENERALISTS —
SHARED KNOWLEDGE

Breadth of Knowledge

- Crossed trained
- Generalist
- Level loading

Changes will not occur overnight. It is important to view any changes in steps or stages.

To support this enabler the content of this book has been broken down as follows:

Part One - Get Everyone Aligned and Started in the Right Direction
Part Two - Create the Structures Allowing Work Flow to Emerge
Part Three - Sustain the Gains to World Class

Part One - Get Everyone Aligned and Started in the Right Direction

Employees today are most likely in control of 80% of the process knowledge, with the manager (or organization) in control of 20% of the process knowledge. Part One of this book will provide a set of Lean tools to initiate transfer of the process control and organizational knowledge to the organization where it should reside for continuous improvement initiatives. This stage also addresses the importance of why process knowledge must be owned by the organization. This initial transfer can take up to six months to complete.

Organizational Control   Worker Control
(20%)   (80%)

Part Two - Create the Structures Allowing Work Flow to Emerge

In Part Two, additional Lean tools will be provided to ensure employees have only 50% control of the process knowledge, thus allowing managers (or the organization) to control the additional 50% of the process knowledge. The tools in this part will enable employees to release more of the process knowledge in a systematic way to the organization, such that all employees participating will experience and understand the benefits of this transfer. This part may take between six months and one year to complete.

Organizational Control   Worker Control
(50%)   (50%)

Part Three - Sustain the Gains to World Class

In Part Three of implementing the Lean Office, the employees will effortlessly contribute daily to continuous improvement initiatives. This will be within a structured Lean Office methodology. 80% of process and organizational knowledge will now reside in a continuous improvement infrastructure. This will enable the new Lean culture to emerge. It would be unrealistic to believe that 100% of the process knowledge will be controlled by the organization. The important point is to begin a gradual process to ensure process knowledge is documented within the organization in a systematic way.

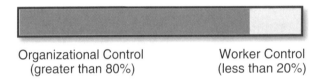

Organizational Control
(greater than 80%)

Worker Control
(less than 20%)

The key to implementing the Lean Office and sustaining it is the continual, daily effort to improve. As behavior changes, you will want to initiate a reward and recognition system to acknowledge the changes that are occurring. Quick adapters to change will embrace this system. They will see the benefits immediately. Slow adapters may fight the system and hold on to old habits. Slow adapters will struggle for a while; however, be patient as the system will speak for itself when implementation is under way and employees start to experience the benefits. Lean is not one step, but many small, incremental steps, each and every day.

Enabler #2: Understanding the Business Case for Lean

To become and remain globally competitive, managers must focus on costs. Administrative or office costs are a major contributor to the cost of a product, good, or service sold. The administrative cost of a product or service is typically 60-80% of the total sales price. Administrative costs are now aggressively being reduced to be competitive. Toyota developed a cost-reduction philosophy. Market conditions (the constant in the equation) set the selling price. Cost and profit became variables. Focusing on internal costs became the philosophical approach leading to improvement initiatives.

Through adaptation of the Lean thinking model and the Lean tools, any organization can reduce internal costs by focusing on waste. Through eliminating office wastes by driving costs out of the process, the business will remain competitive in the global market. To do this, process waste must first be identified before it can be eliminated. To do this, a thorough understanding of what constitutes waste must be understood.

Enabler #3: The Ten Areas of Waste

The purpose of Lean practices is to identify, analyze, and eliminate all sources of process inefficiency. The elimination of waste should be subject to a daily, hourly, or minute-by-minute review. Lean is not meant to eliminate people, but to use them wisely and to make people more valuable to the organization. With that in mind, work elements or job duties will need to be reviewed and modified to accommodate this waste-free environment.

To understand Lean you first need to identify and be aware of waste. It is important to identify these at the micro-level where the waste is occurring.

Waste is anything that adds time, resources, or cost without adding value to the finished product or service. The customer is paying for value; waste is anything that your organization does to a product or service for which the customer will then not pay for. As customers become increasingly sophisticated in determining actual costs, they will expect your costs to be competitive and waste free. Customers want price stability and savings passed on to them. Wastes are a cost to the customer. This contributes to why we have the following:

- Hospital day-rate charges varying significantly from hospital to hospital
- Mortgage application rates and percentages varying from lender to lender
- Higher education systems with a large range of tuition rates
- Credit card companies with different APRs
- Bids on construction projects varying by builder

These examples, plus many more that you probably can relate to, vary by the cost of "acceptable" waste (no matter how the waste is defined).

The following is a pie chart representing the ten wastes and their relationship to value-added activities.

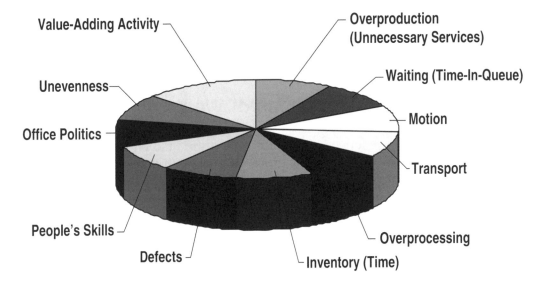

1. The Waste of Overproduction

Producing some type of work prior to it being required is waste. This is the greatest of all the wastes. Overproduction of work or services can cause other wastes. For example, by preparing a quote for a customer without an order being placed, waste is produced in: excessive processing, transport, motion, etc.

The following are some examples of this waste, along with references to the Lean tools that would assist in its elimination.

Examples of overproduction waste are:
- Emailing, faxing the same document multiple times
- Entering repetitive information on multiple documents
- Ineffective meetings
- Producing reports that are not used, or providing additional fields for reporting that are not viewed or used by anyone
- Producing regular reports that the user does not need to view unless an 'exception' occurs
- Performing more analysis than is required
- Unclear expectations of what information is required by whom and when
- Generating performance reports on business processes that are currently operating within normal, acceptable limits (e.g., debtors report, cost-center report)
- Sending completed reports or too much information to the next process without knowing when, or exactly what, is needed
- Too many services, options, or selections in the user interface (or program) than what is required to access or process the information

Tools to eliminate overproduction waste are:
- Takt time
- Pitch
- Proof of Need Survey
- Work standards
- Level loading

2. The Waste of Waiting (Time-In-Queue)

Waiting for anything (people, signatures, information, etc.) is waste. This waste of waiting is "low hanging fruit" which is easy to reach and ripe for the taking. We often do not think of paper sitting in an In-basket or an unread email as waste. However, when looking for the item (document or email), how many times do we search through that In-basket or the Inbox mail folder and try to find it? How many times do you actually touch something before it is completed? It is the finish it, file it, or throw it away system that can help eliminate this waste.

The following are some examples of this waste, along with references to the Lean tools that would assist in its elimination.

Examples of waiting waste are:
- Excessive signatures or approvals
- Mis-matching cross-departmental resource commitments
- Lack of priority in setting work expectations
- Delay in getting feedback/approvals/decisions from peers or higher-level management
- Lack of visual Key Performance Indicators (KPIs) or 'performance dashboards' to highlight exceptions/notifications/deviations, and enable timely corrective actions
- Unacceptable delay (more than 24 hours) in replying to emails
- Delay in starting the next process step because a previous step operates as a batch-and-queue process
- Delay in getting information from another department, customer, or system report
- Wrong methodologies of software development which requires extra steps in processing information due to no user input into the design of the user interface

Tools to eliminate waiting waste are:
- Value stream mapping
- 5S
- Pitch
- Runners
- Lean File System

3. The Waste of Motion

Any movement of people, paper, and/or electronic exchanges that does not add value is waste. This waste is created by poor office layout or design, faulty or outdated office equipment, supply inaccessibility, and movement of information or data that does not add value. The waste of motion is insidious and is hidden in office procedures that have not been reviewed for continuous improvement initiatives. Regardless of the industry, motion waste may appear as someone who is looking "busy" but not adding value to the work or service. Lean tools will assist to identify, reduce, and/or eliminate this waste.

The following are some examples of this waste, along with references to the Lean tools that would assist in its elimination.

Examples of motion waste are:
- Searching for computer files
- Searching for all types documents in file cabinets and file folders
- Hand-carrying paper to another process
- Cross-departmental resource commitments without proper communications
- Excessive email distribution lists and attachments
- Using an excessive number of transaction screens to support decision-making
- Presenting data that is not easy-to-read or not 'user friendly' to support decision-making
- Sending event notifications that do not provide all the details, or do not allow a user to take action without going to another screen/interface for further information
- Selecting additional keystrokes and fields to retrieve information
- Not using default 'speed keys' that can help operate multiple Desktop screens faster

Tools to eliminate motion waste are:
- Standard work
- New office layout
- Pull systems and supermarkets
- Office Quick-Starts
- Kanbans for office supplies
- Document tagging

4. The Waste of Transport

Excess transport affects the time of delivery of any work within an office. Even with internet and email readily available, too often, or not often enough, documents (i.e., files) that provide little or no value are moved downstream regardless of need. Reducing or eliminating excess transport waste is important. Locating all work in sequential process operations and as physically close together as possible will help eliminate or reduce this waste. Transport between processes that cannot be eliminated should be automated as much as possible. Ask questions such as: "Is the office layout optimal?", "Is the release and request for work automated?" and "Is IT aware of the problem and can they help?".

The following are some examples of this waste, along with references to the Lean tools that would assist in its elimination.

Examples of transport waste are:
- Delivering unneeded documents
- Excessive filing of work documents
- Reviewing customer information from another process before it is sent downstream
- Filing/saving documents that will never be used again
- Moving data from one system to another
- Updating customer records in different systems
- Sending and/or requesting unnecessary data to/from the customer (e.g., if you have a self-serve order-entry web portal and still must contact the customer for information)

Tools to eliminate transport waste are:
- 5S
- Value stream mapping
- Lean File System
- Visual controls
- Work load balancing
- Continuous flow
- Standard work

5. The Waste of Overprocessing

Putting more work or effort into the work required by internal or external customers is waste. Excessive processing does not add value for the customer and the customer will not pay for it. This is one of the most difficult administrative wastes to uncover. Some questions to ask to assist in the identification of this waste are: "What are the most basic processes required to meet the customer needs?" and "Is there a clear understanding of the customer's needs?".

The following are some examples of this waste, along with references to the Lean tools that would assist in its elimination.

Examples of overprocessing waste are:
- Duplicative reports or information
- Repetitive data entry
- Unnecessary information being requested
- Constantly revising documents
- Ineffective meetings (e.g., no or poor meeting agendas)
- Processing excessive emails to highlight issues or actions requiring attention
- Using Excel spreadsheets to retain or analyze information 'outside' of the core IT system
- Entering data into multiple systems and/or 'stand-alone' spreadsheets for reporting purposes
- Over-resourcing a process to meet the 'peak demand' rather than investigating work leveling opportunities
- 'Over-checking' an email Inbox for new messages
- Lacking a system to manage incoming emails, causing emails to be read and re-read (again at a later date) before responding

Tools to eliminate overprocessing waste are:
- Data collection techniques
- Standard work
- Predictable output
- Document tagging
- Visual controls
- Lean File System

6. The Waste of Inventory (Time)

Excessive piles of paperwork, computer files, supplies, and time spent searching for documents is waste. They all take up space or require someone's time. There are basically two types of inventory waste related to administrative areas: 1) office supplies and 2) time.

The following are some examples of this waste, along with references to the Lean tools that would assist in its elimination.

Examples of inventory waste are:
- Work awaiting task completion by others
- Obsolete files
- Obsolete office equipment
- Insufficient training of back-ups
- Purchasing excessive office supplies
- Filing unfinished service requests never to be used again
- Keeping multiple copies of reports
- Keeping unused 'required fields' in reports/documents/templates that will not be used in company reports
- Using excessive icons on the Desktop
- Creating excessive document revisions rather than overwriting previous copies
- Keeping excessive 'un-read' emails in your Inbox

Tools to eliminate inventory waste are:
- 5S
- Standard work
- Level loading - heijunka
- Lean File System
- Value stream mapping
- Kanbans for office supplies
- Visible pitch

7. The Waste of Defects

Defect waste refers to all processing required in creating a defect and the additional work required to correct a defect. Defects (either internal or external) result in additional administrative processing that will add *no* value to the product or service. It takes less time to do work correctly the first time than the time it would take to do it over. Rework is waste and adds more cost to any product or service for which the customer will not pay. This waste can reduce profits significantly. If any type of defect is passed along to the customer, customer dissatisfaction will result.

The following are some examples of this waste, along with references to the Lean tools that would assist in its elimination.

Examples of defect waste are:
- Data entry errors
- Forwarding incomplete documentation
- Lost files or records
- Incorrect information on document
- Returning forms/applications due to incomplete data
- Having discrepancies in data content because they are stored in different systems (e.g., customer master database)
- Submitting wrong/inaccurate data
- Creating a document that requires extensive correction by colleagues
- Missing information due to poorly specified information requirements or features

Tools to eliminate defect waste are:
- Predictable output
- Standard work
- Interruptions and random arrivals
- Mistake proofing
- Visual controls
- Lean File System
- Office Quick-Starts

8. The Waste of People's Skills

The under-utilization of people is a result of not placing people where they can (and will) use their knowledge, skills, and abilities to the fullest providing value-added work and services. An effective performance management system will reduce this waste significantly. Use company policies and procedures to effectively place people where they will most benefit the organization.

The following are some examples of this waste, along with references to the Lean tools that would assist in its elimination.

Examples of people's waste of skills and knowledge are:
- Work loads not evenly balanced due to lack of cross-training
- High absenteeism and turnover
- Inadequate performance management system
- Incomplete job skill assessment prior to hiring
- Assigning employees two jobs due to understaffing
- Not providing adequate training while some people are sitting 'idle' due to bottleneck in upstream process, or variable demand

Tools to eliminate people's waste of skills and knowledge are:
- Process capture
- Standard work
- Office Quick-Starts
- Lean File System
- Business Case for Lean

9. The Waste of Office Politics

Additional work that is done (possibly considered as overprocessing) solely to gain favor with management can be considered a ninth waste. This is a delicate subject, but must be addressed, as it has proven to be a real issue within some organizations. This waste is very hard to identify, but must be acknowledged to possibly bring insight into its existence and subsequent elimination.

The following are some examples of this waste, along with references to the Lean tools that would assist in its elimination.

Examples of office politics waste are:
- Creating management reports using incomplete information or estimates (e.g., generating a sales report before end of month when figures are not available, generating a weekly report when only a monthly report is required, etc.)
- Requesting direct reports to consume valuable resources to extract and analyze information for the sole purpose of creating a 'good impression' with peers and/or bosses
- Performing a task that is 'politically motivated' (e.g., organizing an extra meeting just to report the favorable progress of an event or project when a short email could have sufficed)

Tools to eliminate office politics waste are:
- Performance Measurement
- Standard work
- Mistake proofing
- Work load balancing

10. The Waste of Unevenness

Lack of a consistent flow of inputs/information/scheduled work from upstream processes causes many of the other types of waste previously mentioned.

The following are some examples of this waste, along with references to the Lean tools that would assist in its elimination.

Examples of unevenness waste are:
- Not having information ahead of time to meet month-end deadlines, thus causing overtime
- Scheduling all work to be completed at the end of the month and not during the month at even intervals
- Not leveling work adequately
- Having poor office standards/processes causing difficulty in finding documents/reports when staff member is on annual leave (vacation)
- Lacking performance standards (or clearly defined work parameters) from the downstream process (i.e., customer)

Tools to eliminate unevenness waste are:
- Value stream mapping
- Standard work
- 5S
- Work load balancing

Consider thinking about the following questions.

1. How can I communicate these wastes throughout the organization?
2. What are some of the low-hanging fruit?
3. What can be done to immediately improve customer satisfaction?

These questions should stimulate others and promote more open communications regarding waste.

Desktop Waste Audit

The following questions can be a starting point for an individual or a work group to evaluate their current Desktop and networking practices in reference to waste. Reviewing these questions will allow for further understanding of how the wastes just described may be present in your work environment.

Use the following five-level Likert item scale for each of the 25 statements regarding waste in your Desktop environment:

   1 - Strongly Disagree
   2 - Disagree
   3 - Neither Agree nor Disagree
   4 - Agree
   5 - Strongly Agree

1. We have no problems with data entry errors. _____
2. We always have the most up-to-date document version to work on. _____
3. We never struggle with getting the right data from our system. _____
4. We only handle a report once, with no rework. _____
5. We use the same shortcuts and keystrokes to get to the data the same standard way. _____
6. We have a standard file naming convention that everyone adheres to. _____
7. We have all our emails organized in appropriate folders for easy access. _____
8. We never have to search for a file or previously sent email. _____
9. We have our Desktop files well organized with standard naming conventions. _____
10. We have been cross-trained. _____
11. We continually improve our work flow through real-time communications. _____
12. We know our performance standard for the day. _____
13. We never have to recheck or reenter data. _____

14. We have minimum email distribution lists. _____
15. We have established cycle times for our processes which _____
are monitored.
16. We always know when work or information needs to _____
be processed.
17. We always handle an email once, or twice at the most. _____
18. We have a standard way to handle emails in regards to _____
the time of the day emails are read.
19. We have established email rules/filters to immediately _____
identify critical emails in real-time.
20. We have established file sharing features in Explorer to _____
share information within/across department(s).
21. We use file links to avoid sending (file) attachments to _____
multiple users.
22. We can easily locate a file that was created by another user. _____
23. We can block email addresses to avoid or reduce junk email. _____
24. We use visual management principles to provide visibility _____
of work-in-progress (i.e., status of orders, projects, reports etc.).
25. We have a process to share best practices. _____

Total Score [ ]

After your score is totaled, use the following Scoring Guidelines to provide some overall direction in eliminating the wastes identified. The total score could be a maximum of 125. However, if an individual or work group scored an average of 4.0 on the 5.0 scale (80%) they would fit in the **Good Foundation** Scoring Guideline category.

Scoring Guidelines

A score of 90+ - Doing Very Well - Should be sharing best practices via conference speakings, blogs, white papers, etc.

A score of 80-89 - Good Foundation - Must have good IT systems and Microsoft (or applicable software) integration, along with employee engagement already in place, to score at this level.

A score of 70-79 - Some Good Things Happening but More Needs to be Done - Benchmark other organizations; attend conferences that present Lean Desktop solutions. Additional training may need to be done to assist employees to better understand various options within the Microsoft suite of products.

A score of 60-69 - Not Much Happening to Keep Pace with Competition - More efficient and effective information processing may help to grow the business and respond to customers faster. Must ensure Desktop 5S program is implemented throughout the organization.

A score of <60 - Not so Good - Typically, not a passing or satisfactory grade, however, some good things may be happening. Acknowledge the positives and begin a Desktop 5S program immediately, as well as involve IT in the Lean Desktop concept.

If you score less than 70%, then *Lean Office Demystified II* is definitely for you. If you scored above 70% you must already be an avid learner of new techniques for data flow; then this book may provide some additional insights for you to consider. (Guess that means everyone needs this book ☺)

These questions were meant to create an awareness of how wastes can be identified to the management of files, folders, and emails, both the electronic movement of work as well as the physical movement of paper. Information to eliminate many of these wastes can be found in implementing the practices contained in the forthcoming chapters of *Lean Office Demystified II.*

Enabler #4: Applying the Power of Information Technology

Microsoft Office, the most popular and longest running suite of office applications, was first introduced in 1989. Since then, not only have the word processing, spreadsheet, calendaring, and presentation applications themselves become vastly more powerful and feature-laden, the number of users has increased to virtually 100% of the office work force. MS Office, and its many interfacing applications, database systems, along with its integration across the Internet, at times seem to run our lives. Using the principles of Lean will show workers the way to harness the power of Microsoft Office, as well as other applications, and not be overwhelmed by it.

The principles of Lean support software applications in two fundamental ways:

- Many functions within applications may not be realized (or used effectively) until Lean principles have been explained thus enabling a faster method of processing information as well as improving data integrity (error-free).
- The main concepts of eliminating waste and standardizing work can bring new insights into how data and information flow can be improved.

At times it seems the very power of computers invites waste, complexity, and confusion. By keeping the focus on what is really necessary to satisfy customers - with all else being waste - the application of Lean Desktop methods also will help tame the digital beast and bend it to the needs of its masters, the front-line workers and their managers.

Enabler #5: Management Commitment

Companies like Microsoft, Wal-Mart, Federal Express, GE, and Nike have one very important characteristic in common - an undisputed leader at the top to whom members look for guidance and approval. Top managers like Bill Gates, Sam Walton, and Fred Smith are the cornerstones of their organizations. They possess extraordinary vision and have successfully led their companies to become self-perpetuating dynasties.

In John Maxwell's book, *The 21 Irrefutable Laws of Leadership*, he describes his first law, The Law of the LID, by saying, "Leadership ability determines a person's (organization's) level of effectiveness. If leadership is strong, the LID is high. But if it's not, then the organization is limited."

It is vital to recognize that Lean transformation will not work without total commitment from management. A CEO reading Lean in the *Wall Street Journal* on a flight coming home from vacation, and then telling his top manager that "it sounds like a good idea" does not reflect or constitute a long-term desire to implement Lean.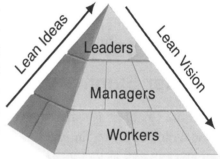

Management commitment must be driven by a passion to improve. The top manager must be totally involved in the implementation of Lean. Even, if that first Lean project involves only 3 people, top level commitment must be present. Management commitment is:

- Committing the necessary resources to the Lean initiatives
- Being present at the first meeting and walking the process area
- Providing coaching and counseling to the team when needed
- Displaying interest in the team's progress by attending meetings
- Rewarding and recognizing the team's effort
- Having empathy when the team is struggling

That is not an exhaustive list, but it does show a general framework for how management commitment can be manifested.

Timelines

Lean Office implementation will take anywhere from a few months to a few years. It will depend on the following:

1. The overall size of the organization. The smaller the organization, the less time it will typically take. For a large organization (500 or more office employees), pilot (or beta) Lean Office projects should be started in a department and then expanded to the other departments.

2. Availability of the tools. This book will provide the detailed road map, forms, templates, and actual examples which the team can use and reference as a benchmark.

3. Understanding of the benefits. Fully understanding the value of cross-training, inter-departmental sharing, the use of generalists versus specialists, discerning and using organizational knowledge, and promoting employee-manager partnerships will all ensure Lean Office success.

Chapter Summary

The Five Enablers for the Implementation of Lean will provide the foundation upon which to create an improvement plan. This plan will allow your organization to realize that the benefits of the Lean Office will make an area or process more productive by eliminating waste and creating positive behaviors. This will improve office productivity and provide a foundation to gain process control.

This chapter focused on:

1. The Behavior, Attitude, and Culture Model, which conveyed that behavior must first change if a new culture is to emerge.
2. The Business Case for Lean revealed the Traditional (Cost + Profit = Price) versus the Lean (Price - Cost = Profit) philosophies.
3. Applying the Power of Information Technology with Lean concepts and practices to optimize the applications.
4. The Ten Areas of Waste which were defined and related to administrative processes and tasks.
5. Management Commitment and how it must be present in all continuous improvement initiatives for success to occur.

Observations from the Lean Office

These observations may assist in further understanding how to apply the concepts and tools contained in this chapter:

- Have as many people as possible read this book. Remember, everyone has different learning styles, some learn by hearing, some by reading, and others by viewing examples. However, the most effective learning for everyone is by *doing*.
- Communicate that this is new territory and for Lean to succeed everyone must contribute their ideas.
- Hold regularly scheduled meetings and prepare short presentations on the various sections of the book.
- Create large posters identifying the ten areas of waste or other graphics that send the message about waste identification and elimination.
- Benchmark a nearby organization that has world-class Lean Office practices.

Application Case Study

Back at Northwind Traders, Andrew Cencini began to study the Lean Office methods as they applied to data and information flow. After conducting a Desktop Waste Audit he and his team could see very quickly several areas where they could immediately improve processes (and thereby eliminate waste). One issue that Andrew (and the team) tackled was the wasteful process for assembling and tracking new business prospects. The problem was that some prospects were generated nationally by his sales team through networking, referrals, cold-calling, and advertising, and were then managed in a simple Access Customer Relationship Management (CRM) database as shown below.

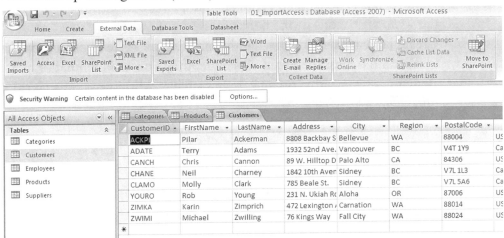

Prospects in Access Database

Two years ago Northwinds replaced its Excel file that it had used for customer tracking with this Access database. Using Access eliminated much double and triple entering of data and allowed the ready cross-linking and reporting of data by customer, employee, product, and suppliers. Most offices today have and use databases – ranging from specialized corporate systems to basic systems such as what Northwind was using – to manage the ever-increasing amount and complexity of information that exists in their business. However, much like Access these larger database systems did not have the advanced charting features that Excel offers. Therefore, many times data needed to be exported into Excel. The effective understanding of this data using the principles of Lean can, as we shall see, yield many benefits to the company. These benefits would include workers having real-time tracking of their performance as well as the ease of data being shared.

Corporate headquarters also sent leads generated through inquiries via the corporate website and by other subsidiaries of Global Winds. The Northwinds team had to re-enter the corporate data that had been sent in the form of an Excel spreadsheet (shown below) into the Northwinds Access database resulting in the waste of overprocessing.

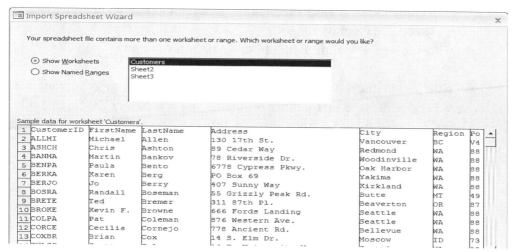

Corporate Prospects in Excel

Andrew and his IT advisor discovered that, with a little planning and simple training, it was easy to import the corporate data to the local database using the Import Spreadsheet Wizard in Access, which simplifies aligning the fields of the Excel Worksheet to the fields of the table in Access, as shown below.

Access Import Wizard Window for Spreadsheets

After the import, the prospect/customer table in Access now includes the leads sent via email in Excel from corporate headquarters – with no manual reentry required, as shown in the following screen shot.

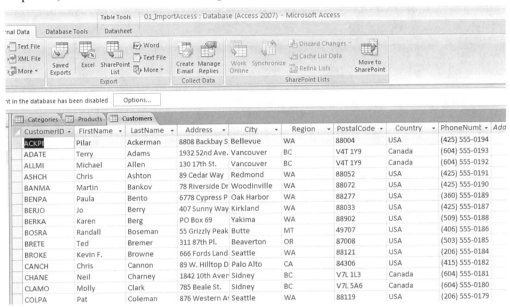

Corporate Data Imported Successfully into Access Database

Doing this eliminated the wastes of:

- Waiting – dependency on others to complete tasks
- Defects – data entry errors
- People's time – eliminating re-entering information

As we will see in the coming chapters, the Northwind's improvement team discovered and addressed many other problems and issues that the Seattle office was having and was able to further improve office productivity and reduce waste using the various Lean Office methods.

Chapter 3

Seeing the Challenge

Effective Teaming is a Must

Chapter Overview

"Seeing the Challenge" in an office or administrative area must involve people at all levels of the office hierarchy. The challenge is to convince employees to not only "see" that change is required, but also to engage them in the forward thinking confidence to build the Lean Office. The more confidence the office leader has in what needs to be changed, the more enthusiasm (and confidence) the team members will have in support of it. Substantive change cannot be dictated to people. It must be packaged as a partnership in a WIN - WIN approach. This chapter provides the basic tools to ensure the team takes that first step onto a solid foundation when building a Lean Office.

The tools and concepts in this section will support the following:

- Respecting the ideas of others through appropriate communications
- Having structured meetings
- Involving the right members for the Lean Office project
- Communicating change as it is occurring
- Understanding team dynamics

Many employees may not realize that a change needs to occur. Some may think the following:

"Our organization has had reductions in the workforce the past year due to the economic crisis and I may be next, so why should I do anything differently now?"

"The company is so large that our small group will have little, if any, impact on organizational improvements."

"I had a good performance appraisal and our departmental goals are on schedule for next year."

"Our office IT systems are out-of-date and in many cases incompatible."

"I know I can do more with MS Office, but I don't want to admit that I have a performance gap in this area."

"We have few competitors in our markets."

"There are no incentives for me to improve, so what's in it for me?"

Also, these types of thoughts may be prevailing:

"We are continually downsizing, so what good does it do me to contribute to a new project or team. I may not be around."

"Our company is continually requesting us to contribute. This is just another program to give us more work."

"I do not see how our small department can have any impact on the organization. We are just too small."

"When one of our team members is out of the office, we find it nearly impossible to find the information needed to cover the absent person's job responsibilities."

"It's very frustrating trying to find a file on our shared directory. Everyone has their own file naming convention."

These are very pessimistic statements, but are true in many instances. Regardless of the type of industry, where the organization is in its life cycle, or what external influences that may play a role, there are numerous reasons why the status quo is perceived to be good enough. However, employees must be made aware that a Lean Office will require change (for the better). Also, if employees have previously been on improvement teams that had little success in their implementation, then an honest dialogue with them must occur to address the many questions that most likely still linger in their minds. Concerns must be addressed early on in any Lean project to promote team unity.

This chapter will provide reasons and justifications required to obtain "employee buy-in" such that everyone can "see and support" the challenges that lies ahead. This will require careful planning to pour that solid foundation for change. Seeing the Challenge has five main areas:

1. Management's Role

Managers must look within their domain and what they know currently of the area or process before any project is defined. Managers must understand and be able to convey to employees the importance of predictable output, which is a key ingredient to the Lean Office. Managers must also have a basic understanding of leadership style. Tool utilized: Management Self-Assessment

2. Predictable Output

Work that has repeatable results based on consistent processes, yields customer satisfaction. Stated another way, predictable output is the ability to complete work in a standard way that ensures customer demands are met every time. This can be an internal customer (the next person or department to which the work is passed on) or the external customer (the customer who ultimately pays for the product or service). Tool utilized: Predictable Output Survey

3. Effective Meetings

Scheduling and conducting effective meetings are critical to the success of any team. Effective meetings can accelerate the team and continuous improvement initiatives. Non-effective meetings can create chaos, reduce team unity, delay, and, many times, terminate continuous improvement efforts. Tool utilized: Effective Meeting Evaluation Form

4. Project Identification and Communication

The Lean project must be meaningful to the office area personnel. Management must provide the necessary support and resources throughout the process. (An explanation of why this may be different from other initiatives in the past may need to be addressed.) A case must be made for "why this and why now?" Tools utilized: Team Charter, Meeting Information Form, Status Report, and Sunset Report

5. The Lean Office Road Map

A detailed road map will ensure a plan exists and thus will provide guidance along the journey. The Road Map will instill a confidence that the team has a proven, effective plan to follow. Tool utilized: Lean Office Road Map

1. Management's Role

The last chapter ended with the importance of management commitment. It is only fitting that we continue with that theme and be more specific in the role management should have when implementing a Lean Office System. Management should provide the following:

- Reasons for moving to the Lean Office
- Resources (i.e., training, benchmarking, meetings, books, videos, workshops, etc.) for the team
- Support in terms of personal involvement, team recognition, and constant communications
- Alignment of the team to the strategic direction of the company

Management's role in contributing to the Lean Office must be one of support and coaching. The manager and the employee will both likely be on new ground, learning the tools, therefore, communication must be open and frequent.

Managers should conduct a Management Self-Assessment to gain insight in their need for personal improvement. This will assist them in learning to ask the right questions when initial communications regarding the Lean project occur.

The Management Self-Assessment should be conducted within the sphere or area over which the manager has control, a value stream or customer issues identified as needing improvement, or an area which top management has indicated requires immediate improvement.

Management Self-Assessment

If you respond NO to any of these, then the Lean Office is needed.
The Lean Office will allow you to reduce costs, improve customer satisfaction, and improve employee well-being, while increasing office productivity.

	YES	NO
1. Do you have any quick adapters of change?	❏	❏
2. Are you satisfied with the productivity in the office area?	❏	❏
3. Do you currently have metrics (measures) in place to understand where you are?	❏	❏
4. Do you have standards of service in the organization?	❏	❏
5. Are most of your processes and organizational knowledge easily transferred amongst the group (i.e., effective cross-training)?	❏	❏
6. Are your processes captured and are they easily accessible to the employee?	❏	❏
7. Is the office stress free?	❏	❏
8. When you have an influx of work, can you easily adapt?	❏	❏
9. Can you operate without overtime or temporary help?	❏	❏
10. Are your customers satisfied with your level of service?	❏	❏
11. Has an Internal Survey been conducted within the past six months?	❏	❏
12. Does everyone follow a standard file naming system?	❏	❏
13. Are employees trained in the latest application software?	❏	❏
14. Are there real-time visuals to monitor work flow and progress?	❏	❏
15. Does the upstream process provide complete information at all times?	❏	❏
16. Is MS Office being used effectively by all employees?	❏	❏
17. Are forms and templates being used?	❏	❏
18. Is all information easily accessible by all employees?	❏	❏
19. Has the Document Management System been improved?	❏	❏
20. Are reports standardized and minimized?	❏	❏

The following is a brief explanation of each of the questions.

1. Do you have any quick adapters of change?

These employees may be your leaders and could assist greatly in the Lean Office process. Remember, no change can be effective and sustained without employees who have the passion to keep it in place.

There are five support levels within an organization going through change. They are:

- People who will make it happen - The Doers
- People who will help it happen - The Helpers
- People who will let it happen - The Followers
- People who are mildly against it - The Resisters
- People who will actively sabotage it - The Saboteurs

The 80/20 rule applies here. Usually, no more than 20% of your employees will fall into the last two categories. Of that 20%, 80% of those people can be converted into supporters (The Doers, Helpers, and Followers), while 20% will never accept the change. Mathematically stated it is: $[.8 + (.8 \times .2)] = .96$ or 96% of the employees will accept change. Focus efforts on the 96%!

2. Are you satisfied with the productivity in the office area?

Be careful here! Just because you seem successful today does not guarantee success tomorrow. It also does not mean that you cannot become much more efficient and profitable than you already are. You might be overconfident that you have a 99.5% internal DPPM (Defective Parts Per Million) metric and do not need to change. Using that logic, if you are a 500-bed hospital with a 0.5% defect rate, you would still have 2,500 incorrect surgical procedures a year. How long do you think that hospital would stay in business believing that was good enough?

3. *Do you currently have metrics (measures) in place to understand where you are?*

This will not keep you from implementing the Lean Office. However, metrics or measurements are extremely helpful in documenting the trend of improvement activities. Metrics, done correctly, will provide an impetus for the employees to continue to improve. It will become a way of life under Lean.

4. *Do you have standards of service in the organization?*

Thomas Edison tried and failed with over 10,000 different processes in trying to invent the electric light bulb. If, after finally discovering the right process, he had not bothered to write it down and standardize that procedure, we might still be in the dark today. Most errors, mistakes, and defects in business are caused by not following the proper procedure (i.e., standard). Too many organizations let employees use the DWFG (Do Whatever Feels Good) method of completing their work. This leads to process variation, mistakes, and hinders any efforts to improve the process.

5. *Are most of your processes and organizational knowledge easily transferred amongst the group (i.e., effective cross-training)?*

Competent employees are those who know how to do their jobs well and are depended upon by all to solve problems. When knowledge becomes the exclusive domain of specialists and work cannot continue in the absence of that "specialist" employee, a problem exists. Predictable output cannot happen when a process is controlled by one person. When this person leaves for an appointment or a two-week vacation, the organization suffers, the work sits, and customers may start to complain. Generally, most offices today have specialists who carry this valuable knowledge in their heads.

Today's workplace cannot afford *not* to have knowledgeable, cross-functional teams working to reduce waste. A smooth-running, efficient office is that way because of teamwork. Team members must share process knowledge and must be cross-trained so they can step into any job if the workload changes or a problem arises.

6. Are your processes captured and are they easily accessible to the employee?

It is not good enough to just have standardized processes. For processes to be effective in the Lean Office, they must be written down (documented) and placed in a location that is easily accessible to every employee who needs them. They must also be documented in a visual and explanatory way such that learning is straightforward and fairly simple. Make sure there is a process for creating, obtaining, and maintaining all processes on the computer. Computers are a great storage place for process information enabling everyone to retrieve and view updates when needed. However, be careful to not allow these processes to be saved on someone's "C" drive. You will lose revision control, which will contribute to people using outdated revisions, improvements being lost, and the maintenance of those process files being out of control.

7. Is the office stress free?

If the stress level is high in your office, people are probably:

- Overworked
- Unsure of how to do the work more efficiently
- Busy, with the work never seeming to get done
- Doing work in "their" own way

The most significant benefit of implementing the Lean Office is the stress reduction employees feel. Once the transformation is complete they feel good being part of a team working in the accomplishment of defined goals. When they go home at night, their desk is clear and their work is done.

8. When you have an influx of work, can you easily adapt?

If unanticipated influxes only happen once or twice a month, there probably never seems to be enough time to cross-train others to help out during those times. As this cycle continues, month after month, everyone becomes a specialist at his or her job. The longer this continues, the less likely it is that people can and will adapt to using the Lean tools to assist when this work volume periodically increases. It is imperative that standards be created to promote sharing work duties when workloads increase.

9. *Can you operate without overtime or temporary help?*

Overtime and temporary help are quick fixes that hide the real issue at hand. If there is a consistency of utilizing overtime or temporary help to get work accomplished, this usually indicates that work processes are inefficient and need to be changed.

10. *Are your customers satisfied with your level of service?*

Many times, organizations ask the external customers how satisfied they are with the organizational level of service. Customer surveys typically are conducted yearly and provide valuable insight into various levels of service that the organization provides to their external customers. Internal customer surveys should be conducted regularly as their processes can impact the level of service to the external customer.

11. *Has an Internal Survey been conducted within the past six months?*

It is difficult to improve processes if the customer requirements are not completely understood. Since organizations are comprised of many departments working together "seamlessly in the customer's eyes" it would be of value to ensure each department is meeting the needs of the other departments. An Internal Survey should be completed every six months.

12. *Does everyone follow a standard file naming system?*

As organizations move to a paperless way of doing business, it is that much more important that a standard file naming system be established. The amount of information sent via emails or put into CRM (Customer Relationship Management) programs can be "lost" if not properly categorized and filed. How many times do we search for a file or ask someone to send it again?

13. *Are employees trained in the latest application software?*

The amount of information that is accessible to the average worker is mind-boggling. Employees must have access to current application packages to be able to properly analyze, format, review, share, and process all the information efficiently.

14. Are there real-time visuals to monitor work flow and progress?

Managers must have real-time information accessible to them on how work is progressing. They cannot wait until the end of the day to determine if work has been completed or not. There are many applications available that can help manage work flow.

15. Does the upstream process provide complete information at all times?

Very few workers are independent of an upstream process. To prevent delays in one department or work group it is critical that the information that is required to be processed is present in its entirely when it is needed.

16. IS MS Office being used effectively by all employees?

Regular training needs assessment should be done to ensure everyone is properly trained in MS Office and other critical applications.

17. Are forms and templates being used?

The organization should have standard templates available on shared drives to ensure standard documents and forms are used to communicate data.

18. Is all the information easily accessible by all employees?

Employees should be well-trained on the Document Management System that the organization is using.

19. Has the Document Management System been improved?

The Document Management System should be evaluated every year and updated to reflect the demands of the customers as well as the needs of the employees.

20. Are reports standardized and minimized?

Reports of all types should be standardized and minimum required information conveyed on those reports.

Managers Must Lead

Any manager can implement the Lean Office. However, this can only occur if the manager engages the process worker in all aspects of the change. We will briefly describe some of the qualities we have found among managers who were good "Lean" leaders in organizations.

The seven qualities of an effective Lean leader are:

1. *Leaders must stand by their values.*
   Without strong values from the leader, a team will waiver and not have the confidence in whatever system or program is being implemented.

2. *Leaders must have courage.*
   Courage allows a leader to stand up to superiors, supported by data, and make a strong case for his or her position, and not waiver at the first sign of confrontation or disagreement.

3. *Leaders must be optimistic.*
   Being optimistic is always attempting to find something positive. Some things in the Lean Office will work easily, while other things may not. Being optimistic, learning from mistakes, and moving forward with a positive attitude is a critical quality of an effective leader.

4. *Leaders must have a plan.*
   Everyone needs direction. A proven plan or detailed road map will provide the leader with added confidence along the journey.

5. *Leaders must team.*
   Leaders must accomplish goals through effective utilization of others. It takes a person with special skills to bring ideas out of people - and get those ideas shared and adopted by others.

6. *Leaders must be good communicators.*
   Communication is the key to project success. A good communicator ensures everyone is aligned with a common purpose and addresses issues as they occur.

*7. **Leaders must show compassion.***

Leaders must continually balance the business needs of the team with the needs of the individual.

Managers who have the desire to change can become effective leaders. The most important aspect is to be yourself, hold consistent standards to personal and organizational values, and have respect for fellow employees. Live by the qualities just listed.

The Management Self-Assessment and a basic understanding of leadership will allow managers to understand their role in implementing this systematic process, both with what can be done with the Lean technical tools and with how one can lead change. The Management Self-Assessment should be shared with employees in the Project Identification phase. The Assessment will also lend support to predictable output.

2. Predictable Output

Predictable output is the expectation that a process which produces a good or service will do it consistently and with no variation (waste). Variation is the root cause of all waste.

Employees must realize that for organizations to be profitable and remain in business, processes must be consistent each and every time. Attaining predictable output from an organization is central to remaining competitive. It is one of the overriding themes in creating the Lean Office.

The following are examples of common activities where we expect a consistent outcome (predictable output):

How frustrated have you become with other types of activities where expectations may not have been met (no predictable output)? Systems like:

Revisiting our earlier example of Thomas Edison, there is a traceable legacy of developing predictable output that spans the time from the first light bulb through to the relentless pursuit of perfection exhibited by modern-day General Electric. The flip of a switch produces light in just about every corner of the world.

If you are a manager, have you ever asked yourself exactly what you should expect from the employees who work for you? If you are not a manager, do you know what is expected of you?

The Predictable Output Survey provides further understanding of what may or may not be required in the Lean Office. This can be completed by the manager and shared with the team, or it can be completed as a team for all to understand and discuss.

Predictable output cannot be achieved without standardizing methods and processes. All employees must learn to follow standardized processes that result in predictable outcomes, ensuring that the quality of work is consistent. Allowing several different approaches to getting the job done creates chaos and unpredictability. Developing best practices for each activity will allow good performance to be duplicated. This can then serve as a basis upon which continuous improvement tools can be applied.

Predictable Output Survey

If you respond NO to any of these, then the Lean Office is needed. The Lean Office will allow you to reduce costs, improve customer satisfaction, and improve employee well-being, while increasing office productivity.

	YES	NO
1. Are there standard methods and processes that ensure the quality of work for each employee or work assignment?	❑	❑
2. Are the standard methods and processes continually improved upon?	❑	❑
3. Are the standard methods and processes made visible and easily accessible to all employees?	❑	❑
4. Are the standards and processes documented to the best practice(s)?	❑	❑
5. Do all meetings for improvements focus on the process and not the person?	❑	❑
6. Are employees able to make changes to the processes based on a systematic process for improvement?	❑	❑
7. Is value-added work evenly distributed?	❑	❑
8. Can workers be assured they are accessing and reading identical versions of business critical documents?	❑	❑

The following is a brief explanation of each of the eight questions:

1. *Are there standard methods and processes that ensure the quality of work for each employee or work assignment?*
   Often a customer is willing to pay more for something simply because of its guarantee of known quality. Consider the following: Sears - Craftman tools; John Deere - garden tractors; Cleveland Clinic - heart surgery. Quality in any good or service depends on the foundation of process control through the standardization of tasks and activities from one employee to another - *error-free.*

2. *Are the standard methods and processes continually improved upon?*
   There is always room for improvement. Predictable output, based on standard methods, can be continually measured and improved upon. Growth and profitability in an organization is based on the continuous pursuit of eliminating waste, removing the process variation, and focusing on the value-added work.

3. *Are the standard methods and processes made visible and easily accessible to all employees?*
   If processes (steps) are not adequately documented, they immediately become unmanageable. Making all processes visible assists in allowing other employees to understand the processes and be trained at the same time.

4. *Are the standards and processes documented to the best practice(s)?*
   Processes must first be documented. For example, if a process is entering customer or patient information, and there are four people doing this on a daily basis, there needs to be a standard method for entering this information. With all the Desktop application tools available, standard work procedures can be only a mouse click away. Begin with the most critical processes to the organization and create a realistic time line to move through all processes in the department.

5. *Do all meetings for improvements focus on the process and not the person?*

Create an environment in which employees feel free to be open and discuss areas of improvement where they see a need. This is achieved when employees know they will not be blamed for honest mistakes; where they are assured that emphasis will always be on improving the process and not on blaming the individual. Concentrate on the data or the facts of the process.

6. *Are employees able to make changes to the processes based on a systematic process for improvement?*

Once the processes have been defined and standardized, ensure that people have the right tools to do the job. Ensure they have a process to improve the process. It is important that employees know that they control their jobs, not that, their jobs control them.

7. *Is value-added work evenly distributed?*

Time is a funny thing. When left to our own devices, we have a tendency to fit the amount of work we have into the amount of time we have to do it. Most of us do not really know if we are being over or under worked. In reality, it is probably both. In a typical office some people will have piles of work on their desk, while others will have little or no work, but both "appear" busy. (This is true even if these individuals have the same job.) Also, some workers will have hundreds of emails to be reviewed, while others have just a few. The natural assumption is that the person with the piles of paper on his or her desk or those hundreds of emails is slow and inefficient while the other person with barely anything on his or her desk is extremely competent and efficient. In reality, probably neither is true. In fact, if you went back through the office a few hours later, you might even witness the opposite. By reducing process variation and establishing business rules (i.e., standards) for the work group or department, you can level the work load. Various software applications can be used to monitor and help ensure the work flows smoothly.

8. *Can workers be assured they are accessing and reading identical versions of business critical documents?*

Communicating effectively in today's office environment is a challenge. There are many CRM systems which help manage data. It is important that standards are created for these systems to ensure everyone is working on the right document at the right time.

Nothing is more frustrating that having team members working together on different versions of the same document. Such lack of predictability introduces errors and wasteful effort reconciling the differing versions.

3. Effective Meetings

Conducting effective meetings does not involve trial and error. The tools and techniques in this section are proven and effective. They have been used by numerous Fortune 500 corporations throughout the world. This chapter provides the necessary steps and guidelines for conducting effective meetings.

Definition of Effective Meetings

An effective meeting is an efficient use of people's time when they are gathered together (physically or virtually through a Web conferencing application) working to obtain a desired result. A meeting, like any process, can be studied and improved upon. A meeting is one process within the Lean Office.

But what makes a meeting effective? Through experience, Lean Offices have learned there are three keys to effective meetings:

1. Identifying clear objectives for meetings
2. Establishing rules and guidelines
3. Having total participation by everyone who must be present

Why Effective Meetings Are Important

Meetings can be one of the most powerful business tools, or one of the least powerful. Common complaints about meetings are that they:

- Accomplish nothing
- Last too long
- Are poorly organized
- Always begin late
- No one is in control
- Waste time because little "real" work is being done
- Are dominated by certain grandstanding workers
- Appear to have pre-arranged agendas and outcomes

However, people need to meet in order to benefit from the collective knowledge and experience of the group. While many decisions can be made by phone, email, or in the hallway, if management truly desires to maximize each person's contributions, all need to *meet* and interact. And, they need to meet effectively.

Effective meetings provide a forum to make necessary decisions and solve problems without wasting time. If meetings are effective, something positive will occur. They will produce a result. People will come on time, participate, offer information and ideas, and have a positive attitude.

It is critical that meetings be productive, enjoyable, and effective.

How to Implement Effective Meetings

To achieve effective meetings, treat them as processes, create standard rules to follow, and then adhere to those rules.

The basic rules for effective meetings are:

- Agree on a clear objective and agenda for the meeting
- Choose the right people for the meeting and notify everyone in advance
- Clarify roles and responsibilities for the meeting
- Adhere to meeting etiquette
- Take minutes and assign action items
- Draft the next agenda
- Evaluate the meeting
- Provide minutes to participants

Clear Objectives and Agenda

Each meeting must have clear objectives and an agenda. Objectives are what you will accomplish at the meeting. The agenda is how you will achieve the objectives.

Objective Type	Example
Awareness/Information	Review and discuss the 10 areas of waste and how they can be applied to sales ordering.
Skill Development	Learn how to update flowcharts when a process has been improved.
Process Implementation	Develop a new sales order form for processing new clients.
Review Responsibilities	Review measures for customer retention and action items from last week's meeting.
Problem Solving	Find the root cause of why 4 patients complained about the wait time for their surgery.

Objectives define the type of meeting to have. Common types of objectives are for:

- Providing awareness and information
- Developing skills
- Implementing a process or procedure
- Reviewing responsibilities and assignments
- Solving problems

Objectives must be brief and easy to read. At the end of the meeting it should be easy for the group to decide whether they achieved the objectives.

Agendas should include the following information:

- The agenda topics (including a statement that defines each item)
- The presenter of each topic
- A time allotted for each topic

Agendas usually include time for the following activities:

- Warm-ups (short activities used to get people focused)
- A quick review of objectives and agenda
- Scheduled breaks to respond to messages (email, text, phone, etc.)
- Review of action items from previous meetings

Advance Notification

Everyone must know what to expect before coming to a meeting. Be explicit about what will happen, how the meeting will be run, who is going to be in what role, and how long the meeting will last.

Within the Microsoft Office Enterprise system, the applications Outlook, Sharepoint Services, and Groove keep calendars, contacts, tasks, and events in sync. There are other applications that accomplish the same functions.

The Right People

The foundation of the Lean Office is waste elimination. That means the right people must attend the meeting to accomplish the objectives. If the right people are not in attendance, time and money are wasted.

How many meetings have been held without the right decision-maker, or without people with the facts? One of the following scenarios usually takes place:

- The group waits while someone searches for the right person to come to the meeting, if that person can even be found
- The group makes a poor decision and is overturned
- The right people for decision making are not in the room

To ensure the right people attend meetings, objectives must be clearly stated. Managers who have the authority to make decisions and who are rich in experience should be included in meetings. Most importantly, people who are closest to the facts should be present at the meeting.

Roles and Responsibilities

Each meeting should have at least six responsibilities assigned. They are: Team Champion, Team Leader, Facilitator, Timekeeper, Tech Rep, and Scribe.

The Team Champion is the person who has the authority to commit the necessary resources for the team. The Champion should "kick-off" the first meeting and then be updated regularly with Status Reports.

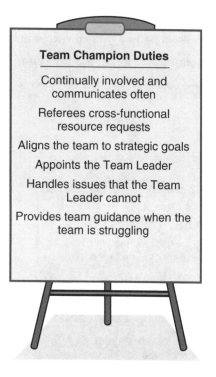

Team Champion Duties

Continually involved and communicates often

Referees cross-functional resource requests

Aligns the team to strategic goals

Appoints the Team Leader

Handles issues that the Team Leader cannot

Provides team guidance when the team is struggling

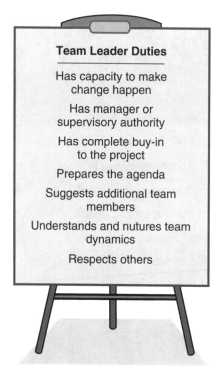

Team Leader Duties

Has capacity to make change happen

Has manager or supervisory authority

Has complete buy-in to the project

Prepares the agenda

Suggests additional team members

Understands and nutures team dynamics

Respects others

The Team Leader is usually the person who arranges for the meeting(s). The Team Leader is responsible for the day-to-day or week-to-week running of the team.

The Facilitator will play a valuable role when there have not been effective meetings in the past. The Facilitator should not have any vested interest in the project, one way or another - other than ensuring the meetings are effective.

Team Facilitator Duties

Keeps discussion focused on topic

Intervenes if multiple conversations are occurring

Prevents one person from dominating

Promotes interaction and participation

Brings discussions to a close

Guides the group in accordance with the charter and agenda

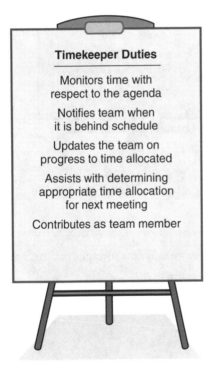

Timekeeper Duties

Monitors time with respect to the agenda

Notifies team when it is behind schedule

Updates the team on progress to time allocated

Assists with determining appropriate time allocation for next meeting

Contributes as team member

The Timekeeper is responsible for keeping the topics on the agenda on schedule, which allows everyone else to focus on issues, facts, and ideas. The Timekeeper can manage the process and agenda. This frees everyone else to produce results based on that agenda.

The Scribe records key subjects, the main points raised, decisions, and action items.
The Facilitator should not be the Scribe.

The Technical Representative (Tech Rep) is the person from IT (or someone with advanced computer application skills) who provides insights into technology tools available and makes the team aware of upcoming technology that may impact the team's mission. It is hard to imagine a meeting today without someone with these skills participating.

Tech Rep Duties

Suggests IT solutions

Trains team on new Desktop applications

Assists with data collection

Looks for ways to streamline all communications

Meeting Etiquette or Rules

Every company culture is different. Therefore, meeting etiquette or ground rules may vary from company to company. However, a few of the more important ground rules to establish are listed below:

Attendance. Management should place a high priority on meetings. They should define legitimate reasons for missing a meeting and establish a procedure to inform the Team Leader if a member cannot attend. The best way to ensure good attendance is to run effective meetings.

Timing. Meetings should begin and end on time. This avoids wasting time and makes it easier on everyone's schedule. Meetings are actually shorter when this rule is enforced. Each team should create specific ways to enforce this rule.

Participation. Every member can make a valuable contribution to the meeting. Emphasize the importance of speaking freely and listening attentively. If unequal participation is a problem, then the Team Facilitator can structure the meeting so that everyone participates.

Basic Courtesies. Everyone, regardless of job description, should use basic conversational courtesies. Listen to what people have to say, do not interrupt, have only one conversation at a time, and respect others.

Breaks and Interruptions. Decide when breaks for phone calls and other interruptions are allowed, and when they are not. Also, decide if text messaging is allowed during the meeting.

Other ground rules. Decide on other ground rules that seem appropriate. For example, what kind of humor is acceptable? What kind of language? What is OK to talk about and what is not?

It is suggested that meeting rules be created at the first meeting and made visible for each meeting thereafter.

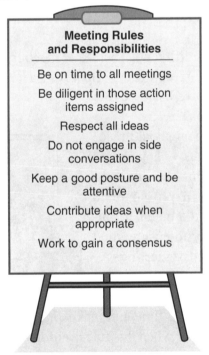

Meeting Rules and Responsibilities

Be on time to all meetings

Be diligent in those action items assigned

Respect all ideas

Do not engage in side conversations

Keep a good posture and be attentive

Contribute ideas when appropriate

Work to gain a consensus

Action Items

No meeting should end without action items. Action items designate who will be responsible for its accomplishment and when the action will be completed.

Drafting the Next Agenda

At the end of each meeting determine the objectives for the next meeting and draft a preliminary agenda. This should take only about five minutes and will save a great deal of "out-of-meeting" time.

Remote Meetings

There are numerous applications that will allow you to share information over the Web, commonly referred to as Remote Desktop Sharing. A version of this is referred to as Web conferencing which allows you to meet online rather than everyone meeting in a traditional conference room. Remote Desktop Sharing can also just mean simply sharing your (and/or your colleagues) Desktop screens. Some common Desktop sharing applications are: Google Docs, Cisco Webex, Gbidge, GoToMeeting, NetMeeting, and Microsoft SharedView, to name a few. Meetings using the Web can save time, resources, and money. Keep in mind the same principles apply whether you are meeting physically or remotely: establish rules and ensure everyone understands and adheres to them.

Meeting Evaluations

Always review and evaluate each meeting, even when other agenda items take longer than expected. The evaluation should include whether the objectives were achieved (and what helped or hindered that process) and what will be done to improve the meeting next time.

Effective Meeting Evaluation

Directions:
1. Spend only five minutes evaluating your meetings.
2. This form is most successful when everyone's responses are shared.
3. Focus on the weak spots, applaud the high ratings.

Rating System: 1 is the lowest score (Poor) and 5 is the highest (Excellent)

	Poor 1 2 3	Excellent 4 5	Score
1. How well did we stay on the agenda?			
2. Are we focusing on the right issues during the meeting?			
3. How well did we look for problems in the process, rather than the person?			
4. How well did we use our time?			
5. How well did we discuss information? How clearly? How accurately?			
6. How well did we all participate?			
7. Was the meeting effective?			
8. How was the pace, flow, and tone of the meeting? (Did we get bogged down or stuck?)			
9. How well did we respond to each other's questions and comments?			
10. In general, were all ideas explored to the extent possible given the time element?			
TOTAL:			
Please provide any other comments or suggestions for improvement.			

The next section provides the necessary forms to assist in developing the effective meeting process, for the Lean Office project.

4. Project Identification and Communication

Project Identification

The Management's Self-Assessment and the Predictable Output Survey generate insight into which area should be the focus of the Lean Office. If there still is some uncertainty, then use the following guidelines:

1. Select the area that will have the greatest impact on the strategic direction of the organization
2. Select the department that is constantly working overtime or constantly behind schedule
3. Select the area that has the most significant impact on the customer
4. Select the area that is shown to be less profitable

Many times the team or manager may require a more sophisticated method of determining the area in which to introduce the Lean Office. If this is the case, further explanation is contained in Chapter 4 - Beginning the Journey - Identifying and Mapping a Value Stream.

Once the project has been identified, proper communication must be developed to ensure alignment of all those connected to the project.

Project Communication

There are four forms utilized in the Lean Office to ensure the free flow of communications exists throughout the project. The four forms or tools are:

- Team Charter - defines mission and deliverables of the team
- Meeting Information Form - provides agenda, meeting minutes, and action items for the team
- Status Report - updates manager/champion on status of the team's progress
- Sunset Report - provides sharing of the team's successes and struggles to future Lean Office teams

Team Charter

Once the project area for the Lean Office implementation has been identified, at least initially, the manager should create a first draft of the Team Charter.

The Team Charter will then be reviewed, discussed, and a consensus will be reached at the first team meeting. The Team Charter has the following attributes:

1. It is the first important step in any Lean project. It ensures everyone is on the same page in reference to the team's mission, scope, and deliverables.

2. It is a living document and will change as conditions occur. It should be updated and posted in a common area.

3. The Team Charter will list the deliverables appropriate to the project.

4. Do not commit to something that is not realistic. Gain a consensus on the Charter from the team.

5. The Team Champion of the team will ensure proper resources are committed. The Champion usually does not attend all meetings. The Champion is available to remove roadblocks, commit necessary resources, provide encouragement, and break down departmental barriers.

6. The Team Leader will be responsible for the day-to-day or week-to-week activities. The Team Leader will schedule the meetings and inform the champion of problems and progress to date.

7. The Team Champion should review the Team Charter and agree to it prior to any resources being committed.

8. The Team Charter duration should be no longer than six months.

Team Charters come in all types and forms. Do not be concerned about how it is presented as much as ensuring everyone is aligned on the team goals and how they are to be accomplished.

Team Charter

Mission
What the team is to do.
How the team will complete its mission.

Deliverables
What specific outcomes can be expected.
What metrics will be used.

Expected Scope/Approach/Activities

Team Resources

Role	Name(s)	Participation Level
Team Leader		
Core Team Members		
Extended Team Members		
Facilitator		
Scribe		
Team Champion		
Steering Body Members		

Team Process

Process Item	Frequency	Audience/Distribution Day(s)/Time(s)
Information Distribution	After meetings	Team members, Team Champion
Team Meetings		
Status Reporting		

External Issues
Outside risks or events that may impact the team mission.

Internal Issues
Internal restraints or events that may impact the team mission.

LAN Location/Revision #   **Company Confidential**

Meeting Information Form

The Meeting Information Form provides the team with a structured approach to effective meetings, including detailed agendas and action items. Listed below are some basic principles that should be followed in regards to the Meeting Information Form:

1. Everyone at the meeting is aware of the agenda, times, and topics
2. Action items are assigned and reviewed at each meeting
3. Project milestones are tracked to ensure Lean project completion

The team leader the Lean Office project should complete a Meeting Information Form and distribute it before the first meeting. This will demonstrate the form in use.

Meeting Information Form

Logistics

Meeting Title:	January Monthly Employee Meeting
Date:	January 12th
Time:	1:00 pm to 2:30 pm
Place:	Learning Center
Purpose:	Review Monthly Measures and Introduce Lean Office plans

Distribution

Participants	Roles
John Wells	President
Gerry Garcia	Customer
Susan Turner	Marketing Director
Barbara Feldon	Training Manager
Chris Perry	Customer Svc. Manager

FYI Copies

Participants	Roles
All departmental heads - ensure all employees receive copy of agenda	Distribute information

Agenda

Time	Item	Who	Duration
1:00 pm	Year end goals, achievements, new goals, admin opportunities to excel	John	30m
1:30 pm	Customer expectations, growth opportunities	Susan	20m
1:50 pm	Newly formed partnership; opportunity for both	Susan	10m
2:00 pm	Pilot project for Lean Office	Chris	10m
2:10 pm	Lean Office training schedule, handout	Barbara	5m
2:15 pm	The Goal Card example and questions	John	15m

LAN Location/Revision #   **Company Confidential**

Status Reports

Status Reports are sent to the Team Champion to communicate the status of the project, that was defined in the Team Charter, on a regular basis.

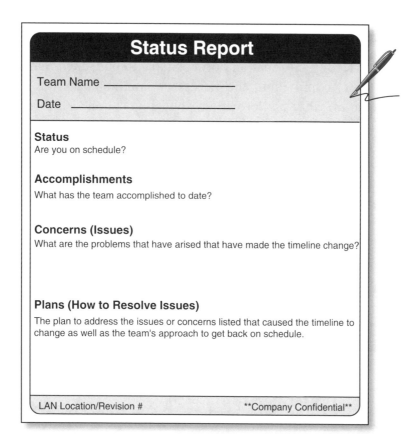

For every area identified as an issue or problem there needs to be a plan for resolution. This gives the Champion confidence that the team has control of the project.

The Sunset Report

Once the team has completed the project, the Sunset Report is the document that contains the knowledge the team gained. It will explain what went well, what tools were most useful, results, and what could have been improved. It is meant to be shared with others. The Team Leader normally fills out the Sunset Report.

Team Charters, Meeting Information Forms, Status Reports, and Sunset Reports are valuable tools in providing the necessary communication for the Lean Office to become a reality and provide a solid foundation. As Management's Role, Predictable Output, Effective Meetings, and Project Identification and Communication are understood, there must be a detailed road map for the Lean Office journey to begin.

5. The Lean Office Road Map

The Lean Office Road Map has three parts or phases for attaining the Lean Office. Each corresponds to a Lean Office milestone. Each part was designed for ease of understanding and practicality for implementation. We recommend you spend the time and thoroughly complete a significant portion of each part before proceeding onto the next one. A Readiness Guide has been provided at the end of each part to assist in determining if you are ready to move forward.

Part One - Getting Everyone Aligned and Started in the Right Direction

The concepts and tools will provide for the following:

- A basic reasoning and understanding of why the Lean Office is required to become a more competitive organization
- A solid foundation for why change must happen
- A basic understanding of waste
- An ability to communicate to ensure strategic alignment
- An effective structure to improve work behavior
- The guidelines to conducting an office kaizen event
- An ability to create a value stream and implement basic Lean Demand tools
- A smooth transition to Part Two

Part Two - Create the Structures Allowing Work Flow to Emerge

The concepts and tools will provide for the following:

- The necessary Lean technical tools to improve work flow
- A method to analyze work loads and level the work
- A standardized process to ensure predictable output
- A standard work process to cross-train employees
- A positive attitude that the Lean changes are effective and working
- A smooth transition to Part Three

Part Three - Sustain the Gains to World Class

The concepts and tools will provide for the following:

- Process control through visual standards
- Culture change to continuous improvement
- Coaching as a daily activity
- Metrics to show positive trends
- Visual controls and mistake proofing devices to ensure the process is error-free

Chapter Summary

This chapter focused on providing the necessary information and useful tools to assist in allowing people to "See the Challenge" that lies ahead. The most important aspect of this chapter is to ensure everyone has a basic level of understanding on the following:

1. Management's Role

Managers must look within their domain and what they currently know of the area before any project is defined. Managers must understand and be able to convey the importance of predictable output.
Tool utilized: Management Self-Assessment

2. Predictable Output

Work which produces repeatable results, based on a consistent process, yields customer satisfaction. Stated simply, this is the ability to complete work in a way that ensures the satisfaction of your customers' needs every time. Promotions, transfers, vacations, and retirements can compromise predictable output and lead to lost business opportunities.
Tool utilized: Predictable Output Survey

3. Effective Meetings

No Lean project will succeed unless rules are in place to assure team cooperation, attention to time, and meeting team member expectations.
Tool Utilized: Effective Meeting Evaluation Form

4. Project Identification and Communication

The Lean project or initiative must be relevant to the office area. Management must provide the necessary support and resources throughout the process.
Tools utilized: Team Charter, Meeting Information Form, Status Report, and Sunset Report

5. The Lean Office Road Map

A detailed road map ensures that a plan exists and provides guidance along the journey.
Tool utilized: Lean Office Road Map

Observations from the Lean Office

These observations may assist in understanding how to apply the concepts and tools contained in this chapter:

- Management must share concerns with the team and vice versa. Management must also realize that changing an area or process and implementing the Lean Office *may* require resources.

- Signs and poster boards posted in the area with examples of predictable output or listing the Ten Areas of Waste, along with specific organization goals, will assist in conveying Lean Office importance.

- Managers should not run meetings alone. It is difficult to run a fair, non-manipulative meeting with a manager running all parts of the meeting.

- One way to ensure that meetings are effective is to expect them to be so.

- Team Charters, Meeting Information Forms, Status Reports, and Sunset Reports should be mandatory. The forms should be posted in a central location of the area being improved.

- The Road Map helps to "see" what lies ahead. It can provide additional support for current activities - keeping the vision of the Lean Office in sight.

We have laid the groundwork in this chapter. Management's role has been defined, predictable output understood, effective meetings defined, project identification and communication reviewed, and the Road Map to a Lean Office explained.

Now it is time to *Begin the Journey*!

Application Case Study

As we have seen, Andrew Cencini, VP of Sales for Northwind Traders, a subsidiary of Global Winds, was put in charge by his manager, Kirk Keating, Executive VP of Sales and Marketing of Global Winds, to lead his office in becoming the first in the company to fully apply Lean Office principles. Andrew was confident of having a structured plan (i.e., the Lean Office Road Map) to guide him and his team along with way.

Every Northwind office employee had on their Desktops at each of their locations around the country various versions of Microsoft Office suite of applications, but they were due for an upgrade soon. Andrew decided it was important to have the upgrade completed prior to his team embarking on the Lean Office project. This would help ensure that added functionality would be available to support any Lean Office improvements when it came to file and folder communications, access, and sharing. The IT department installed Microsoft Office Enterprise 2007 for everyone. Other applications could have performed the same functions, but the Microsoft package had worked well for the organization and it was fairly easy for the team to learn any new applications and functions since they were already familiar with the core Microsoft platform.

Microsoft Enterprise 2007

Andrew felt it was critical to the success of the Lean Office project to show management's commitment to the team by providing the tools and training necessary. In fact, Al Gartner of the IT department, was assigned to support Andrew's team throughout this improvement project as their technical representative (tech rep).

The very first thing Andrew did, once the upgrade was complete and the team had the core training in the use of Microsoft 2007 Enterprise, was to set up effective meetings from the very start. The Enterprise application Groove is designed to support workers who need to share information and collaborate to manage projects, such as the Northwind Lean Office initiative. As described by Microsoft: "Your work in Groove is organized through workspaces that you and other people are members of. In a nutshell, a workspace provides access to information that teams need to share and tools teams need to collaborate in ideas, communicate with each other, and stay organized."

Some of the tools that are available when you set up or become a member of a workspace in Groove include the following:

- Document collaboration tools used to share files and keep files updated
- Discussion tools that let team members conduct online conversations
- Meetings and calendar tools that can advise a team of milestones, meeting times and purposes, and updates
- Custom forms that teams use to collect information in a structured format
- Indicators that tell you who is working in a workspace and whether a team member or contact is online

Other benefits of Groove are:

- Create a Groove workspace right on your computer with two clicks
- Invite your colleagues, partners, and customers without worrying about networks or servers
- Add tools to support your team's evolving needs: file-sharing, discussions, meetings, business forms, and more

Al helped Andrew set up the first meeting using Groove. The following screen shot is the view of using Microsoft Office Groove for the meeting under the Profile tab.

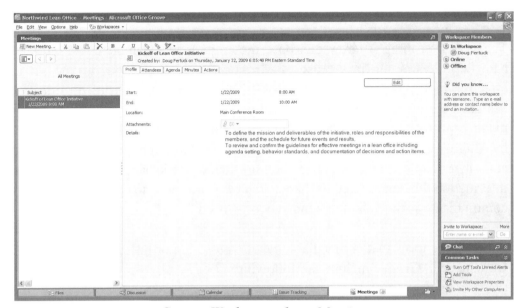

Groove Workspace for a Meeting

Note that this window has tabs near the top for this particular meeting including Attendees, Agenda, Minutes, and Actions. That same information for previous meetings can be quickly accessed by clicking on them in the left pane under All Meetings. Other workspace information can be accessed via the tabs along the bottom including Files, (past) Discussions, (team) Calendar, and Issue Tracking. With all this organized information available at all times to all team members, many sources of inefficiency and waste are eliminated and the best practices for running effective meetings, as described in this section, are fully supported.

Andrew knew that using Groove would get the team off to a great start!

Note: Similar functions can also be done in MS Office 2003 and Windows 7.

Chapter 4

Beginning the Journey

This is the Road Less Traveled

Chapter Overview

Beginning the Journey will require everyone to do some things differently. It *will be* the way of the future. This is the beginning of the process in which the knowledge of the organization is captured and retained. It is not about having people "tic-mark" everything they do. It is about establishing a process that identifies what everyone is working on while identifying waste and bringing everyone's attention to the importance of organizational time. This chapter will also assist to identify best practices, understand how team dynamics work, and provide a tool to document current and future process states.

Beginning the Journey contains four sections: A Solid Start, Getting a Snapshot, Identifying and Mapping a Value Stream, and Problem Solving Made Simple.

1. A Solid Start

There are four stages of team development which every team member must understand. Team members must understand how to minimize the inherent stresses that are involved in the teaming process. Tool Utilized: Understanding Team Dynamics

2. Getting a Snapshot

A snapshot shows a moment in time. The snapshot shows the condition of the department, area, or value stream as it exists currently. It provides a reference point for the team to review and begin to see how work can be improved. The snapshot captures what everyone is currently working on - both the value-added and non value-added activities.

Tools Utilized: Process Capture Form, Interruption and Random Arrival Log, Call Log, and Proof of Need Survey

3. Identifying and Mapping a Value Stream

It is critical to identify processes relative to the customer. This section will have the team understand the qualities of a value stream, as well as how to visually represent the information and work flow. This representation will help you to identify where wastes lie and how Lean tools can eliminate many of those wastes. Identifying and mapping an administrative value stream can be a challenge, but can be accomplished by following the basic guidelines defined in this part.

Tools Utilized: Work Flow Analysis and Value Stream Mapping

4. Problem Solving Made Simple

At the beginning of any Lean Office initiative there may be some issues that need to be addressed. Perhaps there was another project that had not been completed. To get beyond a relatively straightforward issue or problem, simple problem solving may be required to resolve those issues such that they will not interfere with the implementation of the Lean Office.

Tool Utilized: Problem Solving Storyboard

1. A Solid Start

As with any new team or initiative, it is imperative that all those involved in the change contribute their ideas. As new skills are learned, they must be adapted to the particular administrative function or process. This cannot be done in isolation; therefore, a concerted effort must be made to elicit new ideas from the people who are working the processes everyday.

Ideas to Involve Others

Often a group or team will be comprised of people who struggle with group participation. This may occur for some of the following reasons:

- Previous ideas were shot down or not acknowledged
- Previous ideas were acknowledged as good, but that is as far as it went
- Strong managerial control precluded input from the employees
- Fear of public or group speaking
- People taking credit for the ideas of others
- Fear of job loss by improving the processes

For success to occur, everyone must feel free to contribute. Using Lean tools in an office environment will require adaptation and creativity. People must understand the tools as well as have a desire to apply them in their area. By using the Team Charter, and more specifically the Meeting Information Form, the team will begin to see that things are being conducted differently than previously. Attitudes about participation will become more positive. The following are suggestions of how to involve everyone:

- Rotate the functions of the facilitator, scribe, timekeeper, and any other functions among the team members, whenever practical
- Train and practice proper brainstorming techniques
- Constantly communicate that the Lean Office is about improving processes, not eliminating people
- Acknowledge that the Lean Office is a new start for improvement ideas
- The Team Champion should visit the area frequently to recognize progress and lend active support
- Post all communications and documents on Groove Workspace (or equivalent) so that all team members can access them at all times

If, for some reason, an employee refuses to participate, attempt the following:

- Assign the hesitant participant to a more active role
- Have the manager or Champion privately discuss the employee's concerns
- Have the manager or Champion continue to coach the individual in accordance with human resource policies

The Lean Office will not solve all organizational problems. What it can and will do is provide the necessary tools to ensure that proper, waste-free work behavior prevails. As employees experience more waste-free work, which reduces their work load and stress, they will begin to desire this in all their processes and work assignments. Others will begin to model their behavior.

Parking Lot Issues

The Team Charter is meant to keep the team focused on the mission. Many times there will be recommendations that are beyond the scope of the Charter. If this occurs, ensure that the ideas are captured in a Parking Lot list and revisited at a future time. The Parking Lot list can be included in the Action Items section of the Meeting Information Form (i.e.,Groove Workspace or equivalent). If suggestions from the team will improve other areas or processes, the team leader should forward (or post) those ideas to the appropriate manager.

Team Dynamics

The Lean Office cannot be sustained if proper teaming is not followed. Understanding the basics of team dynamics will enhance the entire process by recognizing some basic dos and don'ts about working in groups.

The four stages of team development are:

Stage 1. Forming or Getting Started
Stage 2. Storming or Going in Circles
Stage 3. Norming or Staying on Course
Stage 4. Performing or Full Speed Ahead

Stage 1. Forming or Getting Started

The Forming stage of teaming consists of reviewing the Team Charter, establishing team roles, determining meeting times, and ensuring the right members are on the team.

This is the stage where team members may experience difficulties in transitioning from working as individuals to contributing as team members. There is excitement, anticipation, and optimism. There is also the pride a member feels that he or she has been chosen. The "flip-side" are feelings of suspicion, fear, and anxiety about what is to come. The most important point for this stage, as it will be for all the stages, is to utilize the Team Charter, Meeting Information Form, and Status Report (or information that is posted on the Groove Workspace).

Additional points to consider at this initial stage are:

- Clearly define roles and reach a consensus on all decisions
- Rotate team member roles
- Conduct training activities on teaming or have some members attend a teaming workshop or seminar
- Establish team ground rules and distribute with the Meeting Information Form before and after each meeting (and post on the Groove Workspace)

Forming can last from the initial meeting through the next 4-6 meetings. The Team Leader can remain in control by conducting effective meetings, using proper communications, and respecting team members' ideas.

Stage 2. Storming or Going in Circles

At this stage the team members begin to realize the task is different and more difficult than they first imagined. Impatience about the lack of progress and inexperience on group dynamics may have some team members wondering about the entire project. Also, the team may experience some of the following:

- Continuing to rely on their personal experience of team projects and resisting collaboration
- Arguing among members even when they agree on the real issue
- Being defensive and competitive
- Acknowledging initial goals are unrealistic and voicing concerns about excessive work loads

This stage can be difficult for any team. Teams that do not understand and acknowledge the four stages - especially this stage - most likely will disband.

To get through this stage utilize some of the following ideas:

- Acknowledge the four stages with the team constantly
- Communicate to the team that disagreements are part of the teaming process
- Focus on the team goal
- Acknowledge progress to date
- Request a facilitator to assist with team meetings

- Conduct a round table discussion to get things out in the open
- Always focus on the process, not people or personalities
- Review team norms and standards before each meeting
- Assure that the Team Charter, Issues Tracking (i.e., Action Items), and meeting information details are always up-to-date on Groove Workspace. Demonstrating discipline and attention to detail in this will set the standard for the team for the whole project.
- Request that the Team Champion speak to the team regularly (and comment on something positive that the team is doing)
- If open resistance by one or two individuals creates an uncomfortable atmosphere for the team, a private meeting about this behavior with those individuals will need to be held (avoiding conflict does not work – address it forthrightly and fairly)

With all these issues, many team members may lose the initial burst of excitement and energy. Acknowledge this to the team and slowly focus on what can be done, by whom, and when. This stage may exist for 2-4 meetings, but should quickly be addressed as to not affect the integrity of the entire Lean Office initiative.

Stage 3. Norming or Staying on Course

At this stage, team members accept the team concept. The Team Ground Rules are being adhered to, communication is occurring without disruptions, and visible progress is being made toward the objective. At this stage, everyone feels that the team concept is working. Everyone is contributing in a positive way.

The team may also be doing some of the following:

- Expressing criticism constructively
- Attempting to achieve harmony by avoiding conflict
- Being friendlier during the team meetings
- Confiding in each other
- Exhibiting a sense of team togetherness and common spirit

This stage may exist for the next 2-6 meetings. Communications through the Meeting Information Forms, Status Reports, (Groove Workspace) and giving positive reinforcement will allow the team to progress to Stage 4 and not fall back to Stage 2.

Stage 4. Performing or Full Speed Ahead

By the time this stage has been reached the team can begin to diagnose and solve problems with relative ease. This stage includes:

- Making constructive self-changes
- Achieving project milestones earlier than anticipated
- Coaching by team members in a support role

Teaming in and by itself can be difficult. Utilizing the structured forms (Team Charter, Meeting Information Form, Status Report, and Sunset Report) through your communication channels whether by email, paper-based, or Microsoft Groove will assist greatly in allowing the team to progress through the various stages without a major impact on the overall project. Use these forms throughout your department and organization - not just for the Lean Office project!

2. Getting a Snapshot

Getting a Snapshot is a critical step in establishing a Lean Office after team dynamics are understood. This section initiates awareness in people to the value of time in an organization. It is the responsibility of the manager or supervisor to introduce and explain the significance of the snapshot. It will require office employees to participate by collecting relevant data. Once the data is collected it will then clearly identify what the employees are doing at their desks or work areas.

The purpose of the Snapshot is to:

- Bring attention to time as it relates to the organization
- Involve everyone in collecting relevant data
- Reinforce with everyone the need for improvement
- Begin to share organizational knowledge

The benefits of obtaining the Snapshot will be:

- Increased employee focus and productivity
- Improved quality of the work being performed
- Reduced stress

The information collected in this section will be analyzed to possibly re-define, modify, or update the team's mission and deliverables through the Team Charter (as discussed in the previous chapter). Remember, the Team Charter is a living document and should change as new data or facts are gathered.

To conduct the Snapshot, use a simple Excel spreadsheet to capture, analyze, and report the following:

The Process Capture Form (or Table)
  Use an Excel worksheet to document current work processes and activities for the first month of the Lean Office.

The Interruption and Random Arrival Log

Record in another Excel worksheet how often work is interrupted as it is being processed and who is doing the interrupting. Use this for the first month of the Lean Office, then at six month intervals.

The Call Log

Set up another Excel worksheet to capture all telephone and/or email transactions. Use this in all phases of the Lean Office and only do for a certain period of time to capture what employees are doing with their time. It is meant to ensure employees are working on what they should be.

The Proof of Need Survey

This is meant to increase awareness that standards, process controls, and continuous improvement methods can be improved. Use this during the first week of committing to the Lean Office.

These tools are designed to capture current processes and activities that fill employees' time. They also will create an awareness of organizational time as interruptions that inhibit process work flow are identified.

The Process Capture Form (or Table)

The Process Capture Form is to be filled out by each individual in the group or department. No exceptions. Therefore, managers and supervisors must also be practicing what they preach. The form is meant to capture the processes, not the individual tasks. The form should be used for 30 days to capture what is currently going on and what processes are consuming employees' time. The processes should be categorized as critical or non-critical.

Critical Process

Critical processes are those processes that directly impact the customer or that have a direct financial impact on the organization. The following are some examples of critical processes:

- Entering a customer order
- Invoicing a customer
- Treating a patient
- Transferring money by wire
- Providing information to a customer
- Providing a service at point-of-sale

Non-Critical Processes

Non-critical processes are those processes that are necessary, but do not have an immediate impact on the customer or the financial impact on the organization. Classifying these will provide a solid foundation of process information required prior to the introduction and application of the Lean Office tools. The following are some examples of non-critical processes:

- Obtaining a credit report
- Filling out insurance papers
- Conducting a performance review
- Preparing a budget report
- Attending meetings

- Generating a quote
- Preparing a month-end report
- Ordering/searching for supplies
- Conducting marketing research
- Sorting emails

Use the following form as an example to capture current processes. Brainstorm with the team to generate a list of common processes for the department or the specific value stream (see next section - Identifying and Mapping a Value Stream). This will allow everyone to begin to think in terms of processes. You will most likely not be able to list all the processes, but list as many as possible and leave space on the form for additional (i.e., not commonly used) processes.

Process Capture Form

Name_____ Date_____

Department_____ Job Title or Function_____

Process Name	Date	Critical (C)	Non-Critical (NC)	Upstream Source (supplier)	Downstream Source (customer)

List the processes in the left margin of the Process Capture Form along with the upstream and downstream links. The team can identify the process as critical or non-critical at a team meeting. Use the Process Capture Form for at least one month.

Experience has shown that confusion can exist between defining a process and a task. In the initial stages of the Lean Office do not get too hung up on the difference. Later in this book those will be further classified. At this time, it is only important to document current segments (processes or tasks) of employees' time that comprise their day.

The following process and task definition and examples will assist in providing a framework for understanding the basic difference between a process and a task.

A process is a series of tasks (or steps) required to complete a unit of work or obtain a result. Previous examples of processes were entering a customer order, obtaining a credit report, etc.

Each of these processes are comprised of numerous tasks that lead to the completion of those processes. *A task is a unit of work within a process. Many tasks are required to complete a process.* For example, entering a customer order is comprised of the following individual *tasks* for a customer service representative:

1. Obtaining a customer ID from the database
2. Entering a customer order (each entry into the computer could also be considered a task)
3. Emailing a customer order acknowledgment
4. Updating internal records as to order completion or status
5. Notifying the customer of the shipment date
6. Generating an invoice
7. Sending the invoice to receivables

The Emergency Room triage nurse may perform the following individual *tasks* associated with admitting a patient to ER:

1. Determining the source of pain or discomfort
2. Inquiring about the cause of pain or discomfort
3. Obtaining patient history
4. Obtaining vitals (blood pressure, heart rate, breathing, etc.)
5. Notifying the physician on duty
6. Preparing the patient for physician arrival (gowns, etc.)

Remember, employees will be new at this and most likely there will be a mix of processes and activities (tasks) listed. Work with the team to further define the differences once the initial processes have been gathered. Some tips on creating and using the Process Capture Form are:

- The team may brainstorm on one person's work to create a first pass on what his or her processes and tasks are
- The supervisor or manager may visit each team member and coach him or her regarding how to use the form
- The supervisor or manager may want to provide an initial process list to the team

When filling out the Process Capture Form, it may be helpful to further identify if the process is Generalist Based or Specialist Based.

Generalist Based functions are processes that are written and detailed to the extent that a new person could complete the process with minimal or no supervision. These would include having available: standardized work, flowcharts, visuals, etc. for the process ensuring no deviation from the original process intent.

Specialist Based functions are processes that have minimal or no written detailed information that would allow a new person to complete the process without considerable supervision. Having someone else perform one of these processes would cause deviation from the original process intent. (e.g., if the employee is gone, his/her work cannot be completed). Processes like this are typical of many administrative procedures. The Lean Office will move an organization from Specialist Based to Generalist Based process control.

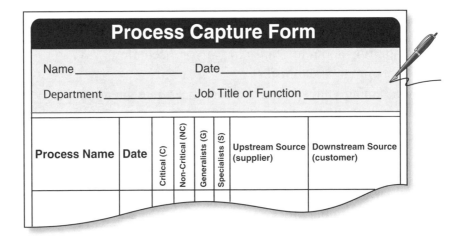

Process Capture Form

Name_____ Date_____

Department_____ Job Title or Function_____

Process Name	Date	Critical (C)	Non-Critical (NC)	Generalists (G)	Specialists (S)	Upstream Source (supplier)	Downstream Source (customer)

It is important to identify whether processes are Specialist Based or Generalist Based. Even though many, if not all, processes have some form of written documentation contained in a quality or service standards manual, they typically are for auditing purposes only. As non-Lean processes are identified, further investigation and focus will drive these processes out of the manuals and into real-time, process control that represents the work being done or service being provided.

The Process Capture Form does not reflect actual process cycle times (cycle time: the time element that comprises a set of tasks or the rate of the process). (See Chapter 8, Cycle Time, pages 249-250 for a detailed explanation of cycle time.) The Process Capture Form is meant to be a high-level analysis of the current work processes.

The Interruption and Random Arrival Log

The purpose of the Interruption and Random Arrival Log is to identify the interruptions occurring throughout the day that prevent someone from working on a process. Almost every time there is an interruption, some type of waste will be generated. An example when an interruption would not be a waste would be when a new customer was calling into the customer service department.

An interruption is defined as a break upon an act in progress. The Interruption and Random Arrival Log will identify how much time is lost out of the day from that "act." It will also identify the following:

- How often interruptions impede work flow
- How much time is consumed or lost when the interruptions occur
- Who or what interrupted the work

It must be noted that although we stress focusing on the process and not the person for all continuous improvement initiatives, here we need to identify the person who is doing the interrupting. (If the process associated with that person can be clearly identified and linked back, be sure to note it.)

Interruption and Random Arrival Log

Name _____   Month _____

Department _____   Job Title or Function _____

No.	Date	Start Time	End Time	Name	Discussion Topic
1					
2					
3					
4					

Interruptions impede process work flow. Interruptions are unanticipated when they occur and many times will affect the quality of work being interrupted. Once a process or job has begun, and is interrupted, many things can occur. Some of these are:

- Having to repeat previous tasks to get back to where you were
- Making a mistake in a hurry to complete the process
- Having a diminished sense of task or process accomplishment

Interruptions are often referred to as Random Arrivals because they are never anticipated. The employee will not have a process for this interruption; therefore, the work flow is upset and chaos can result. This results in wasted time and resources.

Random Arrival	+	Random Reaction	=	Chaos
(External to Process)	+	(No Process)	=	Waste all around

The Lean Office system works to control everything within a work area to ensure interruptions or random arrivals do not occur. Interruptions may very well be required (value-added), but they should be dealt with within a system of control. Again, common sense must prevail when creating a Lean Office. For example, a doctor conducting a yearly physical exam for a patient should be interrupted during the exam if a patient with cardiac symptoms of distress has entered the clinic. Even though both may have been identified as critical processes, this "random arrival" demands a common sense decision. All industries have similar situations.

Logging the interruptions, by person and by topic, may seem strong, but a case must be made for organizational time. When manufacturing a part, the raw material has an inventory carrying cost, throughout all processing, until it is sold. The longer it resides within the walls of the plant, the less profit the part generates. So too with administrative work. The more work that resides or "sits" in an office or on a desk, the more it costs the company. The Interruption Log will start to create a discipline and, most importantly, an awareness of how critical time is to an organization. If someone is telling each person throughout the day about the movie he or she saw recently, it will show up on the Interruption Log. The manager should review the log and take appropriate action.

Complete the Interruption and Random Arrival Log for one month. This will generate the snapshot data required to further focus the team. The Interruption and Random Arrival Log then should be used for a week every six months to reinforce the importance of organizational time.

There is no winner when routine interruptions occur. All tasks or processes are affected by random arrivals. They are unavoidable. Identify, contain, and schedule the company-specific interruptions within a controlled environment (Lean Office system) such that these interruptions occur less frequently, and that when they do occur, there are standards in place to address them.

The Call Log

The Process Capture Form and the Interruption and Random Arrival Log are to be used for the first month of the Lean Office implementation. The Call Log will be an on-going log that is to be used daily. It is used to capture telephone, fax, and email transactions. The Call Log is a valuable tool for improving overall communications within the department and with customers.

How many times do you write down on a memo sheet some information received over the phone or contained within an email? Once this is written down, it is most likely put aside for later action, then to find out:

- The memo slip has been misplaced
- The number or name on the sheet cannot be read
- The email was opened early that day and now you need to go back to get more information from it
- The customer must re-submit the request because it was not filed properly

All these can be eliminated by recording such transactions into the Call Log.

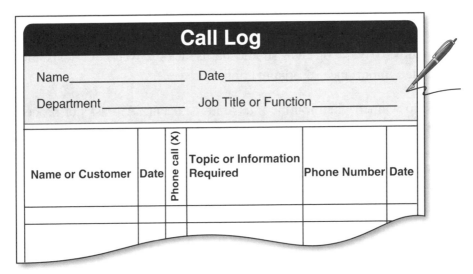

The Call Log is meant to accomplish the following:

1. Ensure standardized recording of information. Each desk or employee will adhere to the Call Log. The Call Log should be located where it is immediately accessible for the employee.

2. Improve customer satisfaction. This initiates the Generalist type of process to be documented. If someone is out of their area, and the customer calls, you can refer to the Call Log and continue the request. This will allow employees to share basic information.

3. Ensure commitments are kept. At the end of the day, a quick look at the Call Log will indicate what may need to be completed.

4. Provide for quick retrieval of information. This will eliminate the need for searching for that memo.

Experience has shown that the Call Log will reflect over 80% of the actual time a person spends on the phone or responding to emails for company business. Be satisfied with the 80%, for you will most likely never achieve 100% compliance.

The Proof of Need Survey

The Proof of Need Survey is an integration of the Management Self-Assessment and the Predictable Output Survey that was discussed in the previous chapter. This survey will continue to enlighten and reinforce employees on the idea that change is required. The survey is meant to reveal that standards, process controls, and continuous improvement methods are essential for the organization to become more competitive.

The survey should be distributed to everyone in the area after the initial Lean Office project meeting. This will give employees an understanding of why change must occur. The supervisor/manager (i.e., the team leader for the Lean Office project) should collect the survey and consolidate the answers. At the next meeting the results should be shared and discussed with the team.

Proof of Need Survey

If you respond NO to any of these, then the Lean Office is needed.
The Lean Office will allow you to reduce costs, improve customer satisfaction, and improve employee well-being, while increasing office productivity.

	YES	NO
1. I know the standards of service expected within my area.	❏	❏
2. I work little or no overtime.	❏	❏
3. Someone not familiar with my work can easily do my job with little or no training due to the availability of well documented processes.	❏	❏
4. When there is an influx of work, I can easily adapt and get it done.	❏	❏
5. The processes I work on are well documented and updated within 30 days of a change.	❏	❏
6. The standards and methods for my processes have been made as a visual aid.	❏	❏
7. The stress level for me is low.	❏	❏
8. There is a systematic process for improving a standard or process.	❏	❏
9. The work loads are evenly distributed.	❏	❏
10. Temporary help is not assigned when I am absent or on leave.	❏	❏

The answer of "No" to any of these indicates a non-Lean situation exists. A "Yes" implies that Lean principles may be at work.

Use this survey as a reference to confirm what the Management Self-Assessment and the Predictable Output Survey revealed. Have an open discussion with the team regarding all the information collected. This will help to ensure alignment on the Lean Office direction and set the stage for creating an open dialogue regarding the upcoming changes in the Lean Office.

The Process Capture Form, Intervention and Random Arrival Log, Call Log, and Proof of Need Survey are used to collect general process information. Further process analysis of the area must now be conducted by creating a current state value stream map.

3. Identifying and Mapping a Value Stream

Depending on the size of the organization, number of employees in a department, number of customers, number of parts/services that are being sold, or number of clients or patients being affected, it may be important to get an overall map of the area which requires improvement. While data is being collected, selected team members should create a current state value stream map.

A value stream is defined as the actions (both value-added and non value-added) that are necessary to deliver a product or service to a customer. A value stream may include a single process or a linked series of processes. It is a visual representation of the information and work required to meet a customer demand. It typically would connect the customer (internal or external) through multiple processes within an organization.

A stream is the flow of water from a spring that meanders down through various land formations to the ocean (or sea). For the Lean Office, a stream is a flow of work from an upstream process (the request from a customer or supplier of service or "spring") to the downstream process (the work or service delivered to the customer or "ocean").

Most rivers have bends and other hindrances that cause the water to not flow smoothly. Offices also have hindrances, such as:

- Seniority issues
- Lack of vision or purpose
- Fear of change
- Job security issues
- Financial constraints
- Departmental (functional) silos
- Government regulations

- Uneven work loads
- Non-standard work processes
- Cost of new technology
- Lack of application knowledge
- Lack of document/file control
- Legal constraints
- Safety concerns

These hindrances in offices may be non value-added activities. It is the goal of the Lean Office to eliminate these activities or office wastes and provide to the customer only what he or she is willing to pay for, the value-added activities. This in turn produces a smooth work flow with no hindrances.

Value is something the customer is willing to pay for. Non value-added is what the customer will not want to pay for. Both are identified on a value stream map with the ultimate goal of eliminating the non value-added work (or waste). The ultimate goal of the Lean Office is to identify and eliminate anything that adds no value for the customer. Lean tools will make this happen.

Identifying a Value Stream

There are a variety of methods by which you can identify a value stream. The most common are:

1. Work Flow Analysis
2. Work Volume
3. Business Conditions
4. Customer Concerns or Mandates

1. Work Flow Analysis

By creating a simple matrix or chart in Excel displaying which work units share common processes, a value stream will be identified. *A **work unit** is a predefined amount of material, information, or service capacity that will flow through a process or between processes.*

To create a Work Flow Analysis, follow these steps:

1. List the customers on the left. These customers would have been documented in the Team Charter.
2. Next to the customers, list volume, total sales, number of patients/clients, etc. for each type of customer over a given period of time. If available, use a minimum of three months of data. Six months to a year would be ideal.
3. Across the top of the chart list the processes in sequence that involve all the customers listed in (1) above.

4. Identify all processes that are specific to each customer.

		Process A	Process B	Process C	Process D
V..	Mission/Sales/Year	Customer Service	Order Fulfillment	Manufacturing	Shipping
Dom : Sales	30	X	X	X	X
Interna. ..l Sales	20		X		X
Aftermark. ˈales	10			X	X

	Patients/Mc ..ly Avg.	·sician ·ferral	Admissions	Prep	Procedure
Radiology	30	X	X	X	X
OB/GYN	20		X	X	X
Ortho	10	X	X	X	X

	Volume$/Mission/Sales/Year	Cred. Check	rocess·	Loan Application	Closing
30-Year Fixed	10	X			X
Refinance	4	X			X
Second Mortgage	3	X		X	X

	Volume$/Mission/Sales/Year	Quoting	Project Planning Board	.hasing	Esti.. r
Government	8	X	X	X	X
Commercial	4	X		X	X
Residential	4	X		X	X

5. Group all customers by those that have identical processes.

		Process A	Process B	Process C	Process D
	Patients/Monthly Avg.	Physician Referral	Admissions	Prep	Procedure
Radiology	30	X	X	X	X
Ortho	10	X	X	X	X
OB/GYN	20		X	X	X

For example, Radiology and Ortho have common processes. These would be identified as the value stream in which to use the Lean tools. OB/GYN would also be a separate value stream because the patient would not have to go through the Physician Referral process.

Improving multiple value streams for an initial Lean Office project is not recommended. See the case study at the end of this Chapter for an example of using Excel to create and analyze a Work Flow Analysis table.

2. Work Volume

List the customers by a quantity (i.e., yearly sales, total patient load, etc.). Domestic and International sales represent over 80% of the total sales in the example below. This would be the value stream if total sales (work volume) were the determining factor. Aftermarket sales would be a separate value stream.

	Volume$/Mission/Sales/Year	**Process A** Customer Service	**Process B** Order Fulfillment	**Process C** Manufacturing	**Process D** Shipping
Domestic Sales	30	X	X	X	X
International Sales	20		X		X
Aftermarket Sales	10			X	X

3. Business Conditions

In today's competitive business climate, with technology and communications playing a major role, it is imperative that organizations continually strive to be the best. Constant attention must be given to the competition. If competition has created a product or service that may decrease a company's market share, then the company would need to identify a new value stream in which to compete.

4. Customer Concerns or Mandates

Many times a customer will request or mandate for a product or service to be improved. This external customer request would have those processes connected as a value stream. These would take precedence over all other methods of selecting a value stream.

Mapping a Value Stream

The goal of value stream mapping is to obtain a high-level, visual representation of a specific set of processes as defined previously.

A value stream map does the following:

- Creates a common visual for everyone to be on the same page
- Provides a visual map for ease of process understanding and communications
- Allows everyone to "see" areas of waste
- Provides the foundation on which to base Lean initiatives from the customer perspective

Do not use value stream mapping exclusively as a management tool. Ensure value stream maps are posted in common areas for increased awareness as improvements are made. Update them as necessary. Value stream maps should be posted next to the Team Charter along with any additional information relative to the Lean project.

Value stream mapping is of two types: current and future state. Current state maps provide a visual representation of the way information and work flow is occurring at the present time. The future state map is the application of the Lean tools as a visual road map displaying how to eliminate the waste identified in the current state. Create the initial maps on a whiteboard or flip chart.

The Current State Map

Value stream mapping begins with creating the current state and proceeds according to the following steps:

1. Use icons to draw a "shell" of the current state, listing the main processes, customers, and suppliers (internal and external).

 Dedicated Process Box - the main process or area where value-added and/or non value-added work occurs (order processing, order quoting, title search, customer credit history, subcontractor's agreements, prepping the OR cart, etc.)

 Shared Process Box - where multiple value streams all interrelate (mail rooms, human resources, banks, admissions, etc.)

 Attribute Area Box - characteristics of the process (cycle times of individual tasks, number of people, internal defects, etc.)

 Truck Shipment - denotes the physical surface arrival or departure of work related to the value stream

 Plane Shipment - denotes the physical airborne arrival or departure of work related to the value stream

 Database Interaction - computer interaction (EDI, e-commerce, email, Web interaction)

 Queue Time - the amount of time, work or information that resides between two processes within the value stream

 Manual Information Flow - physical conveyance of work between two processes within the value stream (hand carrying work to another area or person, courier delivering work to another process)

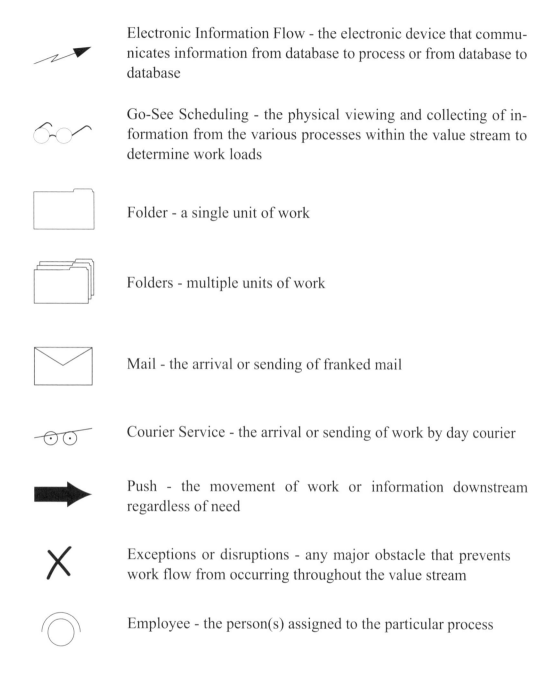

Electronic Information Flow - the electronic device that communicates information from database to process or from database to database

Go-See Scheduling - the physical viewing and collecting of information from the various processes within the value stream to determine work loads

Folder - a single unit of work

Folders - multiple units of work

Mail - the arrival or sending of franked mail

Courier Service - the arrival or sending of work by day courier

Push - the movement of work or information downstream regardless of need

Exceptions or disruptions - any major obstacle that prevents work flow from occurring throughout the value stream

Employee - the person(s) assigned to the particular process

2. Visit the areas, beginning with the most downstream process, and collect the attributes related to the value stream. Gather actual data, use a stopwatch, if practical, and clearly communicate to everyone in the area what you are doing and why.
3. Determine the amount of time that work sits idle between processes.
4. Determine the amount of work that arrives at each process.
5. Determine what is done with the work after each process is completed.
6. List all the attributes on the current state map.
7. Draw all forms of communication, electronic, and manual.
8. Total the process cycle times within the process box. This is typically the value-added time.

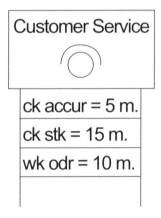

The total value-added time for this process is 30 minutes (10 + 15 + 5).

When drawing a value stream map for the first time, do not concern yourself with whether the main category is a process or department. Work with the team and ensure the main element is the queue time that would separate them.

9. Compile a step graph at the bottom of the value stream map displaying the total cycle time for each process, including the queue time between processes.

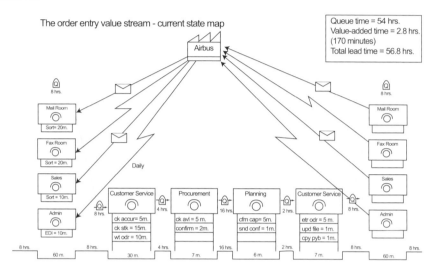

The map should convey the total lead time and total queue time, along with any other key metrics that the team has found to be significant.

Once the current state map has been created, ensure a consensus is reached by all team members regarding its representation. If additional data is required, obtain it at this time. The basis for creating a doable future state map depends on the accuracy of information obtained and displayed on the current state map.

The Future State Map

The future state value stream map is a visual representation of the application of the various Lean tools. It is created by:

- Arriving at a consensus
- Brainstorming
- Problem solving
- Testing tools for practicality and use
- Resource availability

The future state value stream map will never be implemented all at once. It is meant to be adopted over a time period (i.e., six to eighteen months). The following icons can be used to create the future state value stream map.

These icons will again be presented in Part Two, Create the Structures Allowing Work Flow to Emerge, when all basic Lean tools and concepts have been thoroughly explained. These are presented here to have you start thinking in Lean terms.

Buffer Resources - temporary resources to assist work flow when there is a sudden influx of customer demand (temp employees, volunteers, overtime, retirees, cross-training, etc.)

Safety Resources - temporary resources to assist work flow when there are internal issues such as turnover, illness, vacation, etc. (temp employees, volunteers, overtime, retirees, cross-training, etc.)

Cart - a device used to distribute work units throughout the value stream

Kanban - work unit(s) for delivery to a process

Supermarket - a physical location located between two processes to hold work until it is required downstream

U-Shaped Work Area - the arrangement of desks, office computers, fax machines, copiers, etc. to accommodate efficient work flow

Pull - the representation of work being requested from a downstream process

Max = XX

FIFO - a physical location located between processes to hold work sequentially for the downstream process

XOXO

Heijunka Box - a physical device or location used to hold or convey work requirements based on volume and variety

Runner's Route - the route the runner will use to deliver and pick up work (kanbans) throughout the day

Pitch Board - the physical device used to hold work based on volume

Kaizen Focus (improvement activity) - a focused group that improves specific value stream areas within a specified time

The overall goal of creating a value stream map is to clearly identify where waste lies and what Lean tools can be used for its elimination. Future state maps will require numerous iterations as progress is made and will change as team members continually learn from their Lean implementation experiences. The future state map, similar to the Team Charter, is a living document, and will reflect all changes as they occur or are projected to occur.

Process Mapping

Process mapping is another effective (and at many times more practical) tool to visually represent a value stream or process in an administrative environment. When creating a process map, the project team should tackle the activity as if it were doing an investigation: find out exactly what is occurring and what is and is not happening in the process. If a true value stream cannot be identified due to the variability within the processes (many conditions having to be met) then process mapping would be a tool to use. Follow the same steps as in value stream mapping when creating a current and/or future state process map.

The following symbols can be used for creating a process map:

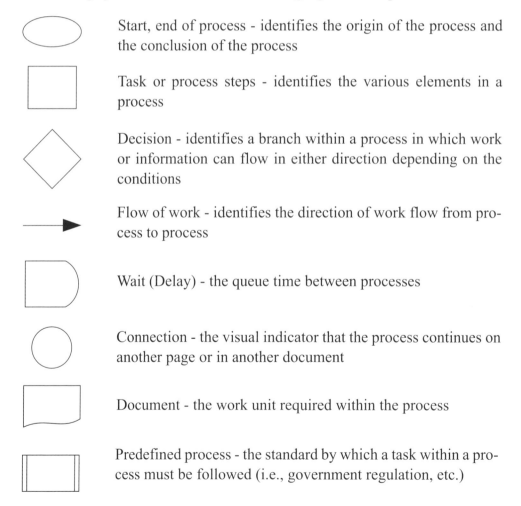

Start, end of process - identifies the origin of the process and the conclusion of the process

Task or process steps - identifies the various elements in a process

Decision - identifies a branch within a process in which work or information can flow in either direction depending on the conditions

Flow of work - identifies the direction of work flow from process to process

Wait (Delay) - the queue time between processes

Connection - the visual indicator that the process continues on another page or in another document

Document - the work unit required within the process

Predefined process - the standard by which a task within a process must be followed (i.e., government regulation, etc.)

The following are examples of process maps.

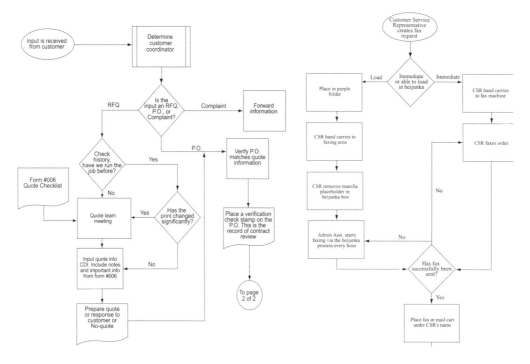

Also, process maps can be simplified (graphically illustrated) to convey what is happening in the process.

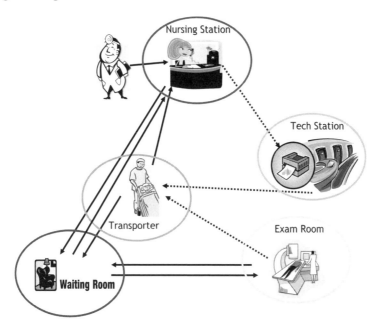

The following is a comparison chart between value stream mapping and process mapping. Microsoft Visio is an excellent application for creating both value stream and process maps and is covered in the case study at the end of this chapter as well as in the Appendix.

Value Stream Mapping	Process Mapping
Makes the waste and source visible	Makes waste visible, can show source by identifying function
New Icons	Familiar flowchart
Fairly new tool	Commonly used to analyze business processes
Requires repeatable sequential processes	Can be done with repetitive or non-repetitive processes
Common process driven	Task/activity driven
How value is created	How the work flows

The goal of creating a value stream or process map is to clearly identify where waste lies and to obtain an accurate portrayal of current work conditions. This is the basis on which the future state will be created. Often, some basic issues arise once the current state value stream map is created. Also, there may be times, for a variety of reasons, that current state mapping may need to be postponed due to the identification of an issue or problem. In that case, address the issue or problem using the following problem solving methodology. Six Sigma, a sophisticated problem solving methodology, can also be used. (See Appendix C)

4. Problem Solving Made Simple

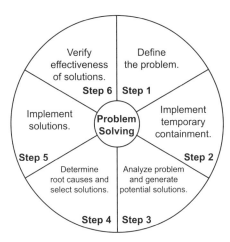

Problem solving is the process or system used to permanently resolve undesirable process variations or conditions. By definition, a "problem" exists when a process that has been producing acceptable results begins producing unacceptable results. When using Lean tools and concepts within a problem solving methodology, greater improvements can be achieved.

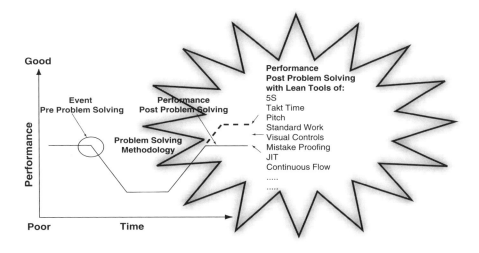

There are several systematic problem solving methodologies that work well. Most are similar and have the following steps:

1. Define the problem.
2. Implement temporary containment.
3. Analyze the problem and generate the potential solutions.
4. Determine the root causes and select the solutions.
5. Implement the solutions.
6. Verify the effectiveness of the solutions.

The six step method described here has several advantages:

*   It is simple
*   It can be used by individuals or teams
*   It can be used at all levels of the organization
*   It provides a common language and approach

1. Define the problem.

This is the most crucial step and should not be rushed. The more specifically defined the problem is, the more likely the solution(s) will be effective. When conducting this step, approach it as follows:

a. Write a statement describing the problem. A good problem statement describes a situation both in terms of your own experience and in measurable terms.

b. The statement should be:
    *   Specific - What is it, and what is it not? How big is the problem?
    *   Time-bound - When did it first appear? How was it first identified? Are other events happening at the same time?
    *   Current - What is the present trend? Is it increasing, decreasing, or unchanging?

The following Is/Is Not form can be used to guide the team in problem identification.

IS/IS NOT

Symptom _____ Date Opened _____

Problem Description_____

Is/Is Not Questions	IS	IS NOT	Deductions About Facts		
			Differences	Changes	Date
What Object					
Where Seen on object					
When First seen When else seen					
How Large How many objects have defects					
Trend Increasing or decreasing over time					

2. Implement temporary containment.

This step is to take the necessary actions to ensure the customer does not experience any of the effects of the problem. It is often a band-aid until a permanent solution can be applied.

3. Analyze the problem and generate the potential solutions.

Use the following Quality Improvement tools to further analyze the problem. These have been found to be the most applicable in solving problems in administrative areas. These 10 tools are:

- 5-Whys
- Pareto Charts
- Histograms
- Scatter and Concentration Plots
- Storyboards
- Process Mapping (previously covered in value stream mapping)
- Frequency Charts and Check Sheets
- Cause & Effect (or Fishbone) Diags.
- Control Charts
- Brainstorming

Many of these tools may also be used in determining the root causes. The following briefly describes each of these tools and provides examples of each.

5-Whys

Symptoms are the apparent indicators that a problem exists. The symptoms are not the problem. Ask "Why?" are the symptoms showing.

Statement of the Problem: too many customers are not receiving exactly what they had ordered.

Why?
Because customer service does not know the exact inventory level.

Why?
The logistics system is 2-3 days behind the actual.

Why?
The information being entered is not entered daily.

Why?
It is always batched to be done twice a week.

Why?
No one has notified the logistics department to request daily or hourly entries.

Frequency Charts and Check Sheets

Frequency Charts and Check Sheets are used to collect, organize, prioritize, and analyze data. They can be used to answer the question, "How often is an event occurring?" They help to "see" the variations in a process.

Frequency Chart		
#	Orders/department	Frequency
1	domestic - fax	|
2	international - fax	||
3	domestic - internet	|||
4	international - internet	||| |
5	domestic - phone	⌗⌗ ||
6	international - phone	|||
7	internal org.	|

Cause and Effect (or Fishbone) Diagrams

Cause and Effect Diagrams are used to clearly show the various factors affecting a process. The problem or effect is on the right and possible causes are listed on the left. If done properly and completely, the cause of the problem appears somewhere in the diagram.

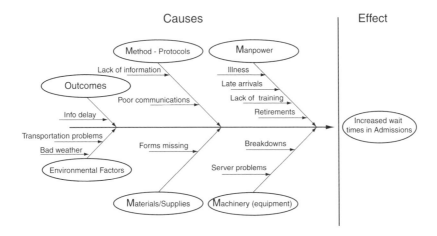

Pareto Charts

The Pareto Chart is a type of bar chart. Issues are listed in descending order of frequency or importance. These charts help to prioritize and break down complex problems into smaller chunks. They also help to identify multiple root causes.

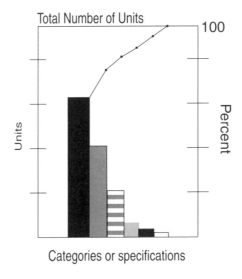

Histograms

Histograms use data to display the spread and shape of the distribution. They are a simple, graphical representation of the dimensional performance for a sample of data. Histograms are a "picture" of sample data.

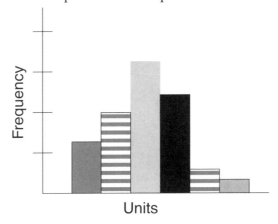

Control Charts

Control Charts are basically line graphs taken over time. The vertical axis contains dimensions or other measures and specification limits. The horizontal axis indicates a specific time interval. They are useful for tracking progress over time.

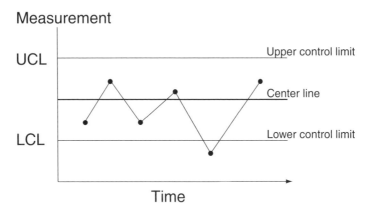

Scatter and Concentration Plots

Scatter and Concentration Plots are used to study the possible relationship between one variable and another. Through visual examination and additional mathematical analysis, relationships between variables can be determined, (e.g., correlation).

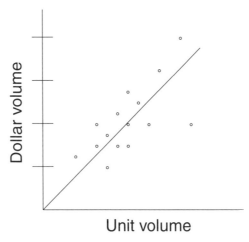

Brainstorming

Brainstorming is used to capture people's ideas and organize those thoughts around common themes. Begin with a topic, then get as many ideas as possible within a 15 minute time period. Use a consensus of the team to prioritize. Do not criticize any idea during the brainstorming session.

Storyboards

Storyboards are graphical representations of a common theme. They are meant to tell a story visually. Teams should be creative and have fun in creating a problem solving or Lean storyboard.

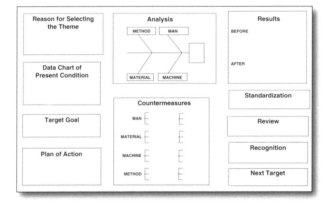

4. Determine the root causes and select the solutions.

In determining a root cause, gather sufficient data to ensure that the most effective solutions will be evident. When identifying the root cause and selecting the permanent corrective action, clarify the constraints that might apply to the solutions (i.e., approvals required, timing, capital, impact on other departments, people, etc.). Do not improve one process at the expense of another.

When determining the root cause and developing a list of solutions, use the following list of questions to guide you through the process:

- Is there a better way to do things?
- Can the root cause(s) be eliminated?
- Can negative forces be minimized?
- Can positive forces be strengthened?
- Have you explored all possible scenarios?
- Have you involved others to get different perspectives - technical experts, customers, clients, etc.?
- Have all consequences of the solution been identified and controlled?

5. Implement the solutions.

The team should agree on the action plan to implement the selected solutions. This should be specific as to who will perform the necessary steps, when, and how. Agreement must involve key decision makers on the circumstances under which implementation will take place. All people who will be impacted by the implementation of the solution should be made aware of any changes. Progress must be monitored and measured against the implementation plan.

6. Verify the effectiveness of the solutions.

Use a monitoring system to determine progress towards solving the problem. The following questions and recommendations serve as a guide in this process:

- Has the problem been eliminated?

- Has the root cause been found and solved? If so, prepare a work instruction or other documentation to standardize the solution.

- Check to see if other areas of the organization can benefit from the solution through communication in the newsletter, monthly meeting, internet site, etc.

- If the problem has not been corrected or you have not correctly identified the root cause, return to Step 1. Learn from what you have done.

The key benefits of this six step method are as followed:

- Facilitates a full analysis of the problem or issue
- Stops a team or individual from jumping to conclusions
- Encourages teams to draw upon the skills, experience, and creativity of team members where appropriate, and draw upon outside resources when needed
- Forces a planned implementation schedule to evaluate solutions, and then "lock-in" the improvements or solutions

Most failures in problem solving are due to improper identification of the root cause. The root cause may have been improperly identified or the wrong solution may have been chosen and applied.

Perform these steps in sequence. World-class organizations have a proven process for problem solving and it is used at all levels. Individuals and teams must be trained in using a problem solving process. Problem solvers must be given sufficient time to solve problems.

Use the following Problem Solving Storyboard form as a visual aid to complete each step.

Problem Solving Storyboard

Department _____   **Start Date** _____

Team Name	Team Members

1. Define the problem. SYMPTOM	2. Implement temporary containment.

3. Analyze the problem and generate potential solutions.

Phase Completion Date: _____

4. Determine root causes and select the solutions.

CAUSE

Phase Completion Date: _____

5. Implement the solutions. REMEDY	6. Verify the effectiveness of the solutions. P A D C Phase Completion Date: _____

The following chart is a summary of the various problem solving tools. It is by no means all-inclusive, but can serve as a catalyst for the initial Lean problem solving teams.

Tools	Applications
1. Is/Is Not Analysis	Defining the problem
2. 5-Whys	Defining the problem - finding the root cause
3. Process Maps	Establishing control - finding deviations
4. Frequency Charts and Check Sheets	Gathering data - establishing control
5. Cause & Effect	Developing root cause - gaining consensus
6. Histograms	Identifying the problem - gathering data
7. Control Charts	Gathering data - holding the gains
8. Pareto Charts	Identifying the problem - finding root cause
9. Scatter Diagrams	Identifying the problem - developing solutions
10. Brainstorming & Storyboarding	Generating ideas - developing solutions - finding root cause

Chapter Summary

This chapter focused on providing the necessary information and useful tools to help teams "Begin the Journey." The most important aspect of this chapter is to ensure that everyone has a basic understanding of these four sections.

1. A Solid Start
Teaming is a critical component of any Lean initiative. Understanding the stages of team development by learning some of the characteristics of those stages will assist teams along the way.

2. Getting a Snapshot
The Snapshot introduced various forms that the Lean project team should use to analyze processes at a higher level. It is important to identify how much time is being spent on interruptions. Interruptions are waste.

3. Identifying and Mapping a Value Stream
Use a detailed road map to "see" where waste occurs. Use the Lean tools to eliminate waste. There are two types of value stream maps: the current state and the future state. Process mapping can also be used if processes are not sequentially linked.

4. Problem Solving Made Simple
It is important to solve problems that may impact a Lean team's project. Teams should utilize the six step problem solving model or a similar problem solving model to ensure root causes are found and eliminated so as to not hinder any Lean initiatives.

Observations from the Lean Office

These observations may assist in understanding how to apply the concepts and tools contained in this chapter:

- Be as specific as possible with everyone's role. If an area has been defined for the first project, communicate to everyone in the department what the project is about. Since most employees will likely be involved in a similar project in the future, it will provide a meaningful introduction to their future.

- Do not underestimate the importance of the Team Charter, Meeting Information Form, and Status and Sunset Reports. They are proven, effective, and easy-to-understand project communication tools.

- Use the Lean Office Road Map as a visual tool to help employees "see" the course that lies ahead. Use value stream or process mapping to obtain an accurate current state. Describe the time and dedication required by the employees involved. They need to realize that change is the "name of the exercise." Reinforce that the Lean Office journey will be accomplished with small, incremental steps.

- Inform employees that collecting data for the Office Snapshot will help them understand what is occurring in their department. It will assist in reducing the stress level that may be present.

- Emphasize the importance of the project's success to the organization.

- Be sensitive to the employees' aversion to change. Empathize with them, but stay true to the course. Do not make exceptions to the Process Capture Form, Interruption and Random Arrival Log, Call Log, or Proof of Need Survey.

- Ideas will flow when you work with the team and achieve a consensus on improvements. Use the Parking Lot concept to document the ideas outside the scope of the project. Stay focused with the Team Charter.

- Positive behavior and attitude demonstrated by team members should be acknowledged and recognized.

- Understand team dynamics. Be positive. Every team experiences the four stages of team development.

Listen to the team members' concerns. Incorporate their ideas into improvement initiatives as much as possible. Every office is unique and some adaptation will be required.

The foundation has been created by applying the tools explained in this chapter. The next chapter will focus the team on specific Lean tools to meet customer demand.

Application Case Study

Andrew Cencini led the Northwind office team in getting started on the journey to the Lean Office. At this data gathering stage, the various Microsoft Office applications provide the necessary tools to gather and analyze their data.

The Process Capture phase is critical to the launch of the project. Again, Andrew and team decided, because of its flexibility, to set up a simple Access database to capture and manage the team's process definitions. Note that in Access, each column is automatically set up with a drop-down menu populated with previous entries for that column; this feature helps eliminate errors of data entry (waste!) and incorrect spelling. The team brainstormed, using the group communications tools of Groove and came up with the processes captured in Access as shown in the following screen shot.

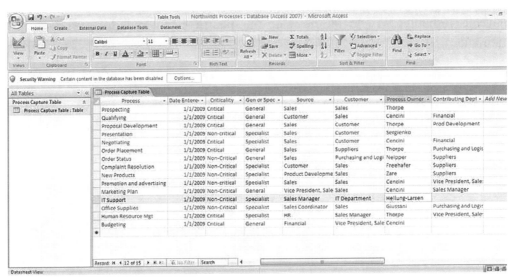

Access Table of Northwind's Processes

It is easy to add additional fields. For example, Northwinds added Process Owner, Customer (i.e., downstream process), Source (i.e., upstream process), etc. This Process Capture Form (or Table) can also be expanded and used later to further document and define the appropriate processes in greater detail.

The Call Log described earlier in this chapter is straightforward for manually documenting and analyzing phone calls, but for emails, Outlook itself provides the tools necessary for categorizing and organizing emails for consistent access and action. A team of employees can quickly establish general guidelines for individual and group files and directories (folders). The team and management can also define access rights so all can view the appropriate files and emails of co-workers. Finally, email directories/folders can also be standardized so that all employees can quickly scan their emails and move each email into one of the suggested folder names:

1. Inbox: Leave emails in the Inbox that can be closed out with an immediate, quick response within the current work session.
2. Work Organization Folder: "Action for expected business, respond within 24 hours". Immediate response is not required, but responsive action is still necessary.
3. Work Organization Folder: "Action for interruption, respond within 24 hours". Immediate action is required, but use this folder to capture work requirements that are outside of a normal process.
4. Non-Action Folders: Set up as many folders as necessary by project, contact, subject, etc. for those messages that are for information and reference only (otherwise, delete them).
5. Reading Folder: For items, not urgent, that require significant time to study and read.
6. Waiting Folder: For emails that require action from others before a response can be completed.

Note that by establishing an Interruption Folder, unanticipated Random Arrivals will be automatically segregated and collected to be addressed systematically as the Lean Office is implemented. The screen shot on the following page shows how an Outlook Navigation Menu for Mail Folders was set up at Northwind Traders according to the suggestions above. In Outlook, each office member easily exported the contents of the Interruption Folder to the office server where the Interruption messages of the other team members were aggregated. This provided a comprehensive listing of all the disruptive email messages coming into the Northwind office.

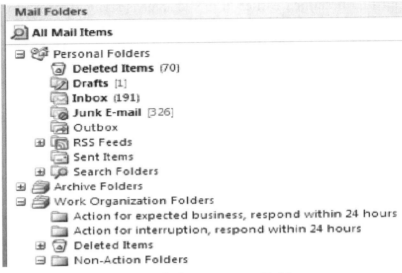

Outlook Work Organization Folders

Excel can be used to set up Northwind's Work Flow Analysis Matrix to show sales by customer (e.g., Acme, Alpha Always, etc.) and by work process (e.g., Prospecting, Personal Sales, etc.) as shown below. Once a similar-type spreadsheet is set up, it is also easy to add other fields, such as product category and sales location to enhance the usefulness of the data analysis tools (i.e., chart functions) within Excel.

Customer Name	Product Name	Sales	Year	Month	Category	State	Prospecting	Pers Sale	Web Sale	Serv	Order	Ship UPS	Ship Other
Acme	Crab Meat	$736,000.00	2006	May	Canned Meat	WA	X	X		X	X	X	
Alpha Always	Beer	$1,400,000.00	2006	January	Beverages	NV	X		X	X	X		X
Alpha Always	Dried Plums	$105,000.00	2006	January	Dried Fruit & Nuts	NV	X		X	X	X	X	
Begin the Beguine	Coffee	$13,800,000.00	2006	March	Beverages	TN	X	X		X	X		X
Begin the Beguine	Clam Chowder	$482,050.00	2006	April	Soups	TN	X	X		X	X		X
Begin the Beguine	Crab Meat	$920,000.00	2006	April	Canned Meat	TN	X	X		X	X		X
Begin the Beguine	Coffee	$230,000.00	2006	June	Beverages	TN	X	X		X	X		X
Cinderella Imports	Clam Chowder	$1,930,000.00	2006	February	Soups	CA	X		X	X	X	X	
Cinderella Imports	Syrup	$500,000.00	2006	April	Condiments	CA	X		X	X	X	X	
Cinderella Imports	Curry Sauce	$120,000.00	2006	April	Sauces	CA	X		X	X	X	X	
CC's Ready Market	Chocolate	$127,500.00	2006	February	Candy	CO	X	X		X	X	X	
CC's Ready Market	Beer	$1,218,000.00	2006	April	Beverages	CO	X	X		X	X	X	X
CC's Ready Market	Fruit Cocktail	$1,560,000.00	2006	June	Canned Fruit & Vegetables	CO	X	X		X	X	X	
Davenport	Dried Pears	$300,000.00	2006	January	Dried Fruit & Nuts	NY	X		X	X	X	X	
Davenport	Dried Apples	$530,000.00	2006	January	Dried Fruit & Nuts	NY	X		X	X	X	X	
Davenport	Dried Plums	$35,000.00	2006	January	Dried Fruit & Nuts	NY	X		X	X	X	X	
Davenport	Chocolate Biscuits Mix	$184,000.00	2006	February	Baked Goods & Mixes	NY	X		X	X	X	X	
Davenport	Marmalade	$3,240,000.00	2006	April	Jams, Preserves	NY	X		X	X	X	X	
Davenport	Long Grain Rice	$280,000.00	2006	April	Grains	NY	X	X		X	X	X	

Work Flow Analysis Matrix

Once the matrix is set up, it can be enhanced using the Pivot Table function in Excel to summarize the information into the listing of those customers to show the total number of times each process is applied and to analyze those companies using the same processes as shown in the following screen shot. Since each customer was involved with the Count of Prospecting field, the team determined that this would be the value stream for Northwind's first Lean Office project.

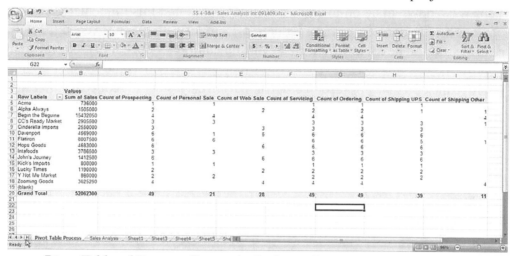

Pivot Table of Process Counts in Defining Prospecting Value Stream

Another great tool to use at the beginning of the Lean Office journey is the value stream mapping capability of Microsoft Office Visio, the flexible diagramming application that is part of the Office family of products. The screen shot on the next page shows Northwind's Prospecting Value Stream. It was generated and mapped in Visio. Visio provides literally thousands of shapes with the capability to connect them in various ways with relevant information allowing for a comprehensive visual document. With a little training and practice, the processes of any office environment can be modeled, documented and optimized using this tool.

Note: Step-by-step instructions for creating a value stream map in Visio can be found in Appendix D beginning on page 372.

Note: Microsoft Excel can also be used to create a basic value stream map.

The team listed the main processes comprising the Prospecting Value Stream as shown below. They broke down the process into five steps ending at "Commitment to Buy." Also, they indicated on the map that not all steps are completed for every prospect, hence the probabilities of proceeding to the next step listed (XX%) at every Wait Time. For example, only 20% of prospects contacted agreed to be interviewed in the Needs Assessment step. The Wait Time between steps was known to be on-average a full day, 24 hours; this immediately was an obvious area to pursue for waste reduction. Similarly, the Value-Added times for each step would be investigated closely using additional Lean tools for efficiency improvements. It is easy to see how this map can be used as the starting point to improve the efficiency of resources spent during each step, to reduce waiting time between subprocesses, and to address how to improve the probabilities of moving the prospect on to the next step.

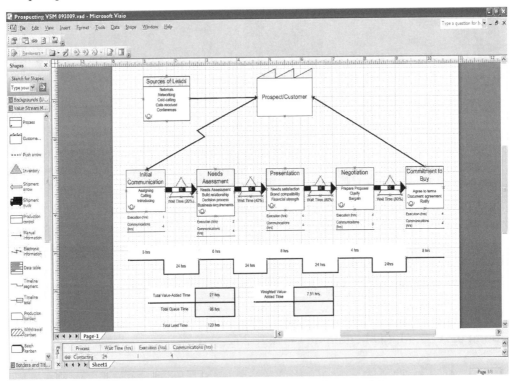

Northwind's Prospecting Value Stream Map

The following screen shot is a larger image of the previously shown value stream map.

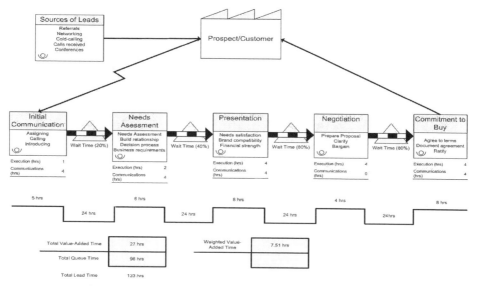

Northwind's Prospecting Value Stream Map (Larger View)

Notice that under each step in the process is shown the time spent in executing that step and the time spent in communication. These two categories can be broken down further as appropriate. For example, under Negotiation, the 4 hours spent on Execution could be broken down into sub-steps, such as:

- Searching for templates or comparable documents
- Entering customer data and requirements
- Developing a pricing proposal
- Reviewing the proposal with finance and management
- Editing and proofing the final document

Opportunities to eliminate waste may emerge from analyzing the more detailed breakdown.

Note: Teams should use the tools as they and their management see fit to identify and understand opportunities for improvement.

Visio can also be used to construct more simple flowcharts and process maps which are valuable in arriving at a common understanding of how work is done and in tackling how to eliminate waste in the processes. The following screen shot shows the flowchart that the Northwind team created to break down the first sub-process of Initial Communication on the value stream map. Again, diagrams such as this can be easily produced and manipulated in Visio to provide insight into how work is really being done.

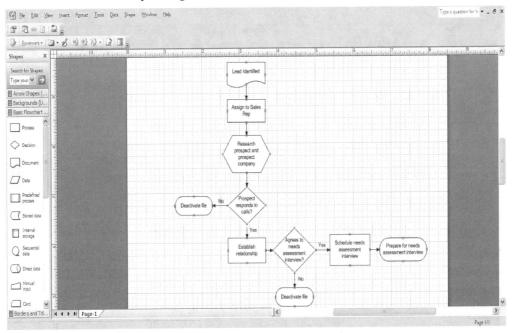

Initial Communication Flowchart

By developing this flowchart, the team surprised themselves by gaining a greater understanding of the importance of properly researching the prospect to help establish an effective relationship before attempting to schedule an assessment interview. These steps came out of comparing the various current methods being used by the team members and documenting the best practices in the final process flowchart.

Andrew and team used these applications and tools to document the status of existing processes, but doing so also made the information visible and easy to understand. Further, the charts would be available to the entire team at any time, with the capability to be updated easily as improvements were to be made. By keeping such documents always available to the team via Groove, no time will be wasted looking for or disputing the latest versions.

A number of templates and built-in capabilities in the Office Suite exist to support several of the problem solving tools identified in this chapter. For example:

- Cause and Effect (or Fishbone) diagram: Visio. The following screen shot shows a breakdown of the causes for prospects not returning or accepting calls during the Initial Communication state of the Prospecting Value Stream. This analysis may suggest some practices Northwind might use to overcome these obstacles and increase the interview rate.

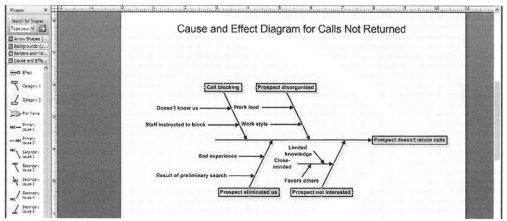

Example of Fishbone Diagram of Why Calls Are Not Being Returned

- Histograms and Pareto Charts: Excel. As shown, the team put together a Pareto Chart of the reasons as to why they lost sales at the last Commitment to Buy stage. They were surprised at the results once they looked at the data, particularly by how frequently it was that poorly understood requirements (Poor Reqt's) cost them business. Based on this finding, the team identified a need to make sure that the Interviewing subprocess be designed to always address more in-depth the specific requirements of the prospect.

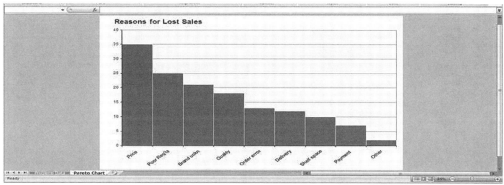

Pareto Chart of Reasons for Lost Sales at End of Prospecting Process

- Scatter Diagrams: Excel. In this case the team thought it might be useful to look at the relationship between the list price of the products and the total sales of each product. The reason they thought this was important is that it would suggest which products, and therefore which leads, should be the highest priority in the Initial Communication process. A Scatter Diagram is useful for this. First, the team open an Excel report showing list price and sales by product as shown below. Notice that the data is very difficult to interpret in this form.

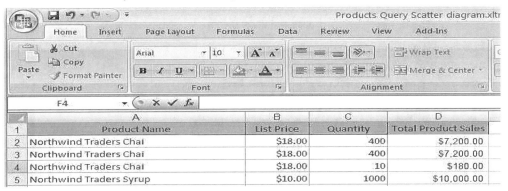

Excel Spreadsheet of Scatter Diagram Data

Then the team created a Scatter Diagram in Excel (one of the available features in Excel 2007 and Windows 7) using the two columns of data for List Price and Total Product Sales. The result showed an apparent sweet spot for sales of products in the $25 to $40 range. This phenomenon was to be further studied to lend insight to the other sales outside of the $25 to $40 range. Understanding this phenomenon may increase the overall probability of the proposed sale proceeding to the next step for all products.

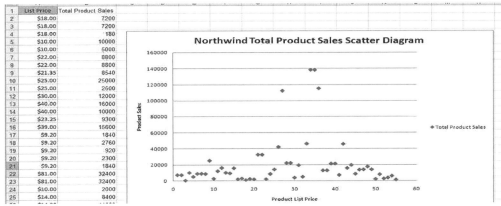

Scatter Diagram of Product Sales by Product Price

- Brainstorming/Mind Mapping: Visio. The team brainstormed all of their sources of leads and prospects for feeding (indirectly) into the Initial Communication process and captured them quickly and in free flow on a mind map in Visio as shown below. Such documents are meant to be quickly produced and unfinished at first so that connections and relationships can be quickly written down by the team and then sorted and prioritized later for more careful analysis.

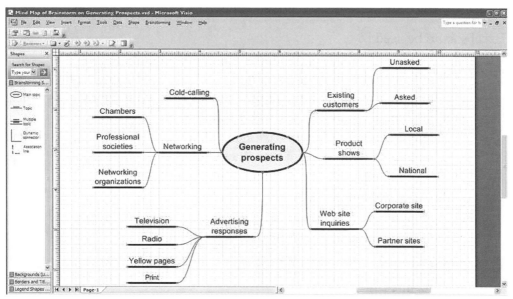

Using Mind Mapping to Organize Brainstorming

Pencil and paper work just fine for some things like gathering data for check sheets. But when the right Desktop application and/or tool is used for the job, it can eliminate the potential wastes of motion, overprocessing, and people's time.

Note: Two of the most widely used applications to create a value stream map are MS Excel and MS Visio. Both have easy-to-use features to quickly and effectively create a value stream map. You may find that MS has bundled both applications into your office software.

Creating a value stream map in Excel or Visio will be determined by several factors. These factors are driven by the limited drawing capabilities of Excel, and the considerable and advanced drawing capabilities of Visio.

Excel should be used if:
- There are a limited (5-10) number of process boxes
- It is a single function value-stream (within the same department)
- There are a minimal number of data sets (e.g. cycle times, wait times, First Time Right (FTR) or quality measures)
- There a limited volume/throughput of work (i.e., documents, orders, applications, etc.) through the value stream
- Limited number of process owners and stakeholders
- It is a repeatable process
- A step graph is required that will sum up total cycle times and queue times from process boxes (using Excel formulas)

Visio should be used if:
- It requires 10+ process boxes
- There are more complex, cross-functional and cross-boundary (with suppliers/customers) value streams
- There are complex data sets (e.g. cycle times, wait times, First Time Right (FTR) or quality measures)
- There is a high volume throughput of work (i.e., documents, orders, applications, etc.), high value ($)
- There are numerous process owners with multiple lines of reporting up the chain of command
- It is a process with a high degree of individual discretion (i.e., decision-making)

Whichever method you use to create a value stream map, ensure the data that is used to populate it is a good representation (i.e., appropriate sample size) of the process.

Note: There are numerous other value stream mapping applications available for purchase.

Chapter 5

Understanding and Deploying the Demand Tools

Always Keeping the Customer in Mind

Chapter Overview

The information up to now provided the following:

- A foundation for understanding Lean - Chapter 1: A History of Lean - Brief
- The ground work required to implement a Lean Office - Chapter 2: Five Enablers for the Implementation of Lean
- The organization's method of communicating the need for change - Chapter 3: Seeing the Challenge
- An understanding of the importance of organizational process knowledge, along with the need for problem solving and the ability to create a value stream map - Chapter 4: Beginning the Journey

The tools described in this chapter will allow the team to continue to build upon the foundation created from the other chapters with the application of basic Lean tools.

The Customer Demand Tools

This chapter introduces Lean tools that will analyze customer demand and how that demand can be met. Lean tools will be used and applied to the current state value stream map. This will allow the current state value stream map to be transformed into a future state value stream map for the Demand Phase only. The future state value stream map will be the road map for the Lean Office.

The tools utilized in the Demand Phase are:

1. Initial 5S
  The improvement process to ensure everything has a place and everything is in its place.
2. Takt Time
  A measure corresponding to customer demand that determines how fast a process or area must work to meet that demand.

3. **Pitch**

A time segment representing the optimal work quantity to move throughout the value stream. Many times it will be a multiple of takt time.

4. **Buffer/Safety Resources**

Temporary measures that help to meet customer demand and are considered compromises to a true Lean system.

5. **Baseline Metrics (Lean Office Assessment)**

Two levels of measurements: one level for the department or organization and the other for the team/employee.

6. **Office Quick-Starts**

Quick, to-the-point, morning meetings that assist in balancing workloads for the day and communicating common goals.

7. **Kaizen Events**

Organized and focused team activities that quickly improve a specific value stream or area using Lean tools and concepts.

8. **The Demand Phase – Future State Value Stream Map**

The representation of the Demand tools on a value stream map.

1. Initial 5S

5S is a process to ensure work areas are systematically kept cleaned and organized, assuring employee safety while providing the foundation on which to build the Lean Office. It is recommended that the first 3S's be done during this phase (Part One) while the 4th and 5th Ss be completed in Part Two - Creating the Structures Allowing Work Flow to Emerge. Changes most likely will be occurring in the targeted work area and it would not be beneficial to create standards (the 4th S) prior to those changes.

The five steps in the 5S process are:

> **1ˢᵗ S** – **Sort** through and sort out.
> *When in doubt, move it out!*
> **2ⁿᵈ S** – **Set-In-Order** and set limits.
> *A place for everything and everything in its place!*
> **3ʳᵈ S** – **Shine** and inspect through cleaning.
> *To be Lean, you must be clean!*
> **4ᵗʰ S** – **Standards** created and set.
> *Standardize to improve!*
> **5ᵗʰ S** – **Sustain** through audits.
> *Sustain the gain!*

5S provides a good foundation for allowing employees to contribute to Lean initiatives. 5S can be applied to an entire department or just to the pilot Lean project. It is simple in concept, easy to do, and gets everyone involved. For detailed information on applying 5S in the office you can obtain *5S for the Office* (Productivity Press, 2006) or the *The 5S for the Office User's Guide* available at http://www.theleanstore.com.

Note: The Application Case Study at the end of this chapter shows an example of how to apply these principles to electronic files and folders.

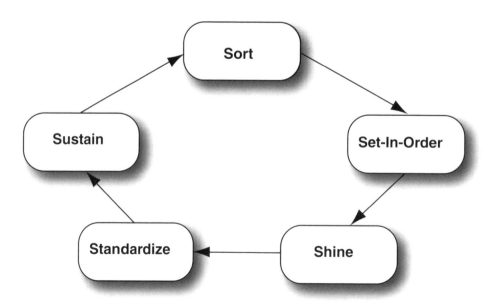

1st S

Sort through and sort out.

When in doubt, move it out!

This is the weeding out of items in the target area that have not been used for a period of time and are not expected to be used again. The team or employee would follow these steps:

a. Define the staging area (temporary location) for unnecessary items.

b. Create guidelines for items not essential to the area. It is recommended that if an item has not been used in 3 months, remove it from the area.

c. Identify items not necessary for the area and place a red tag on them. Note: In healthcare use a different color than red, since that denotes biohazard.

d. Remove tagged items to a staging area.

e. Determine disposition of tagged items. This may include: return to area, dispose of, or donate to charity.

f. Post the 5S visual circle in a common area and place a seal on the first S - Sort.

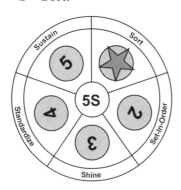

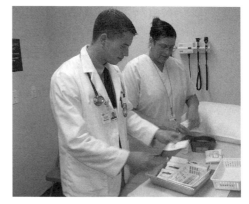

2nd S

Set-In-Order and set limits.

A place for everything and everything in its place!

This S establishes the locations where items belong, by either labeling or visually marking. The team or employee would follow these steps:

    a. Mark off common areas, label drawers, and identify everything within the area.

    b. Create a Criteria Checklist for Set-In-Order as a guide for the team.

Criteria Checklist for Set-In-Order

Target Area _____

Number	Consider These Questions
1	Can multiple items be grouped and placed in one location?
2	Can work be arranged so backlogs do not occur?
3	Have desktops and common areas been considered?
4	

    c. Create a standard for the target area, something to refer to if an item is out of place or not returned. It should be obvious if something is missing. Each item should be labeled so it is obvious where it belongs.

    d. After 1-2 weeks of monitoring, place a seal on the second S - Set-In-Order.

3rd S

Shine and inspect through cleaning.

To be Lean, you must be clean!

This is basic cleaning of the area and establishing a sequence in which the area is kept up on a regular basis. This ranges from cleaning your keyboard to having the floor mats shampooed every month. The team should do a "spring cleaning" and then create a Cleaning Plan. The team and employees would follow these steps:

    a. Set time aside for the "spring cleaning" activity.

    b. Create a 5S Cleaning Plan for the area.

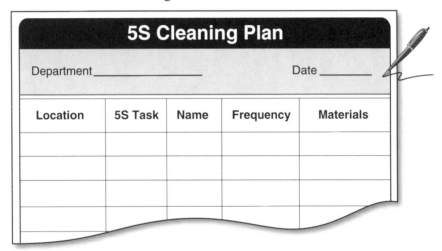

Location	5S Task	Name	Frequency	Materials

5S Cleaning Plan

Department _____   Date _____

    c. Place a seal on the third S - Shine.

5S is a team process, but it also requires the individual employee to commit to the process for his/her own area. The important point is to identify what needs to be cleaned, how it should be kept clean, and by whom. Use a visual chart to ensure the process is followed.

Continue the first 3S's as you create and implement this part of the future state value stream map. At this point we would expect substantial changes in the work areas, for the Lean Office is evolving with many changes. Therefore, it would not be wise to spend time to create the fourth S - Standards, as these other changes are occurring. It is recommended that a strawman (i.e., a process sheet or audit sheet) be created to identify the what, where, and how the first 3S's are to be maintained. It will be a precursor to the 4th S. We will continue to explain the 4th and 5th S for learning continuity. It is also recommended that the New Office Layout in Part II be completed prior to implementing the 4th and 5th S.

4th S
Standards created and set.
Standardize to improve!
Standardize involves creating guidelines for keeping an area organized, orderly, and clean. This also includes making those standards visual and obvious. The team and employees would follow these steps:

    a. Identify the target area.
    b. Decide what the specific tasks are and where they should happen. List them on a sheet of paper.

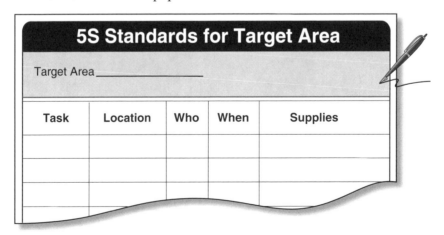

c. Decide who will perform the tasks. List in column.

d. Decide task frequency and supplies required. List in column.

e. Post in target area.

f. Place a seal on the fourth S - Standardize.

5th S

Sustain through audits.

Sustain the gain!

Sustaining involves education and communication to ensure that everyone uses the standards created. The essence of Sustain is found in the saying, "Sustain all gains through self-discipline." This S will allow employees to be trained in this methodology. A learning environment must be created to support those participants who have attended the training sessions. This is vital because the information presented in these sessions may be linked directly to employees' jobs. The team and employees would follow these steps:

a. Create a 5S Training Matrix and maintain documents in Groove (or equivalent shared drive location) so it is available for everyone.

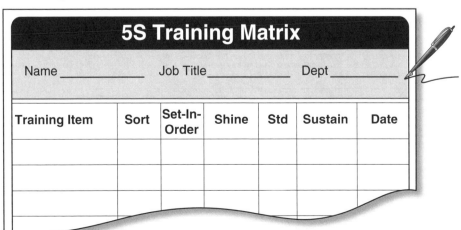

Training Item	Sort	Set-In-Order	Shine	Std	Sustain	Date

5S Training Matrix

Name_____ Job Title_____ Dept_____

b. Regularly conduct a 5S Office Audit and maintain the history in Groove (or equivalent shared drive location).

	5S Office Audit			
Name _____ Work Area _____	5 or more problems, enter 0 4 or 3 problems, enter 1 2 problems, enter 2 1 problem, enter 3 0 problems, enter 4			
Category	**Activity**	**Date**	**Date**	**Date**
Sort	1. Unneeded books, supplies, etc.			
	2. Unneeded reference materials, etc.			
	3. Items present in aisles, hallways, etc.			
	4. Safety concerns			
Set-In-Order	5. Correct places for items			
	6. Items are put away			
	7. Work areas properly defined			
	8. Office equipment locations defined			
Shine	9. Desk surfaces, cabinets free of dust			
	10. Computer screens clean			
	11. Cleaning materials easily accessible			
	12. Common areas looking clean			
	13. Labels, signs, etc. are clear to see			
Standardize	14. Work information is visible			
	15. 5S Standards are posted			
	16. Everyone is trained to standards			
	17. Checklists exist for all areas			
	18. Items in areas can be located quickly			
Sustain	19. An audit sheet has been created			
	20. Audits are conducted regularly			
	21. Improvement ideas for 5S are used			

Offices are like living organisms in that they change and grow. 5S must be a process that adapts as employees come and go, as business conditions change, and as new technology develops. 5S is the foundation for a Lean Office.

c. Place a seal on the fifth S - Sustain.

The benefits of 5S are:

- Allows everyone to be involved in a simple Lean tool
- Provides the foundation for the Lean Office
- Assists in elimination of waste
- Allows for smoother work flow
- Reduces employee stress
- Provides a systematic process for improvement
- Focuses on the process of housekeeping and not the person
- Impresses customers
- Gains buy-in on the importance of standards to be further applied to administrative procedures and processes

2. Takt Time

Takt time is how fast a process must run or how fast area personnel must work to meet a customer demand. Takt time has the following benefits:

- Aligns internal work rate to customer demand rate - similar to a metronome keeping the pace for someone playing a musical instrument
- Focuses awareness on customer demand
- Sets a standard rate that all employees can plan for and be measured against

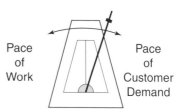

The takt time formula is:

$$\text{Takt time} = \frac{\text{Available daily work time}}{\text{Total daily volume required}} = \frac{\text{Time}}{\text{Volume}} = \frac{T}{V}$$

There are three steps in calculating takt time for a value stream:

1. Gather appropriate data on customer demand. This is the total daily quantity (volume) required. The following is recommended:

    -   Gather historical data for at least 1 month, preferably 3 months
    -   Use data collection techniques to determine work demand over a course of time (a minimum of 1 month)
    -   Use a period of time long enough to reflect variations in customer demand

There are three value streams listed in the Takt Time Data table below. The oil change value stream serviced **3840 oil changes** for the three month period.

Once that number has been determined, proceed to step 2.

Takt Time Data

Department _____   Date _____

Value Streams	January	February	March	Total
Oil changes	1120	840	1880	3840
Transmissions serv.	12	10	8	30
Belt replacement	33	40	22	95

2. Determine the internal resource allocation of available work time.

For example:

Available hours of operation or total hours open:

Monday - Friday 7:00 am - 7:00 pm = 12 hours/day = 60 total hours week
Saturday - Sunday 8:00 am - 6:00 pm = 10 hours/day = 20 total hours week

Total hours for one week = 80 hours

Four weeks per month (average) x 80 hours per week = 320 available hours per month. 320 hours per month x 3 months = 960 hours of available work time or (960 hours x 60 minutes) = **57,600 minutes of work time available** for three months.

The net available work time is the total available work time minus time for meetings, breaks, and any other non value-added activities. A typical day may have the following schedule:

```
8:00 - 8:10    Morning Meeting
8:10 - 9:30    Available  work time (80 minutes)
9:30 - 9:45    Break
9:45 - 12:00   Available work time (135 minutes)
12:00 - 12:30  Lunch
12:30 - 2:00   Available work time (90 minutes)
2:00 - 2:15    Break
2:15 - 4:45    Available work time (150 minutes)
4:45 - 5:00    5S Activities
```

The Net Available work time is:
80 minutes + 135 minutes + 90 minutes + 150 minutes = **455 net available work minutes per day.**

Or you can calculate using 9 hours (8:00 am – 5:00 pm) x 60 minutes = 540 total available work minutes, then subtract:
10 minutes (Morning Meeting) + 15 minutes (Break) + 30 minutes (Lunch) + 15 minutes (Break) + 15 minutes (5S Activities)= 85 minutes
or 540 minutes – 85 minutes = **455 net available work minutes per day**

There will be exceptions to the net available work time. Do not let that be an excuse. Determine the reasonable time that is available for servicing the value stream. The important points about net available work time are:

- Reinforces the importance of organizational time
- Conveys the time that is actually available for value-added work

3. Use the formula to calculate takt time.

$$\text{Takt time} \quad = \quad \frac{960 \text{ hours or } 57{,}600 \text{ minutes}}{3840 \text{ oil changes}} \quad = \quad \begin{array}{c} 15 \text{ minute} \\ \text{takt time} \end{array}$$

The 15 minute takt time represents the time (capacity) the organization must have to service oil changes. Takt time for customer demand must be balanced with the requirements of the other value stream demands to ensure people, equipment, and resources are scheduled appropriately.

Once takt time has been established, all efforts must be focused on meeting that demand. This is accomplished by the continued application of Lean tools.

Takt time for administrative processes is not always an exact science. The key is to find a measurable unit of work that allows you to pace and schedule the work to some measurable amount of time.

The importance of establishing a takt time will give you a sense of what will be needed to meet the customer demand. It also indicates the work load relative to the customer. Once takt time has been determined for the specified value stream, pitch must be calculated to determine how work should be "grouped" or "sized" to begin to design the future state and establish the plan for improved work flow.

The following are examples of takt times from other industries:

Takt Time Examples

Customer Quote - 3 minutes

Mortgage Application (30-year fixed) - 10 days

Life Insurance Policy Application - 5 days

Opening Business Checking Account - 45 minutes

Quoting on Government Project - 21 days

Dental Hygiene Cleaning - 45 mintues

Vehicle Maintenance Upgrade - 1.5 hours

De-embarkation of Ship - 3 minutes per vehicle

Hip Replacement Surgical Procedure - 4.5 hours

Generating Invoice - 2 minutes

Engineering Drawing - 6 hours

Marketing Segmentation Report - 12 hours

Yearly Physical Exam - 30 minutes

Course Registration Online - 10 minutes

The benefits of takt time are:

- Sets the pace for the quantity of work required in the office
- Uses standard work units
- Calculates pitch, which is a more reasonable time period to have work flow
- Balances resources as customer demand changes

3. Pitch

Pitch is the optimal amount of time for moving a quantity of work (volume) through the value stream. Additional attributes of pitch are it:

- Is calculated as a multiple of takt time
- Establishes the right amount of work to flow through the value stream with minimal queue times and other wastes
- Allows for a pace to be established
- Allows for a response to problems much faster
- Improves employee focus and efficiency

Takt time used alone will not be the most efficient and practical way to monitor and control work. Therefore, pitch must be utilized to move the work throughout the value stream at a certain pace. Administrative pitch times are typically in 1, 2, 4, or 8 hour increments. It is important to not extend the pitch time, if at all possible, to more than 8 hours for any administrative value steam. If the actual cycle time of the work (e.g., completing an architectural drawing of a building) is longer than 8 hours, consider how the work can be further segmented into increments of less than 8 hours.

The goal of a Lean Office is to ensure work does not sit for long periods on someone's desk. The Radiology department of a hospital may require 10 minutes for a physician to review a patient's chart, but that chart may sit until the end of the day in an in-process delivery system until it is reviewed by that physician. Consideration may be given to grouping these charts for the physician every four hours and creating a notification signal (visual or auditory via text messages) to communicate that a reading is required. This would establish a pitch of every 4 hours for that physician. The important point regarding pitch is to group the work that is aligned around a specified value stream in meeting a customer demand, thereby reducing the queue time between two processes.

A visual aid can assist in allowing pitch to be incorporated into the organization. This can be accomplished by creating a visible pitch board. The visible pitch board is a physical device that visually communicates the work required for the day at the pitch increments.

Grouping work by value streams will create separate pitch increments. Pitch and the visible pitch board will be integrated into the heijunka box as an advanced Lean tool explained in Part Two.

Do not concern yourself with creating the heijunka box at this stage. Focus on one group of Lean tools at a time. When success is achieved, the application of advanced Lean tools will become easier.

There are three steps in determining pitch.

1. Calculate the takt time (see previous section).

2. Determine the optimal number of work units to be moved through the processes in the value stream.

3. Multiply the takt time by the number of work units.

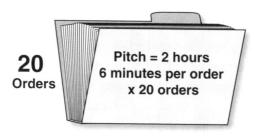

Example: Takt time of 6 minutes X 20 work units to be moved = 120 minute pitch

This means that every two hours the packet of 20 work units (orders) will be moved to the next process.

Pitch must be monitored to ensure that work is being completed on time. Reports can fairly easily be generated out of a database system to monitor if pitch is being met. However, if the database system is not linked to real-time work activities, then an Access or Excel spreadsheet may need to be created. If a problem arises and work cannot be completed during a pitch increment, then there needs to be a process in place indicating what steps will be taken so work can be completed by the next pitch increment. There are different ways this can occur:

- The team or group leader communicates the need for assistance when pitch cannot be met
- The employee who cannot meet the next pitch work increment communicates the need for assistance
- The runner (see next section) communicates the need for assistance

The communication required for assistance can include:

- A pager code to the supervisor or departmental manager
- An alert email to all employees for a round-robin type of support
- A phone call or text message
- A physical meeting with the departmental leader or supervisor

Creating the visible pitch board or real-time computerized report will have employees starting to think and work differently. Just by having the board, there will be a goal to accomplish the work within the pitch increment. This will give the people an immediate sense of satisfaction each time the work is completed. Most importantly, if an employee gets behind, the team can assist to ensure the work gets caught up within the next pitch increment. In Part Two, you will learn exactly how work folders should be arranged and how the information should be presented in the folders to support the concept of pitch.

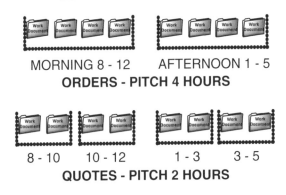

MORNING 8 - 12   AFTERNOON 1 - 5
ORDERS - PITCH 4 HOURS

8 - 10   10 - 12   1 - 3   3 - 5
QUOTES - PITCH 2 HOURS

The benefits of the visible pitch board or electronic report are they:

- Begin to remove the work off the person's desk and into a known process
- Create a visual aid to determine if work is being completed in the pitch increments and not at the end of the day - or not at all
- Allow for immediate problem resolution if a process gets behind
- Provide a foundation on which to create the Heijunka (Leveling) system

4. Buffer/Safety Resources

Buffer and safety resources are *temporary* measures that help to meet customer demand and are compromises to the Lean Office. They should be thought of as band-aids and should be removed once the waste is identified and eliminated.

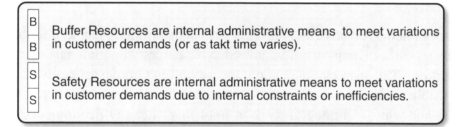

B
B   Buffer Resources are internal administrative means to meet variations in customer demands (or as takt time varies).

S
S   Safety Resources are internal administrative means to meet variations in customer demands due to internal constraints or inefficiencies.

Buffer resources in the Lean Office should be available to meet any variation in customer demand. For example, as interest rates decrease by a 1/4 of a point there will most likely be an increase of new mortgage applications for a certain period of time. This influx of work will be in addition to work already in progress. It would be wise to hire temporary help (a buffer resource) to accommodate this spike in demand. Buffer resources should be agreed upon by the Champion of the team with the appropriate data to justify the additional resource. A buffer resource should have a time line attached to it indicating the length of time it will be required.

Safety resources in the Lean Office should be available when an internal constraint or inefficiency prevents customer demand from being met. Safety resources should be agreed upon by the Champion of the team with the appropriate data to justify the additional resource. A safety resource should also have a time line attached to it indicating the length of time that the resource will be required.

Some examples of buffer and safety resources are:

- Overtime
- Temporary employees
- Civilian employees on contract in the military
- Retirees or volunteers
- Intercompany or departmental temporary assignments
- Managers or supervisors "pitching in"
- Schedule changes - applying "comp" time as in having someone work until 7:00 p.m. for the week and then receive a half-day off

The team should be creative and business wise in determining the need for buffer or safety resources. Employ buffer and safety resources with minimal cost to the organization. The team can maintain a log as well in Groove (or equivalent) to make visible to all patterns over time regarding when buffer or safety resources are used and why. Continue to work to implement Lean Office tools for their elimination.

The benefits of buffer and safety resources are:

- They ensure customer demand is made a priority and *met*
- Kaizen activities are used to eliminate them
- They prevent job burn-out and reduce office stress
- They level the work when volume increases

5. Baseline Metrics (Lean Office Assessment)

Baseline metrics are comprised of two levels: one level is created for the department or organization and the other level for the employee providing the value-added work. They should be aligned. If the dietitian (employee) in hospital food services is collecting data on the number of complaints per floor per meal plan, and the department is requiring data on the number of servings not consumed by the patient (a cost to the hospital), there is a disconnect. There needs to be alignment in the data being collected by the employee to the organization's improvement goals.

The 8 Steps of Metrics

1. Review the Team Charter for strategic direction.
2. Perform a Lean Office Assessment.
3. Determine Lean metrics.
4. Obtain management buy-in for the metrics.
5. Calculate baseline metrics.
6. Select targets for each metric.
7. Make the metrics visual.
8. Continue to measure, improve, and post results.

The following 8 steps are recommended for establishing metrics (or measurements) for a department.

1. **Review the Team Charter for strategic direction.**
   This ensures that the Champion agrees to what is being measured and for what reason. This is critical in any Lean initiative.

2. **Perform a Lean Office Assessment.**

The Lean Office Assessment will provide an overall idea of where you are on the Lean implementation scale. The scores can then be displayed on a radar chart as shown in the following example. In the Application section of this chapter, we will show such a chart generated in Excel by the Northwind team. See Appendix A for the Lean Office Assessment (page 332).

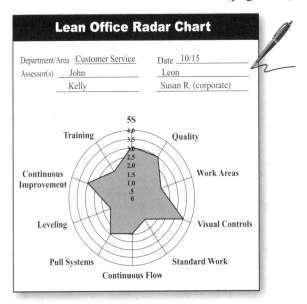

3. **Determine Lean metrics.**

Determining the right metrics for your administrative area depends a great deal on the circumstances of your organization. It may also depend on what the customer is demanding or what the stockholders are demanding for improvement. This should be reflected in what is agreed to by the Team Champion and communicated via the Team Charter.

Lean Office Metric Examples

Patient In/Patient Out	Quality - DPPM
Customer Retention Rate	Nursing Satisfaction
Project Dollars: Budget to Actual	Enrollments - Online
Internal Errors	Online Course Completion Rate
Quote to Firm Order Ratio	Fulfillment Ratio
Profitability	New Client Ratio
Sales per Full-Time Equivalent	Patient Throughput

4. Obtain management buy-in for the metrics.

Use the catchball process between the team (via the team leader) and management to reach agreement on the metrics to be used. In catchball, the team members and the managers "toss" ideas and proposals back and forth, refining them until a consensus is reached.

5. Calculate baseline metrics.

The data from the current state value stream map will have the metrics of total lead time and total queue times. The team must decide the following:

- Who will be responsible for documenting the measurements?
- How often will the measurements be taken?
- What type of form or database is to be used to capture and convey the data?
- To whom will the data be reported?
- Where will the graph or visual aid representing the data be posted?

6. Select targets for each metric.

Play catchball again to gain a consensus. Targets should be realistic and attainable. Creating targets far beyond what is considered reasonable (sometimes referred to as stretch goals) may not be of value. Teams will excel once they achieve results and feel that they have control and input over their work areas.

7. Make the metrics visual.

Measures that are not displayed will fail! Practice "information democracy." Post measures for all to see and make notes on them as appropriate. Visually posting the metrics both on-line and on the wall will also create "buy-in."

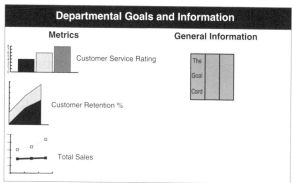

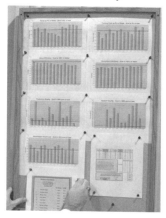

8. **Continue to measure, improve, and post results.**

The benefits of metrics are they:

- Allow team direction and unity toward a common goal
- Create awareness of the importance of continuous improvement
- Contribute to teamwork
- Assist in improving all aspects of the organization with employees being involved

6. Office Quick-Starts

Office Quick-Starts are quick, to-the-point meetings, typically in the morning, used to balance workloads for the day and communicate common goals. They are the constant reminder of what is being measured (i.e., the metrics and any additional support that may be required for the upcoming customer demands of the day).

Office Quick-Starts should begin immediately with the Lean Office project. This will increase communication and involvement. The manager or supervisor should facilitate these meetings at the beginning. As implementation of the Lean Office progresses, these duties eventually will be shared (rotated).

The following are recommendations on conducting Office Quick-Starts:

- Hold Quick-Starts in the morning for no more than 10 minutes. This will align everyone to the daily requirements, potential problems, work issues, as well as who is absent.
- Prepare for the Office Quick-Start the day before or arrive and prepare earlier that morning.
- Rotate handling the phones, early customer arrivals, patient check-in, etc. to ensure good attendance at the meeting. No interruption in customer service should occur.
- State something positive as the first order of business. That may be a metric that was met the day before, a customer visit, or appreciation for someone who exemplified a Lean action the day before.

- Hold the meeting away from distractions.
- Focus the employees on the work for the day, get their minds off of what happened last evening or on the drive into work that morning.
- Review metrics and trends.
- Address any new roadblocks or issues quickly.

Office Quick-Starts are a great way to improve morale and recognize people and their work. As the Lean Office evolves, Office Quick-Starts will become increasingly critical.

The benefits of Office Quick-Starts are they:

- Provide team focus at the beginning of the day
- Ensure issues are discussed at the beginning of the day to prevent many communication problems throughout the day
- Provide an avenue to communicate company news
- Provide an avenue to review metrics
- Provide a forum for training to occur quickly (i.e., new departmental procedure, etc.)

7. Kaizen Events

All Lean Office activities must be organized into a coherent chain of events: Plan, Do, Check, and Act (PDCA). The PDCA cycle is common to all forms of improvement and problem solving activities and has been around for years. A Kaizen Event is the planning, training, and implementation of this "chain of events" of Lean tools and concepts, and is similar in design to the Lean Project initiatives described in Chapter 3.

Kaizen - "Kai" means to "take apart" and "zen" means to "make good." Kaizen is synonymous with continuous improvement.

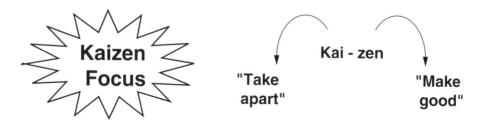

There are three phases to conducting a Kaizen Event:

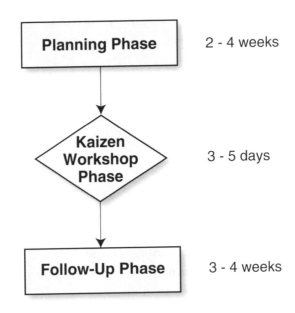

I. Planning Phase

1. Create a current and future state value stream or process map. Use this as the road map to identify problems or areas where waste can be eliminated.

2. Assemble the core Kaizen team. The team should be comprised of a cross-functional group of employees. It is also recommended that someone from another department or value stream be part of the team to offer a fresh perspective. Also, someone from Information Technology (IT) should be part of the team due to our increasing reliance on technology.

3. Complete a Team Charter with the Kaizen team. Identify a project Champion. Post the Team Charter.

4. Obtain approval of the Team Charter from management. Solicit input and update the Charter as necessary.

5. Communicate to all employees (via the Office Quick-Starts) who will be affected by the event well before it begins. Make sure everyone understands how this Kaizen activity will affect them and what may be expected from them.

6. Create a Kaizen Milestone Worksheet, or use the Meeting Information Form described in Chapter 3, to detail the improvement activities. Project tracking can readily be done in Groove with its Project Module. Not every activity is required to be detailed; however, detail as much as possible. It will save time during the actual event.

II. Kaizen Workshop Phase

7. Train the team in Lean Office concepts (if it has not been done previously).

8. Begin the workshop by applying 5S or reviewing current 5S initiatives.

9. Observe the area and document the current way processes are being run. Gather accurate data on cycle times. Develop the Standardized Work Combination Table and Chart (see the next section on Standard Work). Transfer appropriate data to the Kaizen Report Card.

Kaizen Report Card					
Value Stream _____			Start Date _____		
Department _____			Close Out Date _____		
	Kaizen Goal			Kaizen Results	
Measureable	**Before**	**After**	**% Improve**	**Actual**	**% Improve**
Work Area (sq.ft.)					
Cycle Time					
Lead Time					
Cust. Satis.					
Savings					

Kaizen Theme:
_____
_____
_____
_____

Kaizen Team:
_____
_____
_____
_____
_____

Comments:
_____
_____
_____
_____

10. Divide the team into smaller groups to brainstorm how to further improve areas identified on the future state value stream map.

11. Implement immediate improvements and gather results (or estimate results initially). Create an action item list for tasks that could not be completed during the event.

12. Recognize the team for its work during this phase.

III. Follow-Up Phase

13. Report to management the results obtained.

14. Continue to implement ideas. Create standard work once all processes have been verified.

15. Submit regular Status Reports to the champion to communicate project status. Many times the entire project will not be completed during the specific event due to circumstances and issues arising from what is found out while implementing a Lean tool. Therefore, continue to submit Status Reports and continue to meet with the team until the project is completed.

16. Submit a final report when the Kaizen Event is completed.

Recommendations on conducting office Kaizen Events:

- Complete all three phases
- Keep Kaizen Events focused on what is being measured
- Ensure 5S is part of all office Kaizens
- Get management support
- Keep all employees informed of the progress
- The Planning Phase and the Follow-up Phase are just as important as the Workshop Phase

The benefits of Kaizen Events are they:

- Allow for quick implementation of Lean tools and concepts
- Train employees in the application of Lean tools and concepts
- Improve work flow
- Improve office productivity
- Create awareness of the importance of continuous improvement

Note: It is suggested you use the appropriate tools discussed in Chapter 3, Project Identification and Communication, as well as the tools just described, and adapt which ones would best work in your organization.

8. The Demand Phase - Future State Value Stream Map

The Demand Tools explained up to this point should be displayed on an initial pass of a future state value stream map. The first attempts to create a future state map may not be perfect, but do not let that hamper the effort and importance of completing a future state value stream map.

This map will change as more Lean tools are learned and applied. The team must understand the various tools used in each part and create a realistic plan to implement those tools that will impact the measurements. During the mapping exercise, specific Kaizen activities should be identified as such.

The application of a specific Lean tool on the future state value stream map is displayed by drawing a Kaizen burst near the area of the map where the tool will be applied. A Kaizen burst can be an entire Lean tool such as 5S, or it can be a specific activity such as "gather customer data." The Meeting Information Form (or the Kaizen Milestone Worksheet) will further identify additional tasks within the Kaizen burst, indicating the specific application of that tool.

The benefits of creating the demand phase future state value stream map are:

- Ensures the team focuses on the importance of customer demand and what that means
- Emphasizes the importance of 5S
- Improves work flow immediately
- Improves office productivity
- Generates participation and involvement
- Introduces fairly simple and easy to implement tools

At this point, consider using the appropriate icons that were explained in Chapter 4 - Beginning the Journey. Later in Part Two, after all the Lean tools have been explained, additional icons will be presented for updating the future state value stream map. Also consider creating industry specific icons to be represented on the value stream map.

The 30-Year Fixed Mortgage Application Future State Value Stream Map
Demand Phase

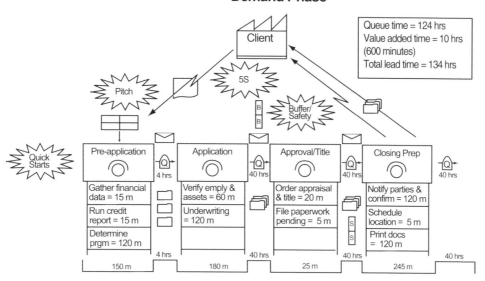

The Order Entry Future State Value Stream Map
Demand Phase

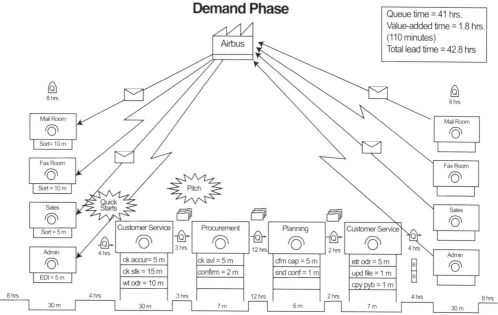

Chapter Summary

This chapter introduced various Lean tools that help meet customer demand. The following is a quick review of the Demand Phase Lean tools.

1. Initial 5S
5S is an improvement process to ensure everything has a place and everything is in its place. It is the foundation for a Lean Office.

2. Takt time
This is the calculation to determine how fast a process must run or a group must work in order to meet customer demand.

3. Pitch
This is the time element for moving the optimal amount of work through the value stream. Many times it will be a multiple of takt time.

4. Buffer/Safety Resources
These are temporary measures to meet customer demand and are considered compromises to a true Lean Office.

5. Baseline Metrics (Lean Office Assessment)
These establish two levels of measurements, one level for the department or organization and the other level for the employee.

6. Office Quick-Starts
These are quick to-the-point meetings to balance workloads for the day and communicate common goals.

7. Kaizen Events
This is a team organized around a common Lean theme that is well-planned to improve a specified area.

8. The Demand Phase - Future State Value Stream Map
This is the first application and utilization of the Demand Tools to be represented on a value stream map.

Many new concepts and tools were covered in this chapter. As important as it is to implement the various tools within the Demand Phase, it is just as important to "steer a steady course." Take the time to collect the appropriate information (data collection). Analyze how the data and information collected relates to the various tool applications. Initiate problem solving where appropriate and create the Demand Phase of the value stream map. All improvement initiatives should be documented on the Team Charter, Meeting Information Form, or Kaizen Report Card to ensure the Team Champion is in agreement. This communication is the responsibility of the team leader.

Observations from the Lean Office

These observations may assist you in understanding how to apply the concepts and tools contained in this chapter:

- Do not rush the implementation of this step. Spend the necessary time, collect the appropriate date, and gain a consensus on how the data should be used.

- Continue to share with the entire department the various aspects of what is occurring. Keep Kaizen Events focused on the application of Lean tools.

- Post the future state value stream or process map in the area where the improvement will be occurring. Explain the map to everyone. Communication is the key to success for any new idea or program.

- The Lean Office System is achievable for any administrative group. The first step is to always spend time, up front, in the planning stages. Ensure the team has a solid foundation in the concepts and tools prior to any implementation.

By implementing the tools contained in Part One, you will have started to change behavior. Remember to reward and recognize the employees often and be specific. Also, address non-participation early, quickly, and privately!

Readiness Guide for Part Two

Many times, teams will continue with the application of Lean without having completed a good portion of what was just covered in the previous chapters. When this occurs, the likelihood of success is diminished. The Readiness Guide prompts the team to determine if it should continue with Part Two or remain in Part One.

The Readiness Guide provides:

1. A review of the critical functions that should be completed prior to learning and implementing Part Two
2. A checklist to ensure all (or most) Lean tools have been completed, which ensures a solid foundation
3. An indication of what the team has accomplished
4. A point in time to acknowledge the team's work and share a form of reward and recognition

The Readiness Guide should be reviewed with the team to ensure a consensus is reached. The team must be trusted in completing the Readiness Guide in the context of organizational objectives, business conditions, and management's directives to determine when to move to Part Two - Create the Structures Allowing Work Flow to Emerge.

Readiness Guide for Part Two

If you respond NO to more than half of these, then you should continue to implement Part One.

	YES	NO
1. Does everyone in the department, group, or value stream have a basic understanding of the Behavior, Attitude, and Culture model?	☐	☐
2. Does everyone in the department, group, or value stream have a basic understanding of the business case for Lean?	☐	☐
3. Does everyone have a basic understanding of the Seven Areas of Waste?	☐	☐
4. Is everyone in agreement that the organization must move from worker specialists to worker generalists?	☐	☐
5. Has the Management Self-Assessment been completed and shared with the group?	☐	☐
6. Has the Predictable Output Survey been completed and discussed by the group?	☐	☐
7. Are Effective Meetings understood and being run accordingly?	☐	☐
8. Has a Team Charter been created?	☐	☐
9. Is everyone aware of the communication forms (i.e., Team Charter, Meeting Information Form, etc.)?	☐	☐
10. Is everyone aware that the Lean Office Road Map will be the basic set of instructions to assist in achieving a Lean Office?	☐	☐
11. Does everyone understand the four stages of team development?	☐	☐
12. Have the processes been captured utilizing the Process Capture Form?	☐	☐
13. Has the Interruption and Random Arrival Log been implemented?	☐	☐
14. Has the Call Log been implemented?	☐	☐
15. Has the Proof of Need Survey been completed and shared with the group?	☐	☐
16. Has the value stream or area to be improved been identified?	☐	☐
17. Has a current state value stream map been created?	☐	☐
18. Has takt time been calculated?	☐	☐
19. Are Buffer and Safety Resources identified and available?	☐	☐
20. Have the first 3S's of the 5S program been completed?	☐	☐
21. Has pitch been established or calculated given the work load volume?	☐	☐
22. Have baseline metrics been established?	☐	☐
23. Are Office Quick-Starts being conducted on a regular basis?	☐	☐
24. Has a Kaizen Event been planned or conducted?	☐	☐
25. Has the value stream or process map been posted?	☐	☐

Application Case Study

Andrew Cencini and his Northwind Trader's team were committed to using the collaborative features and flexibility of Groove to house and share the data, analysis, and reports coming out of their Lean Office initiative. They decided to set up two workspaces in Groove – one to maintain and organize the office documents and files and the other to organize the documents of the Lean Office initiative itself, in effect, a project. Andrew also knew that everyone had local files on their Desktop's C drive and wanted 5S applied to those files and folders. Andrew introduced 5S to the team to incorporate 5S principles while making the much needed changes in the Prospecting Value Stream.

Andrew, as well as each team member, implemented a 5S Desktop program for his or her files and folders. He was not the only one who was always having problems locating files and finding the most recent version. Many times Andrew could not find the right revision and had to request if from someone, which was a bit embarrassing as well as wasteful. The first two S's, Sort and Set-In-Order, directly applied to this problem. Andrew also realized that the third S, Shine, or what he referred to as Scrub, meant folders had to be "cleaned" or reviewed regularly.

The Search feature in Windows Explorer helped Andrew and the team to start sorting through files and folders on their Desktops, locate aged or lost items, and identify actions to be taken with these items. The team agreed to some basic file sorting parameters, as well as some other rules, and deleted most files that were older than 6 months. A group-wide Red Tag folder was created to temporarily locate files for further analysis and archiving or removal.

The following example is of Andrew's Desktop prior to 5S.

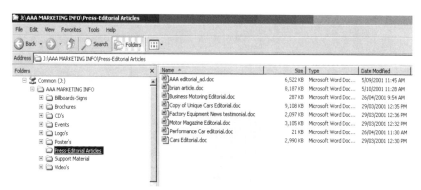

Andrew's Desktop Folders

Examples of some subfolders and files contained in one of Andrew's folders is shown below.

Andrew's Subfolders and Files

Andrew noted some of the key concerns that needed to be addressed:

- In excess of 60 individual folder names (previous page)
- Many folder names that are meaningless to anyone but the creator, such as "KB," "ezaudit," "oft files," and many more
- The letters "AAA" in front of the folder name to ensure it appears at the top of the Explorer screen search
- Business and personal folders in the shared directory
- Different folder names for different revision levels (e.g., "Ops Forecast" and "New Ops Forecast")
- Different folder names for the same activity (e.g., "Inventory" and "Inventory Reduction")
- Lack of standardized naming conventions for files and folders

Andrew, along with reaching a consensus with the team, agreed to apply a basic file and folder naming convention (first for their Desktops, then for the shared folders).

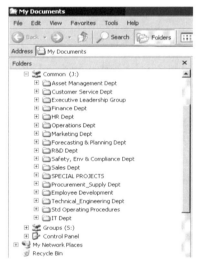

Andrew's New Desktop File System with Sort and Set-In-Order Completed

The above screen shot shows:

- Key departments by name
- All 60 folders have either been deleted, archived, or stored elsewhere

Andrew knew that implementing 5S would allow everyone to immediately see and realize some of the benefits of Lean.

The Lean Office Assessment is critical to starting the project by getting everyone on the same page with a common baseline of understanding how the office is performing. Conducting the audit also opens eyes and makes visible the path to real improvement and a higher level of performance. It becomes the basis for tracking improvement and should be displayed or available online at all times.

The leaders, Andrew Cencini and Steven Thorpe, the Sales Manager, conducted the initial assessment and reviewed it with the team. The team constructively provided their input on the assessment category scoring, which resulted in the lowering of some of the category scores, to Andrew's surprise. The team also suggested assessment targets to be met within a six months time frame. Even though the assessment had a significant subjective component, the team wanted to use it, nonetheless, to track its overall progress. They believed the assessment was good for establishing a baseline score, as well as providing a tool to communicate the need for improvements in certain areas. The following screen shot is an Excel radar chart, which was very easy to set up and modify, that the team posted in the work area and maintained in Groove.

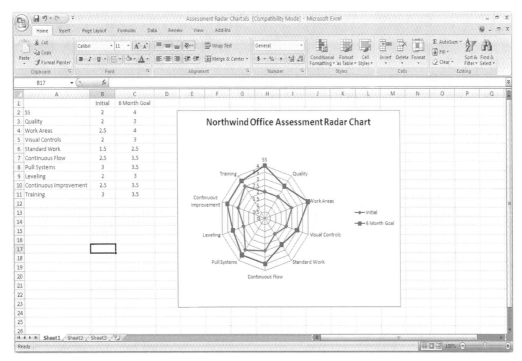

Northwind's Office Assessment Radar Chart

The Lean Office Assessment chart shows both the initial audit and the six month team targets. Note that the team thought that there was no reason why that in six month's time they should not be achieving ratings of 4 for 5S and Work Areas.

Once the Lean Office Assessment was conducted, there was an issue regarding the upcoming trade show and the reluctance of anyone taking the initiative to represent the company. Since the team was still in their early stages of implementing the Lean Office, Andrew knew that cross-training and work load balancing would be Lean tools that the team would need to embrace. To demonstrate support of this concept, Andrew agreed to attend the trade show himself. Andrew, at this time, considered himself a safety resource to the company. This conveyed to the team the importance of teaming and working together to achieve a common goal. Andrew also did not want to over-burden any of the sales reps this early on in the Lean Office project.

Note: Takt time and pitch will be explained relative to the Northwind's case study in Chapter 9 - Making It All Work Through Heijunka (Leveling), beginning on page 284.

Lean Office Demystified II

Part Two.
Create the Structures Allowing Work Flow to Emerge

Making Work Visible

Seeing is Believing

Overview

This chapter will continue with the tools and concepts contained in Part One - Get Everyone Aligned and Started in the Right Direction. This chapter will introduce desktop standards which continue to involve employees and make their work visible by creating a standard desktop layout. Finally, you will see the example of an office supply area as a Lean project to reduce costs using Kanbans.

Desktop Standards

Everyone feels that his or her job requires his or her special expertise, but as we know, if the process (or work) is documented well enough, with proper visual controls and instructions, anyone should be able to perform the task (except for those jobs that require certification, licenses, or accreditation).

This first step in making the work visible requires employees to place their daily work on top of their desk, thus getting the work out of the abyss of drawers and cabinets. This alone is the beginning of capturing process information and transforming it into organizational knowledge.

Making work visible involves the following six steps:

1. Physically get everyone's work on the desktop.
2. Establish a standard naming convention for the desk folders.
3. Create a location for the Work-In-Process (WIP).
4. Organize the folders on the desk.
5. Conduct a desk audit.
6. Acknowledge the need for backup systems.

These steps are considered another phase in capturing the organization process knowledge and ensuring that it remains within the organization. Note: if information is confidential, consider the following:

- Place the confidential information in a separate drawer or file cabinet, secure, and label accordingly.
- Verify exactly what the confidential information is. Establish and follow a standard policy regarding confidential information.
- Create new office procedures with the security company to ensure the office is locked when authorized personnel are not in the area.

Making work visible will later be integrated into the Lean File System (covered later in Part Two) which includes identifying best practices, standardizing to best practice, and training to those standards, thereby supporting the process knowledge residing in the organization.

Note that the principles of making work visible apply to the organization of each worker's computer Desktop and of any office central libraries of files whether they be on an office server, the Intranet of the company, or the Internet (e.g., Google Docs). We will further explore how to organize computer files in the Application Case Study at the end of this chapter. The guiding principle in this chapter is to create a system to have information, in whatever form it exists, readily available.

1. Physically get everyone's work on the desktop.

This will require each employee to relocate all work scheduled for a day, or multiple days, on their desks. This will accomplish the following:

- Ensures the supervisor or manager can identify the type and quantity of work that the employee is working on
- Allows for ease of work that is ahead or behind schedule if the employee is away from his or her desk for any reason
- Creates the first level of process work sharing
- Creates the first step in a visual office, allowing for a transition to improving flow using heijunka (leveling)

Non-Lean

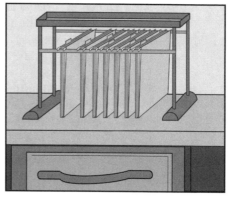

Lean

2. Establish a standard naming convention for the desk folders.

The team should decide on a common naming convention for the folders that will reside on each desktop. One employee should not label a desktop folder as "Quotes" and the adjoining employee label his or hers as "Customer Quotes," "Boeing Quotes," "Customer Quotes - Boeing," etc. A consensus should be reached on a folder naming convention. This allows employees to become more easily cross-trained. It also facilitates meeting customer demand if an employee is temporarily away from his or her desk or absent.

This step can easily be accomplished during a departmental meeting with the outcome being a standard way to label common processes within the department.

The following is an example of a standard naming convention:

STANDARD NAMING CONVENTION

✓ All file and folders must be labeled correctly.

✓ "Quotes-In-Process" is the title for the folder in
which quotes have been entered. If Distributors
and OEMs need to be named separately, then
do so as long as the folder is named as such e.g.,
"Quotes-In-Process - Distributors" or "Quotes-
In-Process - OEMs."

✓ Orders should be filed in folders by the customer and marked accordingly e.g., "Orders
- Customer Name." Quotes should all be
filed together in a folder called "Quotes to be
Entered."

✓ Follow-up folders are for tasks that need to be
done within the next week, but not today. They
can be scheduled at a later date and time.

---

3. Create a location for the Work-in-Process (WIP).

Each desk should have a designated place to put WIP folders. Use a file rack to
ensure the standardization of WIP. This is only temporary. Soon, all WIP will
be located in the Heijunka Box (Chapter 9, *Making It All Work Through Heijunka
- (Leveling)*).

4. Organize the folders on the desk.

Each folder should be located in the rack system in alpha-numeric order. This
will ensure that work is easy to locate and retrieve.

5. Conduct a desk audit.

Conducting a simple desk audit brings additional awareness to all employees. No one in the department should be exempt from a desk audit. It is a self-evaluation tool that should be performed and kept by each individual verifying a proactive approach to the program. The desk audit will identify the following:

- If additional training is required
- Which individuals are participating and which are not
- The areas or processes in which work flow has improved, setting the stage for continued change

The following is an example of a desk audit.

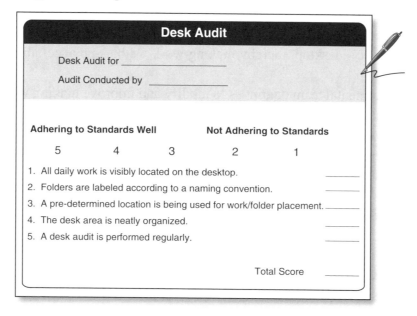

6. Acknowledge the need for backup systems.

The placement of WIP on the desk may be difficult for some. There may be people who create sophisticated and complicated backup systems because they do not trust in the change. Acknowledge these systems and coach those individuals more one-on-one.

The following scenarios may be present or emerge:

- The folders on the desk may not contain all the relevant information
- The employee will only place certain work on the desktop

It is important that as much work as possible be placed on the desktop. Most likely, not all of it will be placed on the desktop at the beginning of the implementation of this tool. Experience has shown that 80% of the work will be made visible and 20% will continue to reside in desk drawers or in file cabinets. Do not be concerned at this time. The Lean Office System will continue to implement additional tools that will ensure nearly all of the work eventually comes into organizational control.

The purpose of making work visible is to gather information (organizational process knowledge) from various individuals' areas into a standardized location on each employee's desktop, thereby making work visible and accessible.

As the departmental team continues to modify and improve making work visible, the team should also implement the Kanban System for Supplies to learn how additional Lean principles can work. The office supply cabinet is a good place to initiate Kanban because it is common to all employees and provides a learning platform for other Lean concepts.

The Kanban System for Supplies

How many times has someone gone to the supply cabinet only to find out something he or she wanted was not there? And then that person places a supply order for an excessive amount to ensure that the supply would be there the next time. Then, when the supply arrives, the "seeker/orderer" takes enough to his or her desk to last a lifetime. Take that situation, multiply it by the number of people in a department, and then multiply that by an accurate cost figure for the supplies. That dollar value can be astronomical!

The Kanban System for Supplies creates a system to ensure the dollars allocated for supplies is substantially less than what the current budget is. Kanban eliminates waste in excess inventory and transport. Kanban is used to create a "pull flow" of material as opposed to the usual "push flow." In "pull flow" an office supply item downstream becomes a demand item to an upstream process. Kanban ensures that a quantity of work, service request, or supply (in this case) is available when it is required and only in the quantity required - no more and no less.

Kanban is a means of communicating via a specific signal to an upstream process precisely what is required, at what time, and in what quantity.

The nine steps to create, implement, and sustain the Kanban System for Supplies are:

1. Understand Kanbans.
2. Conduct a supplies survey.
3. Establish minimum/maximum levels.
4. Create a Supply Order Form.
5. Create the Kanban cards.
6. Create a process flowchart.
7. Conduct the training.
8. Implement the Kanban System.
9. Maintain new standards.

1. Understand Kanbans.

A Kanban is a tool to manage and visually control work flow. It is a signal represented by a card or a visual device indicating the need for additional work or material.

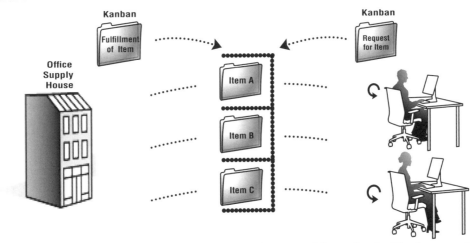

Implementing the Kanban System for Supplies provides a basic Kanban understanding of this Lean tool. Implementing this tool is a good preparation for a broader Kanban implementation in the next chapter when the concept is applied to process work.

You can find the most common Kanban usage in your local grocery store. When you purchase a can of Campbell's tomato soup, as it is scanned, an electronic "signal" or Kanban is generated and sent to the upstream supplier (the Campbell's Soup Regional Distribution Center). When a certain level of inventory is depleted, the specific soup is replenished to a certain stocking level in the next shipment. The loop is self-sustaining and can be applied to office supplies and documents - both paper-based and electronic.

2. Conduct a supplies survey.

The team needs to create a standard list of required supplies that will serve as the upstream process (such as the regional distribution center in the previous example). Create a list of currently required office supplies by conducting an accurate inventory of the supply cabinet. Distribute the list and gather usage information. The following is a sample of a Supply Survey Form.

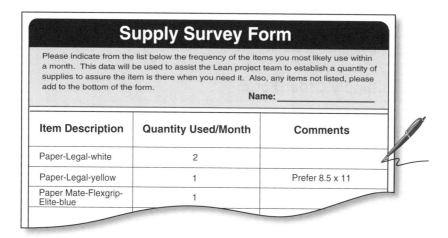

3. Establish minimum/maximum levels.

The team's task is to verify the need for each item on the list, estimate the usage rate of each item over some standard unit of time, and determine a standard required quantity of each to have on hand. This becomes the minimum and maximum levels for each item.

The Lean Office team must gain a consensus on the following:

- The type of standard supply (there are dozens of types of ball point pens, agree on a certain quantity required in each of the types)
- The weekly or monthly usage for the items
- A minimum quantity to have on hand
- A maximum quantity to have on hand

The minimum quantity should allow for enough usage during the time it takes to order and acquire new items up to the maximum level.

Consider these additional points when determining minimum/maximum levels:

- Ensure there is a process to order special items that are not on the standard supply list
- The minimum/maximum level should be reviewed after a few weeks to adjust up or down as necessary to reflect reality
- Numerous office supply outlets deliver daily at no additional charge but have a minimum dollar purchase requirement

4. Create a Supply Order Form.

Once the team has established the type of supplies and the minimum/maximum levels, create a Supply Order Form. The required quantity for each item to be ordered will be the min/max difference. The individual Kanbans from the next step (5) are consolidated on this form. The following is an example of a Supply Order Form.

Supply Order Form

Please fax this form to Staples, 1-888-643-2234 by 5:00 p.m. each day. The supplies will be delivered the next business day. The quantity ordered is located on the Kanban card.

Delivery Location: Penobscot Bldg. 14th Floor   Account Number: ETR556602

No.	Item Description	Item #	Quantity Ordered Max - Min	Unit Price
1	#2 /0.7mm Bic Grip Mechanical Pencils	SP3SM82	2	$7.95
2	Sharpie Permanent Marker 33	SP33656	1	$4.95
3	3M Post-it Notes 2 7/8 x 2 7/8	SP8506A	2	$3.25
4				

The Supply Order Form will include the following:

- Item number
- Catalog page reference or web address
- Cost
- Account or charge number
- Any other information required for ordering

This form may also be set up as an email to an office supply house or directly to an Internet site shopping cart.

5. Create the Kanban cards.

One Kanban card should be designated as the Supply Reorder Kanban for each item. Laminate and color-code a Kanban card for each required item. The color-coding could differentiate between the various supply ordering locations (possibly an internal ordering location versus an external ordering location, e.g., Staples, Office Depot, Inter-company supply outlet, etc.).

The card should be an appropriate size to visually convey all the pertinent information, such as:

- Item description
- Minimum quantity on hand
- Maximum quantity on hand
- Reorder quantity (max minus min)
- Supplier name
- Item number
- Catalog page number
- Kanban card usage instructions

The following is an example of a Kanban card.

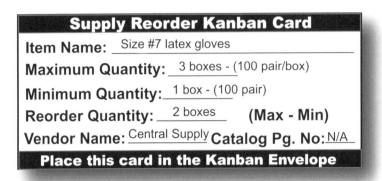

The reorder Kanban cards should all be placed in a Kanban case located outside the supply cabinet. Label the case.

Kanban cards should be attached to the minimum quantity item signaling a reorder of that supply to its maximum level.

Create a Special Order Kanban Card to reorder those special items not on the standard reorder form.

6. Create a process flowchart.

Once the team has completed steps 1-5, the process needs to be documented, standardized, and placed in a process folder (Chapter 8, Creating the Lean File System). Designate one person responsible for the entire supply inventory system (i.e., the process owner).

There are many ways to document the process. A simple flowchart is sufficient or a Standard Work Chart may also be used (Chapter 8, Creating the Lean File System).

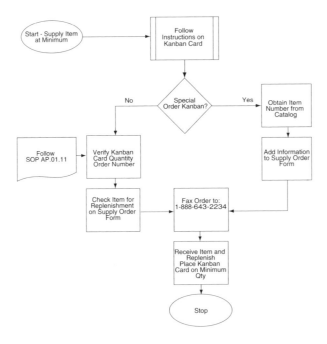

7. Conduct the training.

Complete departmental training prior to implementing the supply reorder system to ensure the integrity of the system.

The training should include the following:

- A brief explanation of the purpose of Kanbans (why it is being done, what the features are, what Kanbans will do for supply ordering, etc.)
- An explanation of how the min/max levels were established while giving appreciation for everyone's input when the supply survey was conducted
- An explanation of how the system will work (distribute process flow-charts or Standard Work Charts)
- An explanation of the two types of Kanban Cards: Supply Reorder and Special Order
- A demonstration at the supply cabinet of how the system will work
- An acknowledgment that this is a pilot Lean project and encourage improvement suggestions from anyone
- Acknowledgement to the team members who contributed to the initial design of this process and project

8. Implement the Kanban System.

After training has been conducted, the Kanban System for Supplies will be ready to use. Begin using the system immediately.

After a month or two review the supply line items. Determine all cost savings. Inform the team and convey the data to management.

Solicit ongoing input to improve and adjust the Kanban System. Every office is unique and will require some sort of modification to the above.

9. Maintain new standards.

Once the system is in place, it becomes a responsibility of the group to maintain and sustain it. The supply cabinet is a common area. Post a schedule on the cabinet door identifying the person responsible for process review and cabinet organization.

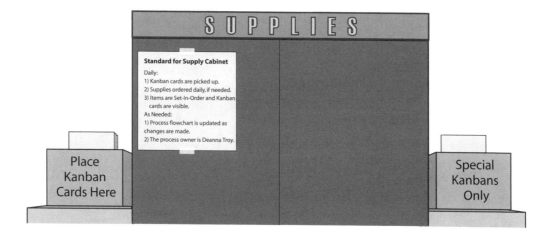

Chapter Summary

This chapter covered Desktop Standards as an important, initial step for placing individual process information in a common area. Kanbans were referenced to improve the inventory of office supplies, while demonstrating a key element of Lean, in regards to the Pull System.

Observations from the Lean Office

These observations may assist in understanding how to apply the concepts and tools contained in this chapter:

- Creating Desktop Standards is the first step in sharing information. Do not overcomplicate this.
- The Kanban System for Supplies will give everyone an idea on how Kanbans work to eliminate excessive inventory and unnecessary transport costs.
- Continue to discuss how Lean tools can eliminate wastes that were explained in Part One.

Application Case Study

The Northwind leadership, Andrew Cencini, VP of Sales, and Steven Thorpe, Sales Manager, felt it was important to organize the computer files and work of the sales representatives (reps) according to the principles of the Desktop Standards described in this chapter. The key was to get everyone's files on the "desktop" with "desktop" representing two locations: 1) the paper-based documents and, 2) the electronic documents. This would then assist management to quickly take the pulse of what was happening each day and subsequently take appropriate action as changes occur.

Since the sales team dealt regularly with customers and prospects that were not using the MS Office business line of applications, Andrew and Steve looked at using Google Docs as the central repository for the files of the reps. Google Docs allowed secure control of access to certain files by customers and clients while providing the sharing and referencing functionality needed for their business communications. Another big advantage of Google Docs is that any file can be put into multiple folders, facilitating flexible structuring of the system.

Note: The following example would also apply if the central library of files was housed on an office server, the company Intranet, or on the Internet via any one of the many other document management solutions available. Whichever option best suits the particular situation for an office will drive a particular solution. The point is to show that sharing knowledge (files) will eliminate the waste of over-processing (i.e., multiple versions of documents floating around and/or working from the wrong version level).

Google Docs can house and organize your uploaded documents and provide controls to assure the appropriate level of access for each user. Word documents, Excel spreadsheets, and PowerPoint presentations, as well as other file types, can all be uploaded to, created or edited within, and downloaded from Google Docs. Multiple people can view and make changes simultaneously within Google Docs, resulting in the ability for a team to easily collaborate and share knowledge - a key to making work visible.

The following screen shot shows how the sales team set up its Google Docs home page to house its shared and common files. One great feature of Google Docs is that a file can be put into more than one folder.

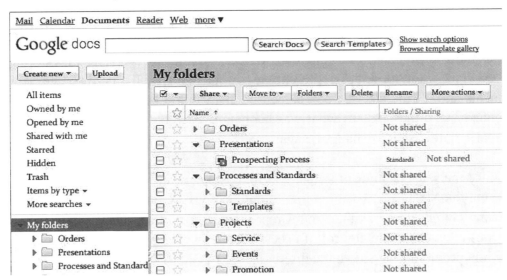

Google Docs Home Page Showing Folder Organization

The following screen shot shows that the file Prospecting Process (see the Folders/Sharing column) resides in both the Standards and Presentations folders. The team established standards for file naming as well as file locations.

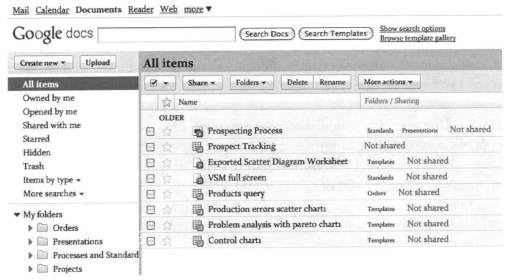

Example of File in Multiple Folders

Chapter 7

Initializing the Flow

Manage By Using Good Data

Chapter Overview

This chapter continues to develop the Lean Office System by introducing new tools to streamline process flow and continue to capture organizational knowledge. Now that standards have been created for 5S and work is visible on everyone's desktop (for both paper and electronic documents), it is time to re-think the current office arrangement. The placement of people and equipment should contribute to the continuous flow of work while capturing data that are required for implementing additional Lean tools. An understanding of continuous flow will be explained and demonstrated by the Lean tools of: In-process supermarkets, FIFO lanes, new office layouts, data collection techniques, and document tagging.

Understanding Continuous Flow

Continuous work flow is a process's ability to replenish a single work unit or service request that has been requested or "pulled" from a downstream process. Pull is often synonymous with Just-In-Time (JIT). JIT ensures both internal and external customers receive the work unit or service when it is needed and in the exact amount.

Excess transport time, queue times (inventory), waiting, and motion waste can be eliminated by properly arranging people and equipment in closer physical proximity to help facilitate continuous flow.

There are different degrees of continuous flow. True continuous flow in an office most likely will not be achieved; therefore, the Lean tools of In-process supermarkets, FIFO lanes, and new office layouts will be used to design work flows for maximum efficiency and effectiveness.

In-Process Supermarkets

The work a customer requires generally will not flow seamlessly from Point A through Point Z without some type of disruption. This may occur because of signatures required, insufficient information, not enough time to process the request, etc. To minimize disruptions and maintain flow, In-process supermarkets can be of value.

A supermarket is a physical device that stores a certain quantity of WIP or service capacity that gets pulled by a downstream user (or customer). In-process supermarkets can be used when there is a difference in the cycle times of the processes (or departments). The In-process supermarket and its associated Kanbans identify transactions (i.e., work) that must occur in an upstream process when the work or service is required by the downstream process. The office supply cabinet described in Chapter 6 is an example of an In-process supermarket.

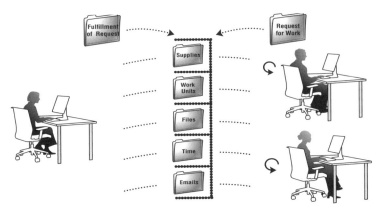

The benefits of In-process supermarkets are:

- Eliminates the need to overproduce work upstream
- Reduces queue times (e.g., piles of paper on the desk or 100s of emails in the Inbox)
- Simplifies identification and rectification of problems
- Reduces the number of hand-offs
- Increases throughput
- Reduces stress
- Improves employee morale and job satisfaction

First-In First-Out Lanes (or FIFO Lanes)

Another way to control the flow between processes is a method referred to as First-In First-Out, or simply FIFO. FIFO is a work control method that ensures the oldest work from an upstream process (first-in) is the first to be processed downstream (first-out).

In administrative areas, each job, customer order, quote, invoice, patient diagnosis, budget report, etc. is unique. Every engineering drawing is unique to that customer. Every diagnostic reading from radiology is unique to that patient. But what is interesting in each of these examples is that each activity can be equated to a time element to complete that process. It may be a rough estimate, but nonetheless, a time can be assigned. Do not let estimates or difficulties in obtaining those times cause the team to stagnate and not reach agreement on obtaining process cycle times. People who are not interested in change will use statements such as "well, that's not for all situations" as an excuse to not attempt to improve a process and not try to establish accurate cycle times.

If an In-process supermarket cannot be utilized, then implement a FIFO system. The FIFO lane is more commonly used in administrative areas. FIFO lanes will ensure smooth work flow and data transaction between processes without undue interruptions.

FIFO Lanes

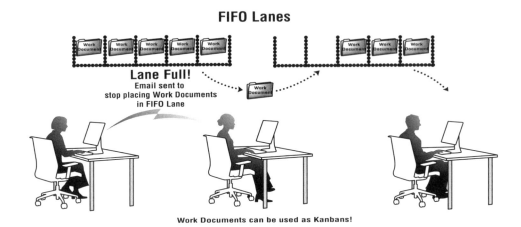

Work Documents can be used as Kanbans!

FIFO lanes have the following attributes:

- Are located between two processes, clearly identified as such
- Have a maximum number of work units placed in the FIFO lane and are labeled as such
- Are sequentially loaded
- Have a system to warn the upstream process personnel when lanes are operating at capacity
- Have visual rules and standards posted to ensure FIFO lane integrity
- Have processes for assisting the downstream process when lanes are full and assistance is required

The team can be creative in establishing a signal method to indicate when the FIFO lane is full. This could be raising a flag or sending an alert email to the upstream process. The signal is to ensure effective notification of the upstream processes to stop producing. When the signal is sent, one or more upstream employees can lend support to downstream employees until the work is caught up. There is no point in continuing to produce upstream when the downstream process cannot accommodate the work. This is known as overproduction - the worst of all the wastes!

There will always be drop-ins, immediate management requirements, or patient or customer emergencies that affect whatever system is in place. Do not let that stop implementation of the Lean Office. Continue to collect data on drop-ins and other work interruptions and work to eliminate them.

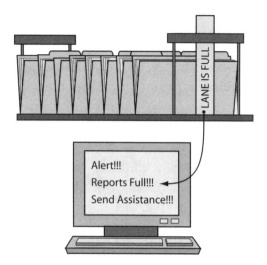

The benefits of FIFO are:

- Lead time reduction
- Queue time reduction (those piles of paper on the desk)
- Problem identification and rectification at the point of occurrence
- Hand-off reduction
- Throughput maximization
- Stress reduction
- Morale and job satisfaction increases

Both the In-process supermarket and FIFO lane are compromises to pure continuous flow. They should be viewed as part of a continuous improvement system and efforts should be made to find ways to reduce or eliminate them in the quest for pure continuous flow. In administration, this can be accomplished by intensive cross-training and work standardization.

New Office Layout

A Lean work area is a self-contained, well-ordered space that optimizes the work flow. Typically, many organizational work spaces are separated by visible, as well as invisible, walls. The purpose of a new office layout is to remove both types of walls, keeping in mind good business sense.

Initially, eliminating walls might be a hard sell, but once people realize that by giving up some privacy they are increasing work flow efficiency, their attitudes will become increasingly more positive.

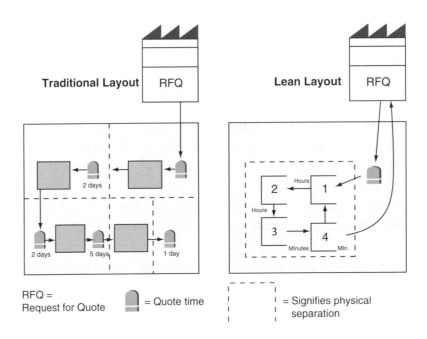

One of the more difficult determinations will be reasoning where to locate specific people. The focus of the Lean Office is to address the process, not the individual employee. Department personnel may not achieve a consensus at the beginning of deciding how to rearrange the office layout.

The manager or supervisor could establish an initial layout by doing the following:

- Locating specialists within an area with the less experienced workers
- Grouping someone who is always working overtime with someone that always has his or her work done at the end of the day

The reasons for a new office layout are:

- Organizational knowledge must be shared and documented
- Everyone must be trained on best practices to reduce work variation
- Work must flow better
- Waste must be eliminated

These continuous flow tools are flexible enough for team members to be creative about their unique office requirements. Continually explain the benefits of improving work flow.

Use the following guidelines when creating a new office layout:

1. Draw the initial layout of the office area on graph paper (desks, people, copy/fax machines, etc.). Review it with the team.
2. Consider locating processes relative to any value stream requirements. For example, if a customer has a mandatory faxing requirement and the worker must continually travel to a central location, consider having the fax machine relocated to his or her area or purchasing an additional machine.
3. Create various work load scenarios or office arrangements with varying demands. Allow for flexibility as business conditions change.
4. Plan how non value-added work or activity can be eliminated.
5. Redraw the layout and post in a common area. Again, a consensus may be difficult at first, but continue to communicate the need for improvements.
6. Consider the new office layout in phases as a compromise if resistance is more than expected.

A new office layout will require employees to share common goals and metrics. This may or may not be included in the Team Charter, depending on the deliverables and score of the project. The department manager must work with any newly created work group when establishing a new office layout in creating appropriate measurements of office productivity. These applicable metrics should be common to the team and realistic to support the departmental objectives. With the metrics established, some things need to occur immediately to begin reaping the benefits of improved work flow:

1. A team leader or coach should be appointed for overseeing the new office layout. This person should be appointed by the department manager. This team leader is someone who has shown a positive attitude to change, is competent in many of the critical and non-critical processes, and, above all, is a good communicator.
2. The Office Quick-Starts, or huddles, led by the team leader or departmental manager should discuss the new office layout and solicit input.
3. The supervisor or manager should give encouragement and positive reinforcement for any positive trends on the metrics due to the new layout.
4. After 1-2 weeks, gather the group together to brainstorm additional ways to improve the layout.

The benefits of the new office layout are:

- Ensures the most efficient layout for optimizing the location of equipment, people, materials, etc. for improved work flow
- Ensures the shortest distance of work movement within the department and value stream
- Allows for flexibility via work sharing and ease of cross-training
- Reinforces and supports small lot work flow
- Creates a team atmosphere for goal sharing
- Reduces the amount of office floor space required
- Increases throughput
- Reduces waste

The eight steps to create, implement, and sustain a new office layout are:

1. Review the current office arrangement and process tasks to determine which wastes occur due to the current layout in terms of travel, motion, and lack of cross-training.
2. Brainstorm to consolidate office arrangements to reduce or eliminate the wastes identified in (1). Processes may need to be modified or standardized, and may need people to be trained.
3. Determine if an In-process supermarket or FIFO lane is required.
4. Prepare a plan, including result expectations, to implement the proposed changes.
5. Obtain management approval.
6. Implement new office layout and/or new process(es).
7. Balance work loads amongst workers.
8. Consider new technologies and software enhancements as you continue to improve.

After everybody involved in a Lean Office project understands and has implemented the appropriate tools of continuous flow (In-process supermarkets, FIFO lanes, and/or a new office layout) it is time to capture customer demand.

Data Collection Techniques

Data collection techniques are used to document process time activity. The data will create a quantitative foundation for allocating and redistributing resources in creating the Lean Office. Data can be collected by using the Data Capture Form, Distribution Report, and Document Tagging Worksheet.

Good data collection techniques:

- Create a good baseline upon which to use Lean tools and concepts
- Create an awareness of group and individual progress
- Document the processes that are currently in progress, as well as "other" duties that occupy people's time

Data Capture Form

There are eight steps in using the Data Capture Form:

1. Brainstorm a list of common processes in the department or what has been determined to be the value stream.
2. Create a Data Capture Form that lists the processes from 1 - XX. Ensure the form provides space to accommodate additional processes.

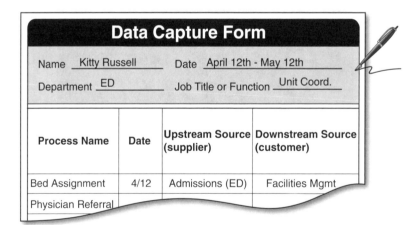

3. Ensure each person within that process is given a copy of the form. Use the form for a specified period of time, not less than 1 month. Time extensions may be necessary to account for seasonal variations.
4. Create a Distribution Report. This involves using historical data to establish customer demand if they are available. Analyze a minimum of 3 months of demand data. After the raw demand data for the value stream processes has been collected, create a Distribution Report. Often times today, these reports exist and can readily be generated by office system databases.

Distribution Report

Department Laboratory   Date   January 1 - March 31

Value Streams	January	February	March	Total
Radiology	450	575	475	1500
Floors	250	330	280	860
Pediatrics	54	48	22	124

Distribution Report

Department   District Office   Date   January 1 - March 31

Value Streams	January	February	March	Total
Oil changes	550	400	330	1280
Transmissions serv.	12	10	8	30
Belt replacements	33	40	22	95

5. Identify common processes and identify value streams.
6. Calculate takt times for each value stream.
7. Create a plan to ensure takt time is met.

8. Create a Demand "Help" tool. The Demand Help tool is a small placard indicating the work requirements for the value stream. The "Help" tool will:
   - Create awareness on the importance of takt time
   - Support work visibility
   - Improve productivity

!! ENTERING ORDERS !!

Takt time will eventually become a common word in your Lean Office. Make takt time visible to all.

Document Tagging

The Document Tagging Worksheet is a form to capture the work elements and steps accurately, as work moves throughout an entire process or value stream. This is the data that is used to create an accurate current state value stream map. Document tagging:

- Continues to create awareness of organizational time
- Involves everyone connected to the process
- Promotes an accurate analysis of the process based on actual times

	**Document Tagging Worksheet**										

Process Name _____   **Start Date In** _____
Tagging Log No. _____   **Start Date Out** _____

Step	Name/Dept.	In		Out		Task/Activity	Delay/Queue Time from Previous Step	Cycle Time	Elapsed Time	Value-Added Time	Non Value-Added Time
		Date	Time	Date	Time						

Notes:
Delay/Queue Time is calculated from the Out Time of the previous step to the In Time of the current step. Day is 8 hours, 8:00a - 5:00p with 1 hr. lunch.
Cycle Time is calculated by determining the total amount of time (in minutes) the work is being transformed into what is required by the downstream process. It is the rate of processing that work unit.
Elapsed Time is the Delay/Queue Time plus the Cycle Time.
Value-Added Time is physically (or electronically) transforming the document into value for the customer.
Non Value-Added Time will be the Delay/Queue Time plus any Cycle Time that does not add value to the customer.

Document Tagging Worksheet

Process Name Order Entry - Domestic Sales   Start Date In 4/10

Tagging Log No. 1   Start Date Out 4/12

Step	Name/Dept.	In Date	In Time	Out Date	Out Time	Task/Activity	Delay/Queue Time from Previous Step	Cycle Time	Elapsed Time	Value-Added Time	Non Value-Added Time
1	Judy/CS	4/10	8:59a	4/10	9:00a	Receive customer order		1	1	1	
2	Judy/CS	4/10	10:00a	4/10	10:10a	Retrieve customer file	60	10	70		70
3	Judy/CS	4/10	4:10p	4/10	4:20p	Verify PO	300	10	310		310
4	John/CS	4/11	8:10a	4/11	8:15a	Contact customer	60	5	65		65
5	Judy/CS	4/11	3:05p	4/11	3:15p	Verify information	350	10	360		360
6	Judy/CS	4/11	4:15p	4/11	4:20p	Send order to John	60	5	65		65
7	John/CS	4/12	9:20a	4/12	9:40a	Verify inventory	130	20	150		150
8	John/CS	4/12	1:10p	4/12	1:25p	Create PO	150	15	165	15	150
9	John/CS	4/12	3:25p	4/12	3:30p	Send PO for approval	120	5	125		125

Notes:

Delay/Queue Time is calculated from the Out Time of the previous step to the In Time of the current step. Day is 8 hours, 8:00a - 5:00p w/ 1 hour lunch.

Cycle Time is calculated by determining the total amount of time (in minutes) the work is being transformed into what is required by the downstream process. The rate of processing that work unit.

Elapsed Time is the Delay/Queue Time plus the Cycle Time.

Value-Added Time is physically (or electronically) transforming the document into value for the customer.

Non Value-Added Time will be the Delay/Queue Time plus any Cycle Time that does not add value to the customer.

The eight steps of the Document Tagging process are:

1. Determine the process(es) or value stream on which data will be collected.
2. Create a Document Tagging Worksheet in Microsoft Word or Excel.
3. Explain to the group specific information that is required on the form. Ensure the tasks are described as a verb-noun combination (e.g., match invoice to shipper, place folder in In-basket, etc.).
4. Initiate the form at the most upstream process in the value stream - the point at which the process originates. This is similar to placing a red dot or tag on a document and following it through all processes until it cycles through the most downstream process.
5. Collect data for four or five complete cycles to ensure accuracy. Require office personnel to collect the following:
   Step - this should be in sequential order
   Name/Dept
   Date
   Time In
   Date
   Time Out
   Task/Activity
   Cycle Time
6. Analyze the data to establish the best cycle time for the process. Once the document has been cycled through the final process, the last person entering data should give it to the team leader to analyze it to calculate the following information:
   Delay/Queue Time: In Time from previous Out Time
   Elapsed Time: Delay/Queue Time from Previous Step + Cycle Time
   Value-Added Time: Time to physically transform the work to provide customer value
   Non Value-Added Time: Elapsed Time - Value-Added Time
7. Create a Standard Work Chart. Brainstorm to establish reasons for variations in overall process cycle times. Use the Standard Work Combination Table and Standard Work Chart for further process analysis and documentation.
8. Train all personnel to the new standard.

Chapter Summary

In this chapter we explained how to use specific tools to assist in increasing work flow and collecting accurate data. In-process supermarkets, FIFO lanes, new office layout, data collection, and document tagging were explained as tools to initialize the work flow.

Observations from the Lean Office

These observations may assist in understanding how to apply the concepts and tools contained in this chapter:

- Be creative in establishing In-process supermarkets and FIFO lanes.
- FIFO lanes are more commonly used for office processes.
- Involve everybody in the new office layout.
- Be deliberate in establishing takt time. Collect the appropriate data.
- Use visual aids as often as possible.
- Focus on the processes in which people work most. Ensure they capture accurate data.
- Be supportive.
- Ensure everyone understands the difference between processes, value streams, and tasks.
- Place a red dot or tag on the process document as it proceeds through the value stream.
- Update the value stream map after document tagging has been completed.

Application Case Study

Andrew and the Northwind team decided that virtual document tagging would be a great way to get a better handle on what was happening within the Prospecting Value Stream (see Chapter 4 and the Value Stream Map), particularly the initial steps required to get in front of potential customers, the Initial Communication subprocess. This first subprocess was determined to be the most critical and difficult – the proverbial foot-in-the-door. They decided to use Microsoft Office Groove, introduced and described in Chapter 3, so that all could easily access the system from anywhere and the results be aggregated instantaneously. This initiative would also serve to get the team working together using the potent collaborative tools within Microsoft Office.

Each prospect is assigned to one sales representative (rep). Each sales rep would be responsible for entering all the information for that prospect in a master document with write privileges to all. By using Groove, only one file exists, not multiple Excel files on each person's Desktop. Sales reps often had to share customer information on prospects even though they were "assigned" to one person because of master contracts, distributor agreements, territorial issues, etc. There was little resistance to this idea because it made sense to everyone on the team. The team realized how much time was wasted in the old way of managing prospects and sales leads (i.e., incomplete, wrong, or inaccurate information on prospects, countless emails requesting further information on prospects, etc.). The team was therefore eager to use Groove for this purpose.

The team decided to start out simply by tracking the initial calls to prospects and recording the date of each call and whether the prospect was contacted or not. This way, the team could keep track of the number of calls required to talk to the prospect and any associated wait time, that is, the time from that first call to any subsequent calls. The spreadsheet was also used to record how much actual, value-added "talking" time took place after contact was made. An unsuccessful call (rejection to setting up an interview), even though contact was made, was counted as non value-added time since no potential sale could result. The following screen shot shows just the first two days of tracking calls for the Initial Communication process. The team made 47 calls to prospects in those two days, including some follow-up calls.

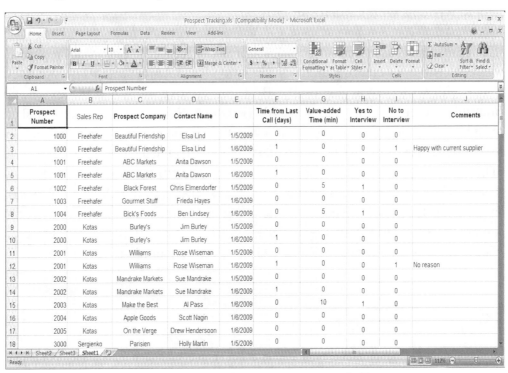

Prospect Number	Sales Rep	Prospect Company	Contact Name	0	Time from Last Call (days)	Value-added Time (min)	Yes to Interview	No to Interview	Comments
1000	Freehafer	Beautiful Friendship	Elsa Lind	1/5/2009	0	0	0	0	
1000	Freehafer	Beautiful Friendship	Elsa Lind	1/6/2009	1	0	0	1	Happy with current supplier
1001	Freehafer	ABC Markets	Anita Dawson	1/5/2009	0	0	0	0	
1001	Freehafer	ABC Markets	Anita Dawson	1/6/2009	1	0	0	0	
1002	Freehafer	Black Forest	Chris Elmendorfer	1/5/2009	0	5	1	0	
1003	Freehafer	Gourmet Stuff	Frieda Hayes	1/6/2009	0	0	0	0	
1004	Freehafer	Bick's Foods	Ben Lindsey	1/6/2009	0	5	1	0	
2000	Kotas	Burley's	Jim Burley	1/5/2009	0	0	0	0	
2000	Kotas	Burley's	Jim Burley	1/6/2009	1	0	0	0	
2001	Kotas	Williams	Rose Wiseman	1/5/2009	0	0	0	0	
2001	Kotas	Williams	Rose Wiseman	1/6/2009	1	0	0	1	No reason
2002	Kotas	Mandrake Markets	Sue Mandrake	1/5/2009	0	0	0	0	
2002	Kotas	Mandrake Markets	Sue Mandrake	1/6/2009	1	0	0	0	
2003	Kotas	Make the Best	Al Pass	1/6/2009	0	10	1	0	
2004	Kotas	Apple Goods	Scott Nagin	1/6/2009	0	0	0	0	
2005	Kotas	On the Verge	Drew Hendersoon	1/6/2009	0	0	0	0	
3000	Sergienko	Parisien	Holly Martin	1/5/2009	0	0	0	0	

Tracking Initial Communication Calls

Once the Excel spreadsheet was being populated with data, Andrew could start analyzing it as shown in the following two screen shots, both views of Pivot Tables breaking down the data. Column B of the screen shot shown below shows how many of the calls were follow-up calls since it counts only those calls that have a number in the column "Time from last call." This count, and the percentage of the total, was bound to increase over time as the number of days tracked increased. With this report, the management team could keep track of multiple callbacks and decide when to shift the effort to other prospects. Column C shows the actual value-added time after two days of prospecting by the six sales representatives. It seems meager, but as any sales person knows, prospecting is not easy and requires persistence.

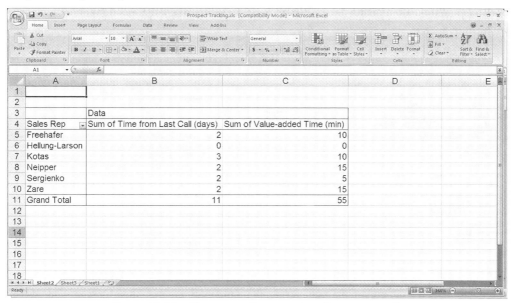

Pivot Table Showing Count of Follow-up Calls

The following screen shot shows the second Pivot Table to keep track of the responses to contacts that were made. So far, the number of prospects agreeing to be interviewed, in Needs Assessment (second subprocess of the Prospecting Value Stream) far outnumbered the refusals: 10 to 4. Having this data aggregated so easily and quickly via a shared spreadsheet showed Andrew how powerful having the right data at his fingertips could be. It peaked his interest in investigating a Customer Relationship Management (CRM) system, which is designed to collect, house, and report data like this and much more. Systems such as ACT!, Goldmine, and many others, including Intranet or Internet applications, are now highly refined and enable a sales team to record, share, analyze, plan, and report on what is working and what is not throughout the whole sales process. We will address what the results of Andrew's investigations into such systems were in Chapter 8.

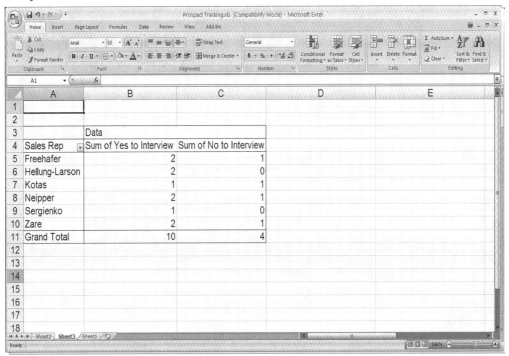

Sales Rep	Sum of Yes to Interview	Sum of No to Interview
Freehafer	2	1
Hellung-Larson	2	0
Kotas	1	1
Neipper	2	1
Sergienko	1	0
Zare	2	1
Grand Total	10	4

Pivot Table Analysis of Responses to Interviews for Needs Assessment

Another tool to manage the data of this example is the concept of the In-process supermarket. In this situation, the contact calls that require follow-up (those that have not been closed by either a "yes" or a "no" to the request for an interview) can be generated by filtering the spreadsheet. This would represent an In-process supermarket for follow-ups. The following screen shot shows the same data shown on the two previous pages (i.e., the Pivot Table examples), but with all yes or no responses filtered out, thus leaving only those prospects which the sales representatives need to continue to follow-up with. Sorting by prospect number, which is tied to the individual sales rep (note the drop-down menu for sorting), shows who needs to continue to make which calls. There is no sorting through scraps of notes and scribbling on note pads to identify the calls for the next day. This In-process supermarket approach will become even more valuable as the volume of calls increases.

This report, as the data accumulates, could be used to automatically flag situations where Andrew would want to take management action, if:

- The number of follow-up calls to any one prospect exceeds five
- It has been more than three days since a follow-up call has been made to any one prospect
- The ratio of no-to-yes closures of prospects by any sales representative did not meet the standard or target

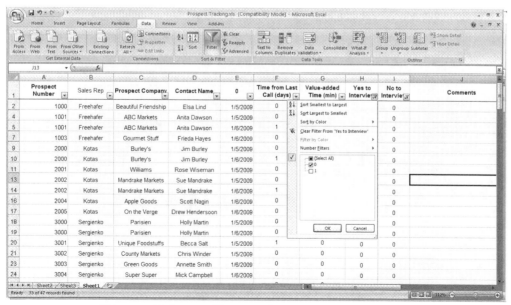

Using a Filter to Show Only Required Follow-ups

Chapter 8

Creating the Lean File System

Get Control of Paperwork

Chapter Overview

In this chapter we will discuss the Lean File System, Work Load Balancing, Standard Work, and Visible Pitch. This chapter is the heart of the Lean Office System. It will be similar to the Kanban System for Office Supplies, which is why that example was covered in an earlier chapter. In that system there was a Kanban card for each office supply item. Once that supply reached a certain predetermined minimum level, the card would be physically placed in a specified location triggering a reorder of that supply to the maximum level. The Lean File System is similar in which it visually triggers how much paperwork (or any other type of work or service) must flow, where it must flow, and when it must flow.

The Lean File System

The Lean File System consists of creating and maintaining three folders: the System Folder, the Process Folder, and the Reference Folder. Each will contain the actual process work or reference required to complete a customer demand.

The six steps to creating the Lean File System are:

1. Create the System Folder or Process Master Kanban.
2. Create the Process Folder or Work Kanban.
3. Establish a Holding Point.
4. Balance the Work Loads.
5. Create Standard Work.
6. Implement Controlled Flow through Visible Pitch.

The above activities require more time to implement than any other section of this book. Do not rush any of these steps. Each are important and must be part of the team's consensus-building process. Be patient in reaching a consensus with the team in these steps because you will be making many critical decisions in regards to how information is processed. This will create the foundation for efficient and accurate work flow. These principles can be applied to a paper-based system of files and folders or the Desktop and networking environment of files and folders. The latter is demonstrated in the case study at the end of this chapter.

1. Create the System Folder or Process Master Kanban.

The System Folder is the "keeper" of all the pertinent information about the processes or value streams identified earlier with the Data Capture Form. The System Folder is the prime reference point for the entire filing system. The System Folder:

- Centralizes all process information
- Creates a visual aid for document control
- Assists in obtaining predictable output information
- Allows process knowledge to be organizationally owned

The System Folder has two parts: the inside and the outside.

The Inside of the System Folder

The inside of the System Folder is the "brain" of the entire Lean Office System. It contains: (a) the Process Master Document, (b) the Process Review Schedule, and the (c) Training Matrix.

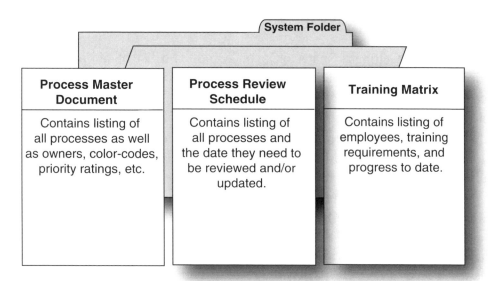

Process Master Document

As with the office supply order form (listing all the various supplies) you also need to define and list the various processes (i.e., supplies) before you can create the Kanban card/process folder for each process. The Process Master Document is a listing of every process required to meet a customer demand for a value stream. These processes may be a subset of all the processes obtained from the Data Capture Form.

The department or unit manager maintains and secures the Process Master Document.

The six steps to creating the Process Master Document are:

    a. Prioritize and classify the processes.
    b. Identify process owners.
    c. Determine color-codes.
    d. Create flowcharts.
    e. Validate the processes.
    f. Train to the validated processes.

Create a Microsoft Word or Excel document for all of the information derived from these steps.

a. *Prioritize and classify the processes.*

In Chapter 4, "Getting a Snapshot," you compiled a list of the processes that people were working on in the department (i.e., the Process Capture Form). It was suggested that you collect data for one month. After collecting this data you now need to prioritize processes as: (a) critical or (b) non-critical within the value stream. You may need to identify additional classifications such as special projects, as needed, meetings, etc. You also need to identify clearly between daily processes and those that are not typically done daily. Your classification of processes (and further prioritization within each category) will allow you to maximize the Lean Office System with flexibility once it is in place.

The first step is to categorize each process according to one of the three process classifications:

1. Critical processes that must be done today (immediately). They have a direct financial impact on the organization or deal with life and death situations.
2. Non-critical processes that can be rescheduled for the next day.
3. Reference processes that are done on a weekly, monthly, or irregular basis.

Critical process examples are customer orders, customer quotes, billing, faxing information to the customer, debit/credit transactions, triage, stat blood work, etc. These processes can further be prioritized as to daily urgency of 1, 2, or 3, depending on your industry or organization. Although all are critical, each may also have a priority assigned. For example, customer orders may be have a daily critical process level of 1 and customer quotes a 2. The entire team should come to a consensus on the reasons for establishing the prioritization scheme of critical processes.

Non-critical process examples are filing information, ordering supplies, scheduling patient follow-up visits, etc.

Reference process examples are completing a capital authorization request, family emergency leave request, trip authorization request, etc.

Once you have classified all the processes, update the Process Master Document by identifying the priority level for each process.

					Critical				Non-critical							

Process Master Document

C= Completed
R = Ready (trained and loaded in Heijunka)
W = Working on

Process Number	Process Name		Critical			Non-critical				
1	Customer Performances		x							
2	Long Term Agreements			x						
3	Contracts						x			
4	Copy Requests						x			
5	Rated Orders									

b. Identify process owners.

Identify the individual owner for each process. The owner of the process is the person who has the most experience or is known to complete that process efficiently and effectively.

Responsibilities of the process owner will include:

- Creating a process flowchart
- Conducting the training for that process
- Ensuring the process is reviewed on the review date
- Notifying the manager of the required updates to the Process Master Document
- Updating all process folders, when required

Total up the entire list of processes, critical, non-critical, and reference. Allocate the total number of processes among the total number of employees working the department. People may volunteer for several processes (giving them immediate ownership and recognition of their expertise) or the processes may be assigned in a round-robin fashion. The person who knows a process the best should ideally be the owner of that process. There may be times when someone volunteers to be the owner of a process but may not be the most efficient owner for the process. In that case:

- Discuss any reservations, privately, with that person, then work to ensure the best process owner is chosen
- Allow the person to keep that process, but monitor it closely
- Allow open group discussion, but address the topic tactfully
- Allow co-ownership of a process for training (be careful not to do this too often)

Update the Process Master Document once all the process owners are identified.

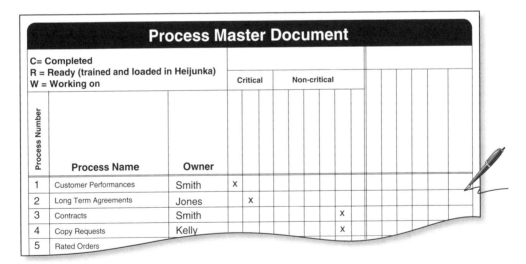

c. Determine color-codes.

It is easier to manage the system by color-coding the file folders. The System Folder that contains the Process Master Document should be white. The team members can decide all other colors. The process categories that need to be assigned a color are:

- Critical (there may be more than one level here)
- Non-critical
- Reference
- As Needed
- Meetings
- Projects

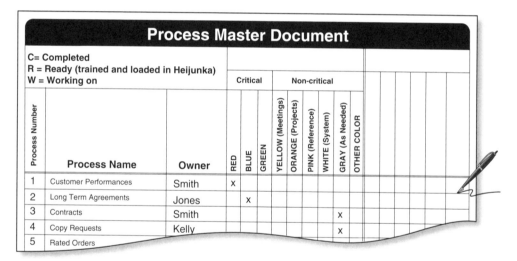

Process Number	Process Name	Owner	Critical			Non-critical							
			RED	BLUE	GREEN	YELLOW (Meetings)	ORANGE (Projects)	PINK (Reference)	WHITE (System)	GRAY (As Needed)	OTHER COLOR		
1	Customer Performances	Smith	x										
2	Long Term Agreements	Jones		x									
3	Contracts	Smith								x			
4	Copy Requests	Kelly								x			
5	Rated Orders												

C= Completed
R = Ready (trained and loaded in Heijunka)
W = Working on

Update the Process Master Document once the processes are color-coded. Place the color-code legend on the front cover of each process folder.

d. Create flowcharts.

Train all team members on how to draw a flowchart. Use software such as Visio or ABC for this task. The flowcharts can also be hand-drawn (not recommended with the ease and availability of flowchart applications today). Team members can also create their documents by listing step-by-step tasks/procedures in a Microsoft Word document. The team members should decide on how they will document the processes. Establish a schedule with the process owners and agree to review at least one process flowchart each week. First, review the critical processes that directly relate to the Team Charter and/or a specific value stream.

e. Validate the processes.

After completing the previous four steps, validate all processes before training people on them. Validate processes by having:

- Various team members review each process and document required changes
- The manager review each process and sign-off

Ensure someone other than the process owner has process review input. Although the owner of the process is responsible for it, and is most likely the expert regarding that process, another person - an auditor of sorts - should audit the process independently. Typical audit standards require that processes get reviewed annually (minimally). The Lean File System requires continual reviewing and updating as changes will occur. This is a real-time process improvement system.

Update the Process Master Document once the process is validated.

Process Review Schedule

Department Customer Service

Location Manager's office and posted on area bulletin board

Time Covered January 1 - December 31

Process Name	Review Date	Owner	Training Needed (employees)	Date Completed	Process Master Document Updated
Contracts	10/15	Matlock	Rubble	10/5	10/10
			Halsey	10/6	

f. Train to the validated processes.

Training employees to a new or updated process may be a first for many organizations. This is a system to capture "real-time" process changes while the actual work is being performed. We will cover that in the Step 2 - Create the Process Folder or Work Kanban section later in this chapter.

There are basically two types of training that can be used for training employees in the new process: (a) competency-based or (b) attendance-based. If the process changes are significant or are critical to the organization, then competency-based training would occur as one-on-one training or as some sort of pre-post test. When the process changes are minor, then attendance-based training can occur.

(a) Competency-based

Conduct competency-based training when the following conditions exist:

- A process is not commonly known
- A process causes customer dissatisfaction
- A process is extremely critical to the business

Competency-based training is typically in the form of a Skills Assessment. The Skills Assessment has an employee demonstrate the process with the process owner or manager/supervisor. The Assessment should be appropriately filed in the employee's records.

(b) Attendance-based

A process owner conducts attendance-based training for individuals or small groups. If the process is common, conduct an overview with employees at an Office Quick-Start. Ensure attendees sign a Training Sign-In Sheet. Update all affected documents to reflect the training.

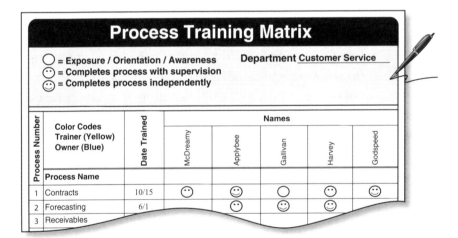

Update the Process Master Document once the training is complete.

Process Number	Process Name	Owner	RED	BLUE	GREEN	YELLOW (Meetings)	ORANGE (Projects)	PINK (Reference)	WHITE (System)	GRAY (As Needed)	OTHER COLOR	Folder Created	Flowchart Created	Approved	Trained	Review Date _Year	Review Completed
	Process Master Document																
	C= Completed / R = Ready (trained and loaded in Heijunka) / W = Working on		Critical		Non-critical							Folder Requirements					
1	Customer Performances	Smith	x									C	C	C	C	4/15	
2	Long Term Agreements	Jones		x								C	C	C	R	6/30	S.J.
3	Contracts	Smith								x		C	C	W			
4	Copy Requests	Kelly								x		C	C	C	R	12/15	
5	Rated Orders	Wagner								x		C	W			3/15	
6	Forecasting	Stetson					x					C	C	C	R	8/31	
7	Order Entry - ABC Company	Parr		x								C	C	C	R	4/15	R.P.
8	Order Entry - DEF Company	Parr		x								C	C	C	R	4/15	R.P.
9	Shipping	Smith			x							W				4/15	
10	WEB Updates	Smith								x		C	C	W		11/15	
11	Internet Sales	Jones	x									C	C	C	R	7/31	
12	Customer Follow-Ups	Parr			x							C	C	C	R	4/15	
13	Packing Slip	Smith			x							C	C	C	R	6/15	J.S.
14	Quotes - Generated	Kelly								x		C	C	W		8/31	
15	Quotes - Follow-up	Kelly								x		C	C	C	R	4/15	D.K.
16	Proof-Reading Orders	Stetson								x		C	C	C	C	10/31	J.S.
17	Credit Check	Jones			x							C	W			11/15	
18	Closing	Smith	x									C	C	C	R	4/30	J.S.
19	Wire Transfers	Jones		x								C	C	C	R	4/15	S.J.
20	Marketing Report	Wagner					x					C	C	C	C	9/30	
21	Credit Hold	Jones			x							C	C	C	R	10/31	
22	Expense Checks	Kelly								x		C	C	C	R	6/30	D.K
23	Ordering Supplies	Jones								x		C	C	C	C	4/14	J.S.
24	Budget Report	Parr								x		W				9/30	
25	Insurance Claim	Kelly			x							C	C	C	R	4/15	D.K

All this information is contained within the System Folder. Each work area or value stream should have a separate System Folder.

The Outside of the System Folder

Display a folder priority rating and the status of the folder on the outside of it.

The folder priority rating, prominently displayed on the folder's front cover, indicates the nature of the time-sensitive importance of the contents as follows: Critical, Non-Critical, and Reference.

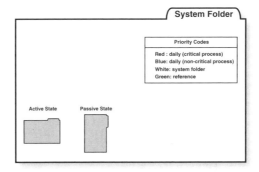

2. Create the Process Folder or Work Kanban.

Now you will organize all of the information that you collected in Step 1 into separate folders: one folder for each process. These folders are referred to as process folders, work Kanbans, or simply Kanbans. Each folder will contain the following:

  a. Value-Added Time Reporting Log
  b. Flowchart of the process
  c. Work required by that process

The process folders should be located near the location where the work will be performed. Process folders contain the working documents to ensure employees follow the process steps consistently, to the standards established by the process owner. The information in this folder will contribute dramatically to improved productivity that is predictable by eliminating work variation and waste.

If different groups work on the same process, create a separate process folder for each group. The process owner is responsible for documenting changes resulting from continuous improvement ideas in each process folder.

The process folder is the "keeper" of all working knowledge for a specific process. It reflects the actual work required by customers. Every process listed in the Process Master Document must have a process folder identified with it. The process folder:

- Details all tasks necessary to complete the process
- Acts as a visual tool to ensure work consistency
- Reduces work variation by promoting predictable output
- Supports continuous improvement
- Allows for organizationally owned process knowledge

The Inside of the Process Folder

The process folder contains the process flowchart, Value-Added Time Reporting Log, and the work that must be completed. The folder is a "Kanban" and is a signal to do work if is placed in the active state. (Later is this chapter you will determine how much work is to be placed in each folder.)

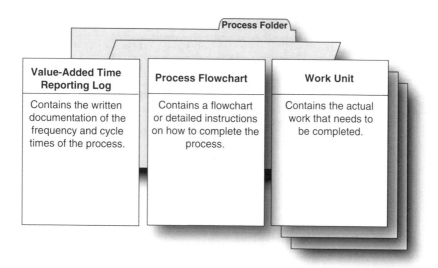

Value-Added Time Reporting Log

Use the Value-Added Time Reporting Log to track process cycle times. This is an ongoing process in the Lean File System. The Log should be located on the inside left part of the folder. Forward the Log to the manager monthly for further analysis and record keeping. The Log provides:

- Accurate, data driven departmental performance indicators
- Up-to-date work analyses
- Continuous improvement ideas
- Justification data for additional employees based on work volume increases

Make Log entries each time a process begins and ends. Initial and date the Log.

Value-Added Time Reporting Log

Process Name _Orders_   Date _August 15 - 30_

Department _Intl Sales_

Quantity in Folder	Date	Start Time	End Time	Initials	Comments
6	8/15	8:30	9:30	MS	
4	8/15	2:15	2:30	RB	

The Outside of the Process Folder

Label the outside of the process folder in two locations: one label on the folder tab and the other on the front cover.

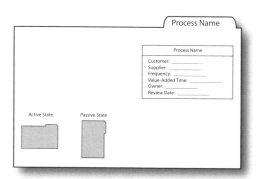

Use this as a visual for quick retrieval. The labels also eliminate wasted "search" time.

Ensure the following additional information is standard on every folder:

Process: The name of the process as listed on the Process Master Document

Supplier: The most upstream process supplying work requirements

Customer: Name of the most downstream entity requesting work to be completed

Frequency: The average number of times the process needs to be completed per time period

Value-Added Time: Total cycle time required to complete the process

Owner: Name of the individual who has process ownership

Review Date: The periodic date on which the process must be reviewed

3. Establish a Holding Point.

Create a physical place where the process folders (i.e., the organizational knowledge) can be placed for general availability. This initial placement creates a visual trigger for all to observe. The following is an illustration of a circular device which would serve to hold the folders.

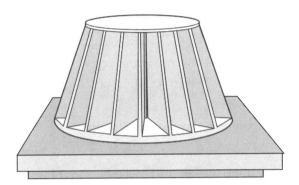

Legends represent the status of the process folders and should also appear on the outside of the folder as a visual aid. Process folders can be in an active or passive state.

An active folder contains work that must be completed and resides in a horizontal position.

Active State

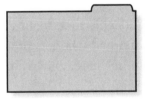

Passive folders contain work that has been completed and are stored vertically.

Passive State

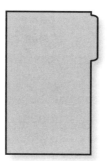

Active or passive state folders are visual cues which accomplish:

- Standardizing communications regarding current work being performed
- Signaling managers when work is behind schedule

The System Folder always remains in the active state.

Process folders start out in the active state since they contain work that must be completed. The folder will move to the passive state once the work in the folder is completed.

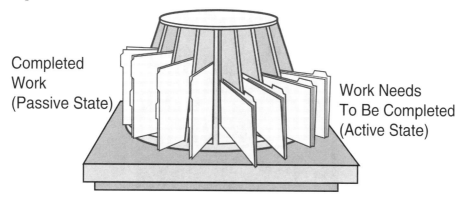

After creating the process folder, the team members need to decide the following:

- The permanent location of the process folder
- The number of process folders that need to be created (dependent on how cells or groups of employees are working together as a team)

Note: If two groups, teams, or areas will be working on the same process, then two identical process folders will be required. If there is only one group/team/area working on a process, then only one process folder is required

Ensure the process folders are made visible throughout the area to which employees have easy access. The process folders will be integrated with Visible Pitch in the next chapter.

The Lean Office Wheel or something similar works well for visibly organizing paper-work. Work should be easily accessible to the employees and should be labeled with the appropriate pitch times for each value stream. This will evolve into the Visible Pitch system and later into Heijunka (next chapter), which becomes the cornerstone for the Lean Office for a paper-based system. However, you will see these same concepts applied in the Application Case Study at the end of this chapter.

4. Balance the Work Loads.

Once the process folders have a location that is central to the area or process where the employees will be completing the work, the work elements must be balanced to promote continuous work flow. Work Load Balancing is a process which determines the optimal distribution of work in the value stream to meet takt time.

Non-Lean offices may have some employees working overtime while other employees may have time on their hands. Work Load Balancing is a process to attain the ideal state where employees are all working evenly on value-added work. Work Load Balancing begins with a current state analysis of the cycle times of a process or set of tasks.

Cycle Time

Cycle time is the time that elapses between the beginning of a work process to the time it is completed. Cycle time is used with takt time in establishing the best combination of work load and task assignments. Administrative cycle times can take between 3 seconds (e.g., for a computer entry) to 1 week or longer (e.g., to create a construction project proposal). Establishing accurate times for processes is critical for the successful application of Work Load Balancing within a value stream.

Cycle time should not be confused with takt time. Cycle time is the rate of a process. Cycle time helps identify the number of people required for a process, value stream, or department (when takt time is known). Cycle time, as well as takt time, should be used in conjunction with Standard Work.

There are three types of cycle times:

(1) Individual cycle time is the completion rate for an individual task or single work operation.

   Examples of individual cycle time are: obtaining a credit report for a mortgage application, dispensing meds to a patient prior to surgery, or entering a customer order.

(2) Total cycle time is the rate of completion of a process or group of tasks that have a common element. This is calculated by adding up the individual cycle times for that process or value stream.

Examples of total cycle time are: prepping a patient for surgery, completing a mortgage application for a client, or selling a piece of real estate.

(3) Group cycle time is the rate of completing a group task or objective. This is the total individual cycle times added together for a project.

Examples for group cycle time are: a contractor building a house, the addition of a new building to a hospital, or building a bridge.

The following demonstrates the various tasks and associated cycle times.

Cycle Time Table							
	Worker 1		Worker 2		Worker 3		Worker 4	
Work Element	Description	Cycle Time	Description	Cycle Time	Description	Cycle Time	Description	Cycle Time
1	Check Accuracy	5 m	Check Availability	5 m	Confirm	5 m	Enter Order	5 m
2	Check Stock	15 m	Confirm Reorder	2 m	Send	1 m	Update File	1 m
3	Write Order	10 m					Copy Payables	1 m
Total Time		30 m		7 m		6 m		7 m

The best tool to balance work amongst employees is the Employee Balance Chart.

Employee Balance Chart

The Employee Balance Chart is a visual representation of the current condition of work activities that make up a process. It is used to determine how to balance the work elements to improve work flow.

The seven steps to Work Load Balancing are:

    a. Choose a process in the value stream.

    b. Obtain individual cycle times for the various tasks in the process. (Information from the Document Tagging process may be used.)

    c. Add the individual cycle times to calculate the total cycle time of the value stream.

    d. Create the Employee Balance Chart of the current state.

    e. Determine the ideal number of employees.

    f. Create the Employee Balance Chart of the future state.

    g. Re-allocate work elements, standardize, and train.

Let us take a brief detour for a minute on where we are. You may be wondering why you are establishing cycle times when you have not established who has the best process to analyze. Use some discretion here. For the value stream and processes that will require this kind of scrutiny and analysis, team members already have a good idea of which employee's processes can be reviewed and used for this activity. For the time being, we are only concerned with improving flow established by simply balancing and re-arranging as much work as possible. Later in this book, we will build on Work Load Balancing, thus allowing the best practice to be standardized.

a. Choose a process in the value stream.

Be very clear about identifying the beginning and end points (or times) of a process. Be explicit about process parameters. The team should have a good understanding of the processes from creating the value stream map.

b. Obtain individual cycle times for the various tasks in the process.

Cycle times should be derived from the current state value stream map and the Document Tagging Worksheet. Re-visit these times to ensure accuracy. Members of the team may want to use a stopwatch to time the various tasks. Ensure the cycle times are accurate. Take the time to analyze the processes. The analysis will provide a good way for team members to understand the wastes that they will discover during the analysis.

c. *Add the individual cycle times to calculate the total cycle time of the value stream.*

d. *Create the Employee Balance Chart of the current state.*

Create a bar chart identifying each process or employee, along with the various individual cycle times. Visually display the chart on an easel or wall so the entire team can review it and make appropriate comments. Use Post-it Notes to represent the tasks associated with the processes. Make the Post-it Notes proportional to represent the time each work element represents. Draw a horizontal line to represent takt time.

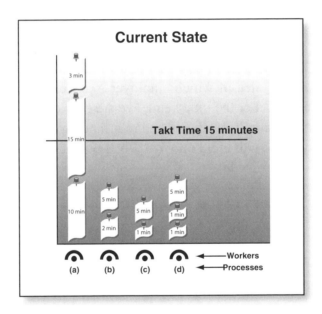

e. Determine the ideal number of employees.

To determine the ideal number of employees needed to meet the requirements of the value stream, divide the total process cycle time by the takt time.

Total process cycle time / takt time = # of workers required

Example: 50 minute total cycle time / 15 minute takt time = 3.3 workers required

The number may not come out exactly even; therefore, the following suggestions may be considered:

a. If the decimal number from the calculation is less than #.5 workers required, balance the value stream to the lesser whole number. Ensure each worker is balanced to takt time and allocate any excess time to one worker. Allocate the additional employee's time to work on Standard Work and Kaizen activities attempting to reduce the cycle times to takt time. Once that has been accomplished, then that person can be used at another position in the organization. Lean is not about reducing the number of people, it is about eliminating waste. Make every effort to place that person in a continuous improvement capacity or elsewhere in the organization. Lean will *never* be accepted if people are eliminated from the organization.

Note: To work on reducing process cycle times to meet takt time, the Standard Work Combination Table and Standard Work Chart will be discussed later in this chapter.

b. If the decimal number from the calculation is equal to or greater than #.5, then balance to the larger whole number. Most likely, you will not be able to eliminate that much waste from the process at this time, but again, make sure each employee is balanced to takt time and have all the excess time allocated to one person.

f. Create the Employee Balance Chart of the future state.

Work with team members to move the Post-it Notes around to balance the various work elements. Attempt to have each employee balanced to takt time while maintaining the flow of work. The ideal situation is to have all employees working towards maintaining takt time.

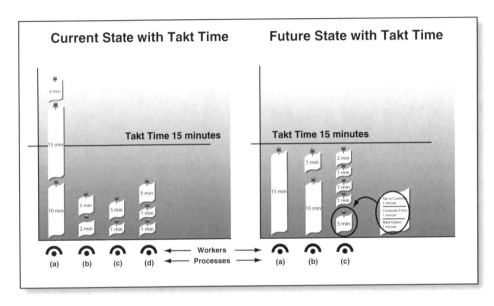

g. Re-allocate work elements, standardize, and train.

Once a consensus has been obtained on balancing the work elements, conduct the proper training, and document what has been done.

In summary, Work Load Balancing will:

- Evenly distribute work elements amongst the employees to improve flow
- Define the order in which work elements should be done in a process
- Determine the optimal number of workers required for a process
- Assist in the work area re-design portion of the future state map

After understanding how flow can be improved by a new office layout, organizing work in the folders, and balancing the work load, efforts must now be used to standardize as much process knowledge as possible to reduce work variation.

5. Create Standard Work.

Standard Work is a set of procedures that control tasks. These tasks are then executed consistently - without variation from the original intent. Standard Work provides a basis for providing consistent levels of office productivity, quality, and safety, while promoting a positive work attitude based on well-documented work standards. Standard Work, done properly, reduces all process variation.

Standard Work is comprised of two main tools: the Standard Work Combination Table and the Standard Work Chart.

The Standard Work Combination Table will:

- Document the exact time requirement for each work element or task in a process or area
- Indicate the flow of all work in an area or process
- Display the work design sequence based on takt time (ideally)
- Demonstrate the time relationship between physical work (computer entries, phone calling, etc.), the movement of work (through walking or digital transmission of documents), queue times, and computer processing time

The Standard Work Combination Table is an important tool for allocating work within the value stream when total cycle times are greater than takt time. Videotaping the process that is being reviewed is a good method to accurately document and time each work element.

The 6 steps for creating the Standard Work Combination Table are:

   a. Break the tasks for each worker into separate work elements (videotape to obtain accuracy).
   b. Time each task from (a) by observation or videotape and review.
   c. Complete the Standard Work Combination Table.
   d. Review each task. Question whether it should be eliminated or if the time can be improved.
   e. Create a new Standard Work Combination Table.
   f. Post in the process folder and work area.

The Standard Work Combination Table is a powerful tool and should be used as the basis for all improvement activities connected with that process. It does require time to thoroughly complete, but will be well worth the effort in the long run. It may seem odd to do this for administrative processes, but it has proven effective when used in office settings.

Standard Work Combination Table

Date	12/10	Value Stream Domestic Orders	Work (physical)
Daily Reqt.	75		Walking
Takt Time	30 minutes	Work Instruction No. 1	Computer Interaction
Process Name	Order entry	Page 1 of 4	Queue Time (waiting)

Processing Times (minutes) — Wrk - Work Physical   Wlk - Walking   CI - Computer Interaction   QT - Queue Time

Step #	Task/Activity	Wrk	Wlk	CI	QT	5 10 15 20 25 30 35 40 45 50 55 60 65 70 75
1	Retrieve mail		5			
2	Separate orders from quotes	15				
3	Determine credit				15	
4	Fax customer confirmation order		2			
5	Update customer file			3		
6	Print hardcopy	3				
7	File hardcopy		2			

Totals: 5 + 15 + 15 + 2 + 3 + 3 + 2 = 45 minutes

The Standard Work Chart illustrates the sequence of the work being performed. It provides a visual training aid for employees. Employees who may not interact with that process regularly can refer to the chart and be confident if they had to complete that process. It should be updated as improvements are made.

The 5 steps for creating the Standard Work Chart are:

    a. Draw the office area layout on the chart. Label all items.
    b. Designate work element locations by number.
    c. Use arrows to show movement of employees.
    d. Fill out all data boxes on the chart.
    e. Post the chart in the work area.

The Standard Work Chart will:

- Display the work sequence, process layout, and work-in-process
- Display the worker movement for each activity, task, or operation
- Identify quality standards, safety concerns, or critical opportunities for errors

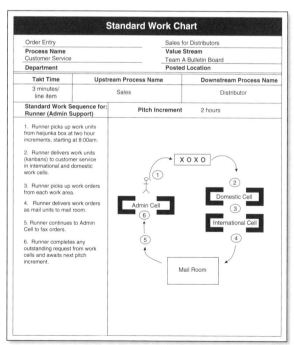

Once the processes are documented and are being performed to the standard, implement controlled flow. Controlled flow is accomplished through Visible Pitch.

6. Implement Controlled Flow through Visible Pitch.

After balancing work loads, improve the overall flow of work by implementing visible pitch. Visible pitch is used to distribute a similar work volume throughout the day using process folders and the Lean Office Wheel (or a similar device for holding work). It is the pre-cursor to Heijunka or Leveling, which will level work by volume and variety throughout the day.

Visible pitch will:

- Provide the first level for controlled work flow
- Become a visual to identify problems as they arise
- Distribute work evenly throughout the day, reducing overtime and stress
- Reveal the need for cross-training and an increase in generalist work

The six steps for controlling work flow through visible pitch are:

a. Determine the critical processes to be 'beta' tested.
b. Balance critical process total cycle times to the new office layout and capacity.
c. Determine pitch increments and label the work holding device (Lean Office Wheel) accordingly.
d. Determine the distribution of process folders.
e. Implement the use of visible pitch.
f. Monitor and adjust as necessary.

Pre-determine the amount of work placed in a visible pitch device. This device is similar to a mail box and resides in a pre-defined location that separates value stream work from other work that may need to be completed. The work will initially be a subset of the critical processes.

The following are examples of visible pitch devices.

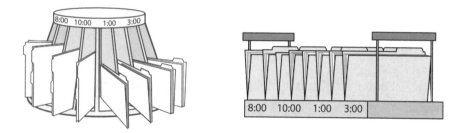

The visible pitch device must be monitored to ensure work is completed as scheduled. Creating a visible pitch device is a pre-requisite to operating a Pull System and Heijunka.

The device should be labeled according to the pitch increments of the value stream. The process folders or Kanbans should be distributed at these pitch increments by the Team Leader or supervisor who allocates process work. This is to ensure the work (i.e., process folder) is distributed and collected as scheduled according to the pitch increment.

Visible pitch is a great tool to get everyone used to the rhythm of takt time. It places emphasis on completing a certain quantity of work in an allotted time to meet customer demand. It further gives the team a common purpose of maintaining this "demand." After approximately two months of using visible pitch, other value streams can be added to this device, thus evolving to Heijunka or Leveling.

Chapter Summary

We covered many Lean tools in this chapter. The Lean File System is the over-all system to create and maintain three types of folders: the System Folder, the Process Folder, and the Reference Folder.

The System Folder is the "keeper" of all pertinent information about the processes or value streams identified. It is the main reference point for the entire filing system.

The Process Folder or Kanban holds the actual value-added work to be performed.

The Reference Folder contains the references required when value-added work is to be performed.

The Employee Balance Chart is used to create a visual representation of the current condition. It can then be used to determine how to balance the work within the value stream to a proposed future state.

The Standard Work Combination Table and Standard Work Chart are tools to document and improve to best practice. Finally, implement the visible pitch device as the "test drive" for visually controlling work throughout a day. This will later evolve into Heijunka or Leveling.

Observations from the Lean Office

This chapter required the most time to complete. It is a long and winding road to get through its essence, but the results are worth every minute. The tools will keep you on the road, but expect some bumps along the way.

- Do not underestimate the importance of standard work. There will be questions with which the team will struggle. Keep focused on the elimination of waste.
- The Lean File System must be completed prior to implementing visible pitch and then moving to Heijunka.
- Any department in any industry can implement what is contained in this chapter.
- Continue to improve the cycle times of the work elements by reviewing the Standard Work Combination Table. Update the Standard Work Chart as necessary.
- Make as much work visible as possible.
- Be creative with how to use the internet, the intranet, and Desktop computer programs to create virtual file systems having the same capabilities explained in this chapter.
- Just get going! Do not attempt to have every question answered at this time.
- The only real failure is if you do not try to do this.

Application Case Study

After studying the principles of the Lean File System, Andrew Cencini and his Sales Manager, Steven Thorpe, saw that every step could also be executed within their office computer systems. The System Folder and the Process Folder could all be housed within the Groove workspace already set up and described earlier. As shown on the following screen shot, the Files tool of Groove (see Chapter 3 for the explanation of this collaboration application within Microsoft Office) shows, looking at the Folder hierarchy on the left, the Sales Process folder has two subfolders, the Process Folder and the System Folder. Within the Process Folder are kept the Value-Added Time Reporting Log, the Process Flowchart, and the Work Unit Files (folder). The Work Unit Files folder contains the working files. The System Folder contains the Process Master Document, Process Review Schedule, and the Training Matrix folder, each housing all of those specific documents (similar to those shown earlier in this chapter); this makes that information easy for all team members to find and use.

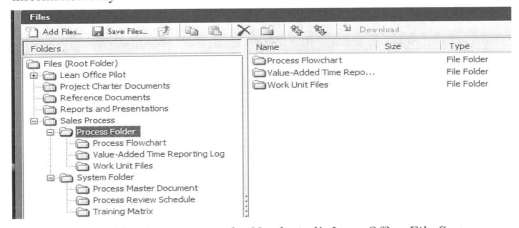

Groove Folder Organization for Northwind's Lean Office File System

Setting up Microsoft Access or Excel to perform the actual work tracking and the data required for the Value-Added Time Reporting Log would require significant IT resources, which is not feasible at this time. Fortunately, for the Prospecting Value Stream, an off-the-shelf software application known as CRM or Customer Relationship Management, could be readily adapted to perform the necessary improvements to their files and folders.

Any of a number of different applications could serve the purpose. They all perform the same basic functions of:

- Making sales data and forecast information all immediately accessible
- Enabling the sales team to view leads on the computer screen and then track what happens to each prospect
- Enabling improved follow-up and customer service
- Providing accessible decision-driving information to management

After some study and with the advice of the IT team, Andrew chose ACT!, a relatively straightforward, affordable, and flexible package that can be used for implementing the Lean File System in a single office. Some other systems that they looked at were Goldmine, Oracle, SalesForce, Microsoft Dynamics, and vTiger, which is an Open Source application. ACT! seemed suitable to start with given Northwind's situation.

Some of the features of ACT! that weighed heavily in Andrew's decision:

- Ease of use, well-designed training modules, and strong service and consulting support
- Flexibility for customization, if necessary, since ACT! is targeted for smaller teams of users such as the Northwind sales force
- Built-in integration with Microsoft Office
- Strong built-in module to manage new opportunities and prospects
- Reasonable and competitive cost overall

Other systems offer more features and power, but usually with the trade-offs of higher cost and complexity. Andrew decided to keep his CRM system relatively simple while still having the necessary features to manage effectively all customers and prospects.

The first step was to acquire and install the system for everyone in the Northwind sales team and then provide the necessary training for all users – not a large investment given the benefits to be realized. Next, the existing data for staff and customers needed to be imported into ACT! This turned out to be straightforward since the data that the Northwind team already had in their Access database was easily imported into ACT!

The following screen shot is the result of the data that was pulled from the Microsoft Access database into ACT!.

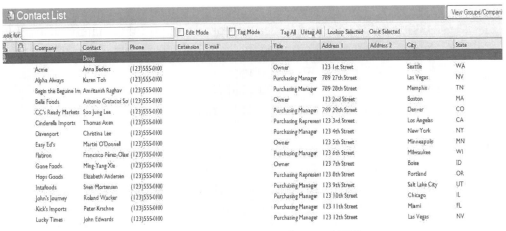

Contact Data Imported into ACT!

ACT! has a built-in opportunity or prospecting tracking feature that was adapted to the Northwind sales process as shown below. The number of steps, the names of the steps, and the probabilities of closure at each stage can be customized for any number of separate processes.

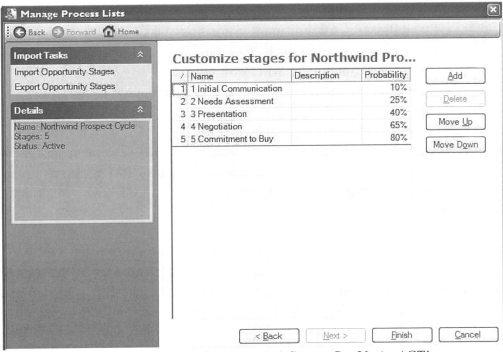

The Prospecting (or Opportunity) Stages Set Up in ACT!

Each time an action takes place in any one of these steps that creates an opportunity with a customer, it is entered into ACT!, as shown in the following screen shot. Note that included in the tracking information are the number of calls required to complete the step in the sales opportunity process and the amount of time directly spent. The date the opportunity was initiated, the current date, and date closed, if applicable, are also captured.

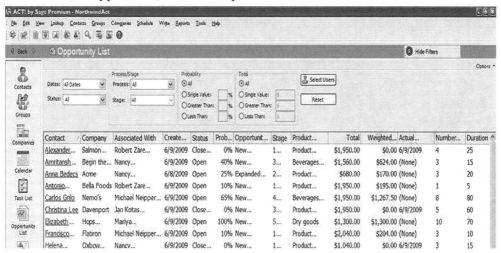

Documenting Actions in ACT!

ACT! has a number of built-in standard reports that can provide valuable management information. The following screen shot shows one such report, the open opportunities generated so far for the month. However, the power of such systems comes in their flexibility to provide the basis for customizable slicing and dicing of the data.

Opportunities by Record Manager

Date Range: All Dates   Total for Date Range: $23,515.00

Record Manager   Andrew Cencini   Number of Opportunities: 10   Total for Record Manager: $23,515.00   % of To

Status	Contact	Company	Name	Process/Stage	Prob.	Est. Close
Open	John Edwards	Lucky Times	New Opportunity	Northwind Prospect Cycle 2 Needs Assessment	25%	6/9/2009
Open	Soo Jung Lee	CC's Ready Markets	New Opportunity	Northwind Prospect Cycle 4 Negotiation	65%	6/16/2009
Open	Martin O'Donnell	Easy Ed's	New Opportunity	Northwind Prospect Cycle 2 Needs Assessment	25%	6/9/2009

Built-In ACT! Report on Opportunities by Record Manager

For ACT!, one such tool is the ability to export the opportunities list to Excel (shown partially in the following screen shot) where it can then be used to generate any number of analyses (e.g., using the Pivot Table capability in Excel).

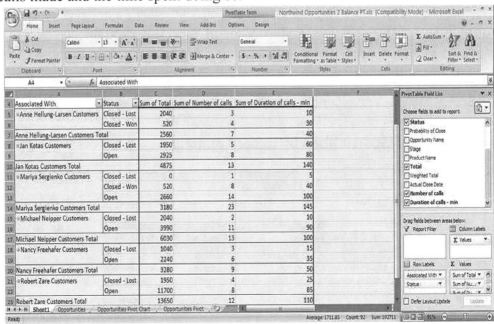

Export of Opportunities Data to Excel for Easier Analysis

The following screen shot is one example of such a Pivot Table. This particular Pivot Table summarizes a number of the fields by sales rep including number of calls and duration of the calls in total making it easy to compare the number of calls made and the time spent doing so.

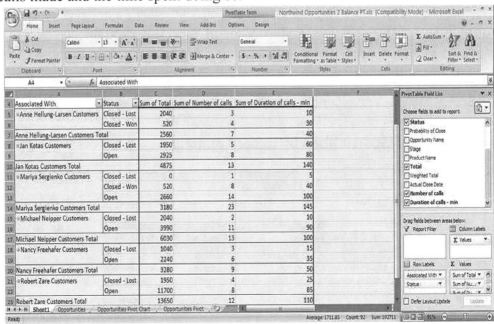

Pivot Table Analysis of Sales Representative Calls

Another important report that can be generated from this data is the Value-Added Time Report for sales, lost sales, and opportunities still open. This data, once additional days of input data have been compiled, will be used by Andrew and the team to pinpoint where they are losing opportunities and how much time they are spending on lost sales and on each step of the process.

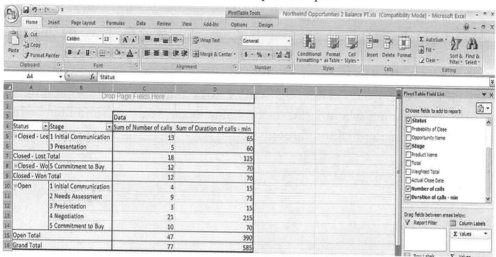

Pivot Table Analysis of Call Time by Process Step

ACT! has many other features, but one particularly useful one is the Opportunity Pipeline Report which is a visual representation of the number of open opportunities at each stage in Northwind's sales process as shown in the following screen shot. This analysis could be helpful to identify bottlenecks or discontinuities in the sales process.

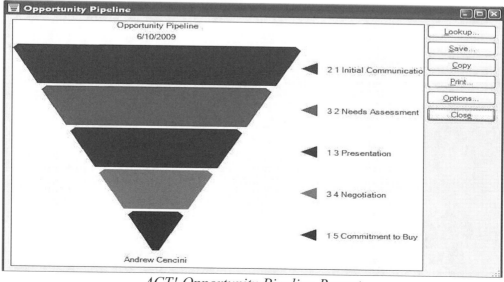

ACT! Opportunity Pipeline Report

Many other reports can be generated from ACT!, from Excel spreadsheets exported from ACT!, or from separate, specialized database mining applications such as Crystal. However, describing such tools is beyond the scope of this book. The point is that such analyses can be readily automated once the data is entered with discipline every day.

Just as CRM systems have evolved into powerful tools for tracking and measuring sales team performance, similar systems exist for other administrative processes as well. The key is to commit to using such systems to capture all the relevant data every day. Then, that data can be made available to appropriate staff for determining where issues or problems occur real-time and thus be used for effective decision-making throughout the day.

Chapter 9

Making It All Work Through Heijunka (Leveling)

Simplify Through Leveling

Chapter Overview

Heijunka or leveling is defined as balancing work by volume and variety during a period of time, typically a day. The day is further broken down into more manageable units of 2-4 hours (previously discussed as Pitch).

In the previous two chapters, work flow was improved through Work Load Balancing, Standard Work, and creating a "living" Lean File System. In this chapter we will incorporate additional Lean tools - the Runner, Leveling, and the Heijunka System - into the Lean Office System.

Leveling

The purpose of leveling is to ensure:

- Work is evenly distributed amongst workers by volume and variety
- No work is waiting in queue
- No work is released upstream that is not required downstream
- A pull system of work is established
- Continuous flow is achieved
- A visual aid that identifies when and where work is behind schedule

Leveling is a simple concept, but it can be difficult to understand and implement. The main principle of leveling is scheduling. Initially, leveling and scheduling may seem similar, but they are distinct. Scheduling is a significant component of leveling and is used in all industries. The following are some examples of scheduling:

- When you schedule a car tune-up, time is allocated depending on the make, age, and problem of the car.
- When you schedule a yearly physical exam, time is allocated according to your age, number of tests required, and previous health issues.
- When you dine in a restaurant, time is allocated according to the size of your party, type of party, etc.
- When you schedule a mortgage closing, time is allocated according to the closing agent's time.
- When you schedule a dental or surgical appointment, time is allocated according to the specific procedures anticipated.

Leveling, in the Lean Office System, is a more sophisticated form of scheduling. From our previous examples, scheduling is the designation of work (or providing a service to a customer) at a fixed time slot. Leveling is the distribution and allocation of the work to fulfill a customer demand over a defined period of time. The difference may not seem like much, but it is significant. Scheduling does not take into consideration customer demand, and most importantly the application of Lean principles, to meet that demand.

Lean tools and concepts place the customer first, at the forefront of what must be done to satisfy that demand. Leveling ensures every customer's demand is met each and every time.

Let us continue from above with further analysis on how leveling may occur in those examples.

Example one: When a car is scheduled for a tune-up, the customer is given a time slot for the expected work to be done. That time slot may not fit your schedule. The scheduler will then attempt to fit you in at some agreed upon time. The Lean approach would be to increase capacity to meet customer demand by doing one or more of the following:

1. Determine historical demand, by the month, and create capacity for what the historical trend has been (tune-ups, brake problems, electrical problems, oil changes, etc.).
2. Cross-train more employees to handle the higher volume service jobs.
3. Increase daily capacity by reducing cycle times for repairs (this could be by implementing a bonus program based on the performance times of repair jobs, evening hours, additional shifts, etc).
4. Create capacity in bays where usage is not high by purchasing additional testing equipment, using part-time employees, etc.

Auto service facilities have well-documented data (i.e., standard work) for servicing cars. They are ahead of many industries in that Lean tool application.

Example two: When a dining reservation time is given by a restaurant, the nearer it comes to the date and reservation time, the less likely that time will be available due to an increase in customers, lack of wait staff, customers staying longer than expected, etc. When you and your guests arrive, you most likely will be told of a 15-30 minute wait. (A Seinfeld episode represents this situation well. Jerry and Elaine were at an airport. Jerry had reserved a vehicle, but despite the reservation, there was no car available. Jerry proceeded to "lecture" the woman at the counter that they are good at "taking" reservations, but not so good at "holding" reservations.) Lean (and leveling) is about doing both!

The Lean approach would be to increase capacity to handle this by doing one or more of the following:

1. If it makes good business sense, open up another area of the restaurant. This would involve tracking the customer demand and determining what percentage of customers missed their reservations by not calling and canceling ahead of time.
2. Create additional tables or re-arrange current seating.
3. Possibly increase staff (i.e., bussers) to turn the tables faster.
4. Create larger tables, maybe 10 to 15 per table, dining family style (not likely).

These examples illustrate the differences between common scheduling and customer-oriented leveling. Leveling is a practice or tool that places at the forefront the resources required to meet a customer demand. Many times, for practical business reasons, many of the solutions from the two previous examples may not work; however, it is important to understand the difference between scheduling and leveling.

COMPARISON OF SCHEDULING AND LEVELING

Scheduling

- Common in offices
- Capacity fixed
- Based on volume
- Lean tools not used
- Continuous flow not key to improvements

Leveling

- New in offices
- Capacity based on customer demand
- Based on volume and variety
- Lean tools used
- Continuous flow required

The eight steps to leveling are:

1. Calculate takt times.
2. Determine pitch for each value stream.
3. Create a scheduling sequence table or chart.
4. Determine the runner's route or other method of distributing work.
5. Create a heijunka box.
6. Create the Standard Work Chart and post on the heijunka box.
7. Load the heijunka box.
8. Implement and adjust as necessary.

The team members will need to use their creativity to design a leveling system best suited to their processes.

1. Calculate takt times.

Recall, the formula for calculating takt time is:

> **Takt Time Formula**
>
> Takt time = Net available operating time / total daily quantity required

Your team probably has been working 6 months or more collecting and analyzing data. You should have fairly accurate takt times for multiple value streams by the time you are ready for this activity.

The following are some examples of takt times:

			Takt Time Examples		
Industry	**Monthly Time Available (minutes)**	**Monthly Volume of Work (units)**	**Value Stream**	**Time/Volume**	**Takt Time (minutes)**
Manufacturing Administration	8400	840	Customer Orders - ABC Co.	8400/840	10
Manufacturing Administration	8400	280	Customer Orders - DEF Co.	8400/280	30
Healthcare Lab - Blood Draws	12600	840	Lab - blood draws from ER and floors	12600/840	15
Financial Services New Home Apps	9000	100	New Home Applications - 30 Yr. Fixed	9000/100	90
Education Registration	9600	1200	Incoming Freshmen On-site Registration	9600/1200	8

2. Determine pitch for each value stream.

You have established pitch and created and implemented a visible pitch device for a single value stream, which should have improved work flow. Now it is time to add multiple value streams to the pitch board. Calculate pitch for each value stream.

The following are some examples of pitch times:

		Pitch Examples			
Industry	**Takt Time (minutes)**	**Value Stream**	**Optimal Number of Work Units to Flow**	**Takt Time X Optimal Number of Work Units**	**Pitch (minutes)**
Manufacturing Administration	10	Customer Orders - ABC Co.	12	10 X 12	120
Manufacturing Administration	30	Customer Orders - DEF Co.	8	30 x 8	240
Healthcare Lab - Blood Draws	15	Lab - blood draws from ER and floors	8	15 x 8	120

3. Create a scheduling sequence table or chart.

A scheduling sequence table or chart is a matrix which shows each work unit or service request, when it is required, by whom, and in what quantity. The table illustrates the customer's demand at a glance and should be posted by the heijunka box. It displays the work sequence via the process folders (or Kanbans). The sequence table should be updated as customer requirements change. The time elements (pitch increments) do not account for any breaks, daily meetings, or other diversions from the work day. The times represent the actual time the work must move. Breaks, meetings, etc. must be calculated into these times.

Scheduling Sequence Table											
Value Stream	Pitch (minutes)	Daily Pick-Up Times with Number of Units									
		8:00a	9:00a	10:00a	11:00a	Noon	1:00p	2:00p	3:00p	4:00p	
Lab - blood draws - Walk-ins	120	12		12		12		12			
Lab - blood draws - Pediatrics	240					8				8	
Lab - blood draws - ER and all other floors	120		8		8		8		8		

4. Determine the runner's route or other method for distributing work.

A runner is an employee who ensures and maintains pitch integrity. Using a runner frees transport time for the people directly involved in value-added activities. The runner covers a pre-defined route within the pitch time period, picking up process folders (i.e., Kanbans) and delivering them to their appropriate places.

If a work unit or Kanban is not ready for pickup at the heijunka box or from the upstream process that is replenishing the heijunka box, the problem is immediately apparent. The runner can notify the appropriate person to remedy the problem.

The qualifications of a runner are:

- Understands value stream requirements
- Communicates well
- Understands Lean Office concepts
- Understands the importance of takt time and pitch
- Works efficiently and effectively
- Is innovative and resourceful to continually improve the route

Runners play an important role in proactive problem solving in the Lean Office System. Runners must continuously monitor the flow of work and be attuned to customer requirements. They are in a unique position to assist in preventing small problems before they become big problems that may negatively impact the customer. The team must work with the quantity of work that the runner will be distributing and create an appropriate device to move the work when it is required.

A runner's cart transports the process folders from the heijunka box and is delivered by the runner to the process.

As with all Lean Office implementation initiatives, be creative when applying the tools. It most likely will not be practical for an office to have a dedicated runner, as sensible as the runner may seem. Brainstorm with the team to determine how the runner's duties can be incorporated into a rotational team function. Consider the possibility of having an administrative assistant or a supervisor be the runner when required.

5. Create a heijunka box.

The heijunka box is the post office for the value streams and the runner is the mail carrier. There are many different ways to create a post office or heijunka box. It should be kept simple (e.g., a common location with a stand or rack identifying the times for pick-up). It may be something as simple as a modification to the visible pitch device.

The heijunka box can even be the circular file system known as the Lean Office Wheel (left photo) or can be a horizontal row of folders (right photo).

This example shows Friday's work (T + 1) as well as Monday's work (T + 2). T stands for today, + 1 stands for tomorrow, etc. Friday's and Monday's work have different colored folders (not shown). This system balances the work loads from numerous value streams.

This example shows paperwork that is organized by the hour in an administrative setting. This heijunka box (circular file cabinet) contains three distinct value streams.

Whichever type of heijunka box is used, ensure it is capable of handling variations of work loads. Once everyone has experience with the heijunka box, it is likely they will place more work in it.

6. Create the Standard Work Chart and post on the heijunka box.

The process folders or Kanbans are placed in the slots corresponding to the pitch increments in which work units are to be released to the downstream process. In the heijunka box, the Kanbans or folders that contain the work will be placed initially in an active state (Chapter 8).

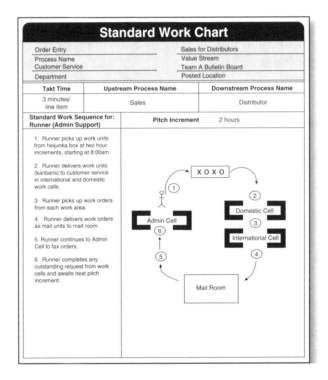

7. Load the heijunka box.

Place the process folders in their time slot. Follow the procedures on the front of the process folders.

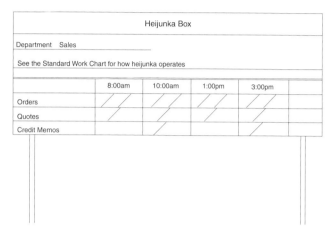

8. Implement and adjust as necessary.

Leveling occurs after achieving continuous work flow. It is a refinement to the Lean Office.

The Flow Phase - Future State Value Stream Map

Update the future state map as you progress. If an office process or activity is not represented by an icon, be creative and create additional icons.

The 30-Year Fixed Mortgage Application Future State Value Stream Map
Flow and Leveling Phases

Standard Work · Client · Folder System · Queue time = 34.5 hrs / Value added time = 2.12 hrs (127 minutes) / Total lead time = 36.62 hrs · XOXO · Kanban Supplies · Cross Training · Leveling · Mortgage Service Cell · 5S · Interoffice credit report/work verif = 60 m · Order title = 15 m · WEB appraisal = 30 m · 30 m · Admin Support · Heijunka · Admin Support / Org. app = 2 m · 2 hrs · Max = 24 FIFO · Schedule Support = 20 m · 2 hrs · 2 m · 105 m · 30 m · 20 m · 32 hrs

The Order Entry Future State Value Stream Map
Flow and Leveling Phases

Queue time = 12.5 hrs / Value added time = 1.67 hrs (100 minutes) / Total lead time = 14.17 hrs · Runner · Airbus · Folder System · XOXO · Kanban Supplies · Cross Training · Standard Work · Technical Support Cell · 5S · CT = 60 m · 30 m · 4 hrs · Admin · Heijunka · Admin / EDI = 10 m · 4 hrs · Max = 24 FIFO · EDI = 10 m / Support = 20 m · 4 hrs · 10 m · 4 hrs · 60 m · 30 m · 30 m · 4 hrs

Chapter Summary

Heijunka or leveling in the Lean Office System is the culmination of using Lean tools to ensure your team meets customer demand with the most efficient use and flow of people, work, and resources. Heijunka/leveling is the heart of the Lean Office System. Continuous improvement must be the goal of the people associated with either delivering work to the processes (i.e., the runner), filling the heijunka box with work orders (the supervisor or team leader), or completing the work in the folders (the value-added worker). Everyone is connected through the heijunka system in the value stream. Update the future state value stream map as a visual display and road map for implementing a Heijunka System.

Observations from the Lean Office

These observations may assist in understanding how to apply the concepts and tools contained in this chapter:

- Do not push too much work into the heijunka box at once.
- Do not overcomplicate the times and value stream requirements.
- Ensure the runner and all others understand pitch times.
- Continually monitor and make adjustments. Create new standard work.
- Document as you make changes. Ensure a future state value stream map is created and posted in a common area.

Readiness Guide for Part Three

Many times teams will continue with the application of Lean without having completed a good portion of what was just covered in the previous chapters. When this occurs the likelihood of success is diminished. The Readiness Guide prompts the team to determine if it should continue with Part Three or remain in Part Two.

The Readiness Guide provides:

1. A review of the critical functions that should be completed prior to learning and implementing Part Three
2. A checklist to ensure all (or most) Lean tools have been completed to ensure a solid foundation
3. An indication of what the team has accomplished
4. A point in time to acknowledge the team's work and share in a form of reward and recognition

The Readiness Guide should be reviewed with the team to ensure a consensus. The team must be trusted in completing the Readiness Guide in the context of organizational objectives, business conditions, and management's directives to determine when to move to Part Three - Sustain the Gains to World Class.

Readiness Guide for Part Three

If you respond NO to more than half of these, then you should continue to implement Part Two.

	YES	NO
1. Has daily work been made visible by everyone in the department?	☐	☐
2. Has a naming convention been determined for the desk folders?	☐	☐
3. Have the office supplies been placed on a Kanban system and everyone trained?	☐	☐
4. Does everyone understand the importance of continuous flow?	☐	☐
5. Have In-process supermarkets or FIFO lanes been implemented to improve flow?	☐	☐
6. Has the office layout been reviewed and improved upon?	☐	☐
7. Has enough data been collected to create a Distribution Report?	☐	☐
8. Have the processes been documented using the Document Tagging Worksheet?	☐	☐
9. Have critical and non-critical processes been defined?	☐	☐
10. Has a Process Master Document (or similar-type) been created?	☐	☐
11. Have process owners been defined?	☐	☐
12. Have processes been flowcharted or documented to current best practice?	☐	☐
13. Have color-codes been determined for processes?	☐	☐
14. Has a Training Matrix been created?	☐	☐
15. Has a System Folder been created?	☐	☐
16. Has a Process Review Matrix been created?	☐	☐
17. Has a Value-Added Time Reporting Log been created and put in use?	☐	☐
18. Has a Cycle Time Table been created for critical processes?	☐	☐
19. Has Work Load Balancing been done to alleviate work flow problems?	☐	☐
20. Has standard work been implemented with correct documentation?	☐	☐
21. Is there a location for the folders (or physical work) defined by pitch?	☐	☐
22. Have additional value streams been identified?	☐	☐
23. Has a runner been deployed to assist flow, if applicable?	☐	☐
24. Has a heijunka box been created and put in use?	☐	☐
25. Has work flow improved?	☐	☐

Application Case Study

Once Andrew and the Northwind's team understood the Prospecting Value Stream and how ACT! can be used to house and manage sales data, the next step was to begin to apply the principles of leveling to the office environment.

Note that in this case, the leveling of the work load will be between externally generated work (i.e., the service calls) and internally driven work (i.e., the prospecting process activities). All types of offices are going to have similar internally generated work elements. Takt time can still be calculated for each value stream. This is one way the office environment differs from the manufacturing environment, but in the end, both types can create "pull systems" that will allow work to be leveled.

Calculating takt time for internally generated work must, at times, be based on performance objectives, not, as is usual, the external demand. By taking into consideration the sales objectives set for the team based on the trend of historical improvement, Andrew calculated, given his sales target (volume of work required) of 240 closed sales per month, a takt time for the Prospecting Value Stream to be 120 minutes (assuming each of the 6 sales reps spend 50% of their day, 4 hours, working on prospecting). This was calculated using the following data: given available time of 20 work days per month = 6 reps x 4 hours per day x 20 days per month = 480 rep hours per month as total available work time. 480 rep hours to generate 240 sales per month yields a takt time of 480/240 = 2 hours or 120 minutes per closed sale. Andrew set the pitch for prospecting at 120 minutes since there was no particular optimum number for the flow of prospecting work units. In fact, according to how the process runs as conveyed by the process map (or flowchart) that was created previously (Chapter 4, page 144), multiple prospects were shown to be moving through the process simultaneously.

The next value stream the team added for leveling purposes was the Service Orders Value Stream. Service orders were the tracking reference for calls and complaints that each customer service rep had to deal with on a daily basis. Andrew wanted to balance the work across these two streams for the sales representatives. Northwind was receiving service calls on an average of 12 per day from existing customers, which also happens to constitute approximately 240 per month. Andrew budgeted for each of the sales reps two hours per day to handle service issues which, at two hours per day, resulted in a service takt time of 60 minutes. The ideal or optimal flow for the service calls is to complete each call as soon as possible (no need for batching work flow) resulting in a pitch for service calls (orders) of 60 minutes.

Andrew set up a spreadsheet to lay out the pitch times for these two value streams for his sales reps - given the work flow for prospecting at two completed closed sales per day and for service calls at two closed calls per day. This pace for each sales representative balanced job activities with the need for timely attention to the two value streams.

Value Stream	Takt Time (min)	Optimal Work Flow Units	Takt Time x Opt Units
	Pitch Time for Service Rep Call Sets		
Prospecting	120	1	120
Service calls	60	1	60

Pitch Time for Service Calls

This means that each representative is paced to spend 240 minutes per day (30 calls given the average of 15 calls per closed sale) for prospecting plus 120 minutes per day handling calls and complaints service calls (orders). The remainder of the work day (480 minutes available in 8 hours minus 240 minutes for prospecting and minus 120 minutes for service calls leaving 120 available minutes) would be used for planning, training, and administrative tasks.

The leveling sequence table for this initial simple application is shown in the following screen shot. The team decided to concentrate most of the prospecting calls in the morning and early afternoon and to spread the service calls throughout the day since service for customers is a top priority. Also, this leveling scheme provided time at the end of the day for catching up on administrative issues and for planning the calls for the next day via ACT!.

The team was happy with this design in that it reflected a balanced load across the team – all had the same sequence – and it balanced the work of each representative within the day. Andrew would be able to check the status of everyone's work throughout the day by counting the closed sales and closed service calls being entered into the company's financial database. Andrew usually checked the status of closed sales and service calls at noon and 5 PM each day. He expected, on average, per sales rep to see one sale completed by noon and one more by 1500 (or 3:00 pm) since the sales effort was to be front-loaded during the day. For service calls, which spread throughout the day, Andrew expected to see one service call closed by noon and one more closed by the end of the day.

	A	B	C	D	E	F	G	H
1				Expected Completion Time				
2	Value Stream	Pitch Time	8:00 AM	10:00 AM	12:00 PM	3:00 PM	5:00 PM	
3	Prospecting	120			1	1		
4	Service Orders	60			1		1	
5								
6								
7								
8								
9								

Leveling Sequence Table

Lean Office Demystified II

Part Three.
Sustain the Gains to World Class

Leadership and Motivation in the Lean Office

Accomplishing Goals Through Others

Chapter Overview

Once the Lean Office team and work area employees have been trained to use the Lean tools (and most of the tools are being applied), sustaining the gains will be accomplished through effective leadership. Employees will become motivated to set and achieve new performance standards to sustain the gains. This can only be accomplished with effective leadership through Total Employee Involvement (TEI).

Leadership

Leaders create and communicate their "vision" of the organization and inspire others to be motivated to work to accomplish tasks consistent with achieving that vision. The focus of the organization should be on "doing the job right" or identifying "where" to go when information is needed to complete the work.

Supervision or management is narrower than leadership. Successful managers and supervisors are tasked with doing things "right," whereas successful leaders do the "right" things. Leaders envision the great scope of situations and seek to have others follow their lead willingly.

There are certain tools required to create the "vision" of the organization. Most strategic planning models cover the "long-term" vision. While this is necessary for an organization to succeed, most people need the "long term" vision broken down into more manageable, "near term" time frames. The shorter time frames include activities such as: work standards, schedules, and objectives used to connect the vision to day-to-day tasks. The leader's vision acts as a compass, always pointing in the right direction. These daily objectives help achieve the vision. By communicating the vision and linking it directly to daily tasks, the successful leader creates an environment where employees motivate themselves to achieve daily or weekly objectives. To do this effectively, a leader must understand his or her leadership style.

Leadership Styles and Situations

After decades of research on leadership styles, the facts show that there is no one best leadership style. All styles can be effective; however, some styles are more effective in certain situations than others. It is best to adapt your leadership style to the situation at hand, also known as situational leadership.

To acquire a better understanding of your leadership style, read through the descriptions on the next few pages, then select the style that best describes you. It is possible to split your leadership style between two or three, but usually one style is dominant. Use this knowledge to capitalize on specific strengths and compensate for your weaknesses. Consider working with someone who is effective in situations where you are weak to improve your overall job (and leadership) effectiveness. More than likely, you have found someone with whom you work well with and who also complements your capabilities.

For team building in the Lean Office, ensure each team member identifies his or her dominant style. This analysis can be used to improve communications between team members. Communication problems can often be traced to leadership style differences.

The following pages provide situational qualities of leadership styles. Use this as a guide with the Lean Office team.

Task and Speed Driven

You Want: To be in control.

You Need: To be obeyed; to be appreciated for your accomplishments; to be given credit for all your abilities.

Strong Points: You are a take-charge person. You can take charge quickly and your "snap" judgments are usually correct (which irritates the rest of us).

Weak Points: You can be bossy and impatient. You do not like to delegate responsibility. You do not like to give credit to others. You can be insensitive to other people's needs and feelings. You do not listen well.

You Get Depressed: When you feel things are out of control and those around you will not do things your way.

You Fear: Losing control of anything - your job, a promotion, your health. You also fear having people around you who are rebellious and unsupportive.

You Like: People who support your ideas of how quickly things ought to be done. You like people who cooperate quickly to make things happen. People need to give you the credit or at least let you take it.

You Don't Like: People who are lazy—meaning they do not work all the time or at least as much as you do; people who question your authority and methods; people who become too independent-minded and people who are not loyal (according to your definition of loyalty).

When Under Stress: You become more controlling; you tend to work harder; exercise more. If you have to, you will get rid of any perceived slackers.

As A Leader: You have a natural and intuitive feel for what will work well, and you believe in your ability to get things done. You have a tendency to overwhelm less aggressive people.

Your Values At Work: You can accomplish more than anyone else in less time and you are usually right, but you do (tend to) stir up trouble.

You Tend To Marry: Stability and harmony types who quietly obey and do things your way, but you feel that these people never accomplish enough or get excited enough about what you consider to be important.

Other Characteristics: Driving, impulsive, controller, big mouth, strings attached, people catalyst, type A personality, fire eater, Lee Iaccoca type.

Stability and Harmony Driven

You Want: To do it the easy way and have peace.

You Need: To be respected and have an environment which promotes your self worth; to be supported emotionally and you need harmony.

Strong Points: You are a balanced person and have an even disposition. You have a dry sense of humor that acts as a defense mechanism. Overall, you have a pleasant personality.

Weak Points: You are not the decisive one in a group nor do you have an abundance of enthusiasm or energy. You have no obvious flaws. When you feel you have been too accommodating you demonstrate a hidden will of iron and a steel backbone.

You Get Depressed: When there is too much conflict or you have to confront someone; when no one wants to help you; and when too much of the responsibility falls on you.

You Fear: Having to handle a major personal problem alone; being left "holding the bag" in any situation. You are afraid of major changes that you always see as creating conflict... no matter how beneficial the change may be.

You Like: People who will make decisions - you want to be consulted but do not want to have to make the final decision. You like people who will recognize your strengths and will not ignore you.

You Don't Like: People who are pushy and expect too much of you (meaning—expect you to carry more than what you feel is your fair share of the load).

Under Stress: You bury it with diversions: watching TV, reading a book, and perhaps eating.

As A Leader: You are calm, cool, and collected. You do not make impulsive decisions. You do not come up with the brilliant ideas.

Your Values At Work: You cooperate with almost everybody and tend to bring calmness to the situation. You keep the peace and mediate between people who tend to argue. You are objective in the way you solve problems.

You Tend To Marry: Task and Speed driven types because you are attracted to their strength and decisiveness, but you get tired of being looked down upon and pushed around.

Other Characteristics: Democratic, supportive, reserved.

People and Persuasion Driven

You Want: To have fun, to influence.

You Need: Attention, affection, approval, and acceptance. Key phrase: "You are wonderful."

Strong Points: You can talk about anything, at any time, for any length, with or without prior information. You have a bubbling personality and are the optimistic one. You have a great sense of humor and can relieve tension. You are a "people person."

Weak Points: You are disorganized—except when you want to look good and have people think you are wonderful. You do not remember details or names. You exaggerate to make yourself, or your story, sound better. You tend not to be serious enough for other personality types. You trust others to do the work. You can be gullible and naive.

You Get Depressed: When life is not fun and when you think that no one thinks you are wonderful.

You Fear: Being bored or unpopular. You do not like to be tied to a clock. You are not good at keeping money records.

You Like: People who listen to you and approve of what you are saying, laugh at your humor, and express approval of you as a person.

You Don't Like: People who are too critical, who focus on details that you think are minor, and who seem to be negative and throw cold water on your ideas.

Under Stress: You leave and change your environment to make yourself feel better. For instance, you go work-out, go shopping, hunting, fishing, etc. You tend to blame others for what happens. You create excuses.

As A Leader: You come up with creative ideas and can see the whole picture. You are a cheerleader for others, especially when they get discouraged. You have energy and enthusiasm but need to work with detail-oriented people.

Your Values At Work: You should be valued for your colorful creativity, your optimism, and your light touch. You come up with ideas when the "well" of others runs dry.

You Tend To Marry: "Perfects" because you are drawn to their sensitive nature. That balances you. You do not like having to cheer them up all the time. They can make you feel stupid and inadequate.

Other Characteristics: Late arriver, emotional, talker.

Perfection and Analysis Driven

You Want: To have things done the way they "ought" to be done; you want things done the "right" way.

You Need: A stable, predictable environment. You need your space and you need to have "peace and quiet" to recharge your battery. You need sensitive and supportive people around you.

Strong Points: You are a great organizer and are detail oriented. You are good at setting long-range goals and seeing pitfalls before reaching them. You are analytical. You have high standards and ideals.

Weak Points: You tend to spend too much time analyzing and preparing (you want to do it "right"). You can be obsessive about details. You remember negatives and are suspicious of others' motives. You get depressed easily.

You Get Depressed: When your life is not orderly and you cannot meet your standards (and when those around you do not meet them either). It's even worse if they do not seem to care.

You Fear: Making a mistake or being told you did something wrong, being asked to compromise your standards, and no one understanding how you feel.

You Like: People who take life seriously and think intelligently; people who can carry on a deep and sensible conversation (according to your standards of sensibility).

You Don't Like: People who are not serious enough, who are disorganized and forgetful, who do not care about details, who are unpredictable, and who exaggerate (you call it lying).

Under Stress: You withdraw by getting lost in a book or going to sleep. You revisit the problem again and again in your mind. You just give up.

As A Leader: You organize well. You are sensitive to what others need. You are creative at a deep level; you want and achieve high standards of quality.

Your Values At Work: You are valuable for your sense of details, your love of analysis and your follow-through, and your high standards and compassion for others.

You Tend To Marry: People-driven types because you like their personalities and social skills. You do try to quiet them and get them on a schedule. This produces depression because they do not respond.

Other Characteristics: Resident genius, record keeper, neat, self-reliant.

Once you understand leadership styles, you will also learn that leadership and power must coexist to get people to do what you want them to do. You can either "push" people or "pull" people to get things done.

Pushing people means making others do something through force, coercion, power, or fear. This is often referred to as "the stick." Pulling people means inspiring others to perform a desired action. This is often referred to as "the carrot." Both techniques have their place in leadership, as well as in implementing Lean. Good leaders know how and when to use each approach. Look back at the various leadership styles. How would each style be applicable to pushing or pulling?

Motivation

It is important that a leader applies the appropriate leadership style as the situation requires. To do this effectively, a competent leader must understand what motivates people. While implementing the Lean Office you must find ways to create the right environment in which people are motivated. They need to fully understand the need for this change and it is the leader's job to assist in that endeavor.

Motivation is the desire of a person to complete tasks based on the desire to fill needs. Motivation is directly proportional to the perceived leadership effectiveness. Improving leadership improves employee motivation. Which approach would motivate you more?

"Good luck and don't mess this up."

"Here are the work instructions. Let me know if you need any help."

People respect those who treat them with dignity, *especially* when things are not running smoothly. Effective leadership is critical to a highly-motivated work group. It has been stated that leaders cannot motivate others, but they can create an environment in which people can motivate themselves to high levels of achievement.

Before learning how to create a motivational atmosphere, it is important to understand why people work willingly. They respond positively to:

- Being appreciated for work done well
- Belonging to a supportive group
- Being recognized as having individual worth
- Having interesting work
- Promotion and growth opportunities
- Management's loyalty to employees
- Good working conditions
- Tactful discipline

The following pages summarize key motivational theories. Understanding these and practicing them will lay a foundation for good leadership and creating an environment for highly-energized and self-motivated employees.

There has been much research done on human motivation. Two important theories to understand for leaders are Maslow's hierarchy of needs, and Herzberg's two factor theory.

Maslow's hierarchy of needs states that people work at fulfilling their needs from lower level basic physical needs to higher level conceptual needs (i.e., from survival to security, belonging through to self-esteem, and then finally to self-actualization). Additional information can be obtained using Google or Yahoo. This is a site that has a good illustration of the five levels: http://www.netmba.com/mgmt/ob/motivation/maslow/.

Herzberg's two factor theory states that there are basic needs, which if not satisfied, causes de-motivation (hygiene factors or dissatisfiers) and additional needs that act to motivate (satisfiers). Also, the following site will provide additional information for Herzberg's two factor theory: http://www.tutor2u.net/business/people/motivation_theory_herzberg.asp.

In motivation theory, the "Hawthorn Effect" is the motivation that people exhibit from having leaders simply pay attention to them. Pleasantly greeting employees each morning as they arrive at work, and taking interest in them as people, will have a positive impact on their motivation.

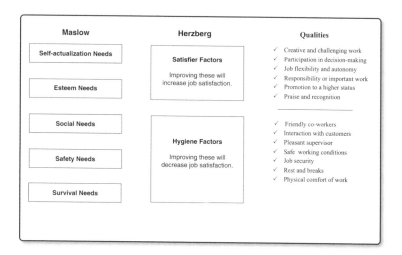

Motivation in Action

Like it or not, people ask the question "What's in it for me?" before they become motivated to perform work. People ask…

1. Is the vision or goal possible?
2. What's in it for me if I do, or do not, act?
3. Is this reward fair or can I accept the consequence?
4. How badly do I want the reward or need to avoid the consequence?

Leaders must address these issues to create the environment for self-motivated employees.

People consider positive rewards to follow:

Do well => Receive Reward => Do Well Again => Get Reward Again

Reward the behavior you want to continue.

People consider negative rewards to follow:

Do Poorly => Get Reprimand => Do Well => Avoid Reprimand.

Five ways to destroy motivation

1. Offer meaningless reward(s) not tied to performance
2. Not be specific, timely, or genuine with praise
3. Use threats and fear to get things done
4. Break promises
5. Treat employees in a non-personal way, instead of as individuals

Six ways to improve motivation

1. Have team members take the employee survey on page 300.
2. Tabulate the scores and protect the team members' anonymity.
3. Identify individual strengths and weaknesses.
4. Develop individual plans to improve.
5. Show commitment to improve.
6. Follow-up with another survey in 4-6 months to check progress.

The following twelve activities can set the stage to increase employee motivation:

1. Provide regular, constructive feedback. Publicly acknowledge employees for any job well done.
2. Ask employees for input. Involve them in decisions that affect them.
3. Establish easy-to-use communication channels. Listen attentively and honestly.
4. Learn and adapt what each individual employee is motivated by.
5. Recognize the power of being physically present.
6. Conduct morale-building events to celebrate group success.
7. Make work meaningful. Provide the tools and information to do the job correctly.
8. Recognize employees' personal needs.
9. Promote employees on performance and competency. Promote from within the organization when possible.
10. Demonstrate a long-term commitment to employment stability.
11. Foster a sense of community.
12. Pay people fairly and competitively. Provide incentives that work.

Your Lean Office will only be as good as the motivation level of your employees and their desire to improve. Leadership and motivation must coexist as a real activity for a Lean culture to emerge. The Lean tools will provide a solid technical foundation, but it will be the people and their desire to improve that will provide the solid ground upon which to build the Lean Office. Chapter 11- Creating the Goal Card will assist you in creating a performance-based system as part of the organizational atmosphere in which your employees will be positioned for success.

Employee Survey

Instructions: Read each statement carefully and circle the response that best expresses your feeling about the statement right now.

	Strongly Agree	Agree Somewhat	Neither Agree nor Disagree	Disagree Somewhat	Strongly Disagree
	5	4	3	2	1
1. I believe my personal work efforts contribute to this organization's Lean initiatives.	5	4	3	2	1
2. Promotions within this organization are based on job-related criteria and on merit.	5	4	3	2	1
3. The work rules and policies of this organization are fair and sensible.	5	4	3	2	1
4. Safety is a major concern in this organization.	5	4	3	2	1
5. Discrimination in this organization on the basis of race, color, religion, national origin, or status does not occur.	5	4	3	2	1
6. I usually understand upper management decisions, even when I may not agree with them.	5	4	3	2	1
7. I am encouraged to go to my supervisor or manager with issues.	5	4	3	2	1
8. My supervisor is competent and knowledgeable.	5	4	3	2	1
9. The goals and objectives of my department are aligned with the goals and objectives of the organization.	5	4	3	2	1
10. Communication within this organization is generally good.	5	4	3	2	1
11. I understand and usually agree with the goals and objectives of my department.	5	4	3	2	1
12. I usually get recognition from my supervisor when I do a good job.	5	4	3	2	1
13. The relationship between management and employees is generally good in this organization.	5	4	3	2	1
14. I have had my job duties thoroughly explained to me and I know what I am doing.	5	4	3	2	1
15. I understand the work rules and policies of this organization, even though I may not agree with some of them.	5	4	3	2	1
16. I feel there are opportunities to learn new skills in this organization.	5	4	3	2	1
17. I feel there are reasonable opportunities for advancement in this organization.	5	4	3	2	1
18. I have opportunities to provide continuous improvement ideas in this organization.	5	4	3	2	1
19. This is a well-run organization.	5	4	3	2	1
20. The results of this survey will be used honestly and constructively by this organization's management.	5	4	3	2	1

Do not sign your name. All responses will be kept strictly confidential.

Chapter Summary

It is important to understand that just one leadership style will not fit all situations. Each situation may require a different approach. Leaders should be compassionate about the situation, but also should provide a solid foundation of expectations to their employees for implementing the Lean Office. Most individuals will need to know "what's in it for them" before significant Kaizen success occurs. It is the job of the leader to motivate and coach the team (and individuals) in terms of their Lean goals.

Observations from the Lean Office

These observations may assist in understanding how to apply the concepts and tools contained in this chapter:

- Gain a good understanding of the various leadership styles.
- Understand that all employees need to know "what's in it for me." Be honest and communicate short and long term Lean Office goals and objectives.
- Share with the team the various leadership styles and ensure they understand their style.
- Realize that Lean Office will only achieve to the level of passion you (the leader) have for it. Employees will look to those in charge and "sense" their commitment to the Lean Office initiatives.
- Assist others to have the passion for Lean Office by listening and implementing their improvement ideas through Kaizen activities.

Application Case Study

The power and capability of computers to house and analyze data can complement or enhance the leadership styles of anyone. That capability can also invite abuse and waste if not harnessed wisely or if not kept in alignment with the goals of the organization. The impulsive and controlling Task and Speed Driven leader can be tempered and controlled by "going to the data" in the Lean Office System before making assumptions or rash decisions. The Stability and Harmony Driven leader can use the data to help and support the team members and to engage the team to suggest improvements. The Task and Speed Driven leader and the People and Persuasion Driven leaders should check themselves by testing their seat-of-the-pants ideas and decisions against the numbers; such leaders must first embrace the power of complementing their particular skills with the easily gathered and analyzed information generated by their IT systems. Finally, the Perfection and Analysis Driven leader can be expected to use their IT systems like a duck-to-water. However, such leaders must be careful not to paralyze themselves or their organizations with too much data, too many measures, or too many scenarios and alternatives.

Andrew Cencini's leadership style was a mix of all four types, as most people's are, but, similar to many managers and executives, his Task and Speed Driven characteristics tended to dominate. Therefore, Andrew resolved his weakness of drive, taking control, and driving for results with a more supportive and personal approach towards his team by using the data to speak. He eliminated making decisions solely from his gut or from unfounded conclusions about performances.

For example, as noted previously, two of Andrew's primary areas of focus were to generate more sales opportunities and to increase the successful rate of closure for those opportunities. Again, ACT! provides the tools for Andrew to track and attain the realization of that strategy. The following screen shot shows the expected dollar value of the opportunities generated one week by Andrew's team. Using this overview graph, Andrew quickly can see the value of the opportunities being generated.

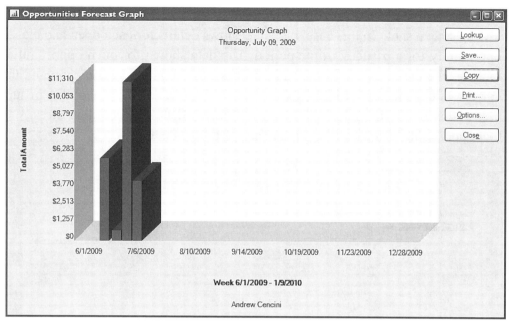

Graph of Expected Value of Opportunities

Andrew wanted more detail, standard reports, such as the one shown in the following screen shot. In this case, the table shows details for each open and closed opportunity for a particular time period. The data shown for open opportunities includes the current stage in the sales process, the estimated close date, and the current value of the opportunity given its closure value and the probability of success at that point. If Andrew wanted even further detail, he could go directly to that opportunity in the database and examine all the details.

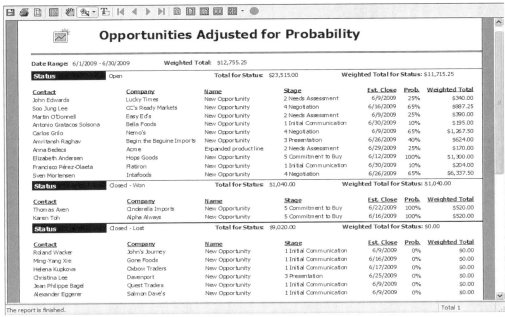

Detailed Report of Status of Sales Opportunities

Leaders must use data wisely to ensure that:

- Not too much is collected and analyzed which could get lost in the weeds and lose focus
- Not too little is collected and analyzed which would then be no true representation of the process(es)
- It is used for supporting process improvement and not for punishment and generating fear
- It is used for objective measurements

It is a truism, what gets measured gets done. Use your MS Office and other applications, with your leadership skills, to help you obtain the desired results.

Chapter 11

Creating the Goal Card

Getting Everyone on the Same Page

Chapter Overview

This chapter, even though it is being explained in Part Three, can be incorporated anytime during the implementation of the three parts of this book. It is particularly placed in Part Three to assure that smaller, incremental gains have been made prior to attempting to involve the entire organization. Creating the Goal Card should be used to align everyone's daily efforts and activities within the organization to the overall strategic direction of the organization. The Goal Card is an excellent tool that links the Balanced Scorecard or corporate targets to where the work is being performed on a daily basis. This chapter is only seven pages, plus the case study, but do not underestimate the power it can have on an organization.

Understanding Goal Cards

People feel responsible for and take pride in their individual work when they have control over the processes governing their jobs. There must be a system in place to assure that the process employees are working to improve is directly related to what is important to the organization in terms of profitability and success. This alignment and the setting of personal and team goals is the first step in developing a high-performance workforce.

If a person plays golf, it is natural to set a goal for playing a round of 18 holes. If a person is a bowler, it makes sense to set a personal goal for a series score. Goal setting establishes a target in our business life.

People are best motivated by setting their own goals; however, when setting personal work goals in a company, people must understand the direction in which the company is heading and that their personal goals must support departmental, team, and organizational goals. Goal Cards will help to align all goals and objectives within an organization.

What is a Goal Card?

A Goal Card is a tool for individuals, teams, and departments to determine how they can contribute to continuous improvement over a particular time period, usually one year. It allows employees to embrace the strategic direction of the organization by creating a visual office contract defining the work of a department and the individual goals that will contribute to it. Goal Cards are also a way to communicate the company's Lean strategy and goals to everyone in the organization.

The Goal Card is the product of a process that unites the company's goals with department and individual goals. It is the first step to Total Employee Involvement. Only by involving everyone, especially those who know their job best, can an organization achieve its Lean and business goals. Ultimately, it is each individual that will make the difference. The Goal Card helps in that endeavor.

Overall Design

A typical Goal Card measures 8" x 11" and is made of card stock. It is folded into three sections, allowing for six panels on which to display information.

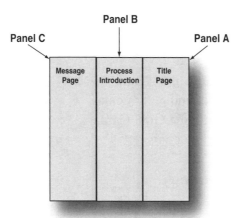

Management prepares the three exterior panels. Panel A is the front of the card when folded and acts as the title page. Panel B introduces the process of the Goal Card and is usually written by the senior manager in the organization. Panel C is the back page and will contain references to the strategic plan.

The interior panels contain the company's strategy and Lean goals, the business unit goals [division or department], and a place where each individual can list his or her own personal or team goals. Whether the employee lists team or individual goals will depend on the organizational system for reporting measurements.

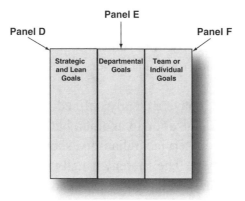

It is important when designing Goal Cards that the design follows usability. All Goal Cards must be simple and easy to read and use.

Creating a Goal Card requires seven steps:

1. Articulate a Lean strategy.
2. Identify Lean goals.
3. Create the Goal Card.
4. Present the strategy, goals, and process to everyone.
5. Integrate personal and team goals.
6. Post and distribute the Goal Card.
7. Monitor and review goals.

1. Articulate a Lean strategy.

Strategic plans have been around for many years, but only in the past 20 years or so have these strategic plans for an organization been shared with the employee. The Goal Card focuses explicitly on all the business processes that drive the organization to achieve success through its strategic plan. A Lean Office strategy may be different from other business system strategies for the following reasons:

- Its purpose is to design and develop a competitive advantage.
- It bases this advantage on system-wide improvements.
- Improvements must be continuous.
- Improvement focuses on elimination of waste from a customer perspective.
- Success is achieved by involvement of all stakeholders, including employees, customers, and suppliers.

A world class company will have a clearly defined business strategy. The strategy will differ from one organization to another, but will focus on such issues as growth, quality of product or service, reliability, short lead times, flexibility, and customer and job satisfaction. The strategy usually consists of a short statement (stating the core competency of the company) and a few major goals. It will also include stated principles for implementation that must be consistent with the overall business plan of the company.

If a strategy cannot be printed on one page, it is too long. If the front-line employee cannot understand it, then it is too complicated. A strategic statement should only cover key issues; it should act as a guide for everyone in the organization. It will be the foundation for the identification of Lean goals.

2. Identify Lean goals.

A strategy is useless without direction. A few solid goals that lend themselves to ease of measurement assist to provide organizational direction. Most organizations have had success using the following four basic types of goals based on the widely adopted Balanced Scorecard:

- Improve customer satisfaction
- Increase financial (business) growth
- Improve process design (process improvement)
- Develop organizational learning

There may be one or two more which are specific to an industry. For example, healthcare may include patient satisfaction, patient safety, mortality, morbidity rates, etc.

It is useful to divide process improvement into three elements that include quality improvement, productivity, and cost saving initiatives. Goals provide an outline for a corporate strategy. They must therefore be quite specific. For example, a goal might be "To improve customer satisfaction." But everyone wants to do that. So a well-stated Lean goal should give direction to the organization by including quality, delivery, and time expectations. For example, if the goal is patient satisfaction in healthcare, then some Lean goals may be:

- Decrease patient wait time by 10% within six months
- Improve patient scheduling for 24-hour service to less than a 10% cancellation rate within 3 months
- Decrease patient billing errors to less than 2% by December 31st
- Improve nurse satisfaction by 20%

The last goal, improve nurse satisfaction, may not seem like a goal to improve patient satisfaction, but there is direct correlation between how an employee (nurse) "likes" her or his job and the impact that can have on a patient (customer).

Goals should be completed and agreed upon by management and each individual employee.

3. Create the Goal Card.

The following should be considered when developing a Goal Card:

- Include the senior manager's introduction to all employees
- Create specific Lean goals at all levels of the Goal Card
- Create a panel for team and/or individual goals
- Print the Goal Card for organization-wide distribution

The Goal Card process is ready for organization-wide implementation.

4. Present the strategy, goals, and process to everyone.

Process improvements, effective teams, and quality products and services do not occur by accident. Success comes from a sense of purpose towards improving those products and services. Without a clear communication of strategy, goals, and how everyone will work together to achieve the goals, most people will not care to participate, and many of those who try to participate will have so little information that they will become frustrated or even hostile. An organization cannot expect its employees to be mind-readers. By explaining the Lean purpose, goals, and processes, managers can save a great deal of time and energy.

This process should be communicated to all employees at a monthly employee/ staff meeting. The information, in an abbreviated form, should immediately be posted on the company intranet site, in newsletters, and on bulletin boards that are available to everyone (i.e., employee entrances, cafeterias, etc.).

5. Integrate personal and team goals.

Depending on the size and structure of the organization, this step may involve identifying department, unit, or team goals before individuals articulate their personal goals. Whatever the situation may be, the principles of effective goal setting are the same. The following guidelines will help keep personal and team goals understandable and useful.

Well-stated goals must be:
Measurable: Quality, delivery, and time (two out of three is not bad)
Observable: Observer must be able to see progress on a regular basis

Characteristics of well-stated goals are that they should be:
Short-term: No longer than one year
Challenging: But not so challenging that they seem impossible to meet
Achievable: People must believe that "they can get there"
Flexible: To allow for adjustments in time or delivery requirements - not quality
Mutually-agreed upon: If either party is hesitant or unsure, the goal will not be accomplished

It is reasonable to expect that some departmental team members may desire to have only individual goals and not team goals. Ensure that when team goals are established everyone on the team understands "they own a piece of the collective pie."

6. Post and distribute the Goal Card.

After personal and team goals are written and shared, they should be posted near the employee's desk or in a common area. The posting of these goals will provide a visual reminder of what each employee must do to support the overall direction of the organization.

7. Monitor and review goals.

Do not underestimate the power of personal and group recognition. High performance exhibited by an employee many times is the result of positive reinforcement from his or her superiors. People need to feel responsible to their peers as well as their leaders. Monitoring and visually reporting progress creates a culture of sharing, teamwork, recognition, and mutual responsibility.

Chapter Summary

The implementation of the Goal Card is an excellent tool for creating a continuous improvement culture. It connects Lean and other business initiatives to team/individual performance and integrates them with organizational goals.

Observations from the Lean Office

These observations may assist in understanding how to apply the concepts and tools contained in this chapter:

- Create time lines for creating Goals Cards and implementing them throughout the organization.
- Create new Goals Cards annually.
- Keep goals realistic and obtainable.
- Reinforce positive performance with recognition.
- Goals Cards *can allow* an organization to take a giant leap in their continuous improvement journey.

Application Case Study

The Northwind team put together their Goal Card using one of the many brochure templates in Microsoft Word. Each team member would not only have available a card stock copy to print and use, but also have the Goal Card in digital format readily available on their Desktop or via the office server.

The following two pages show the front and back of Northwind's Goal Card. Note that the goals for the departments roll down from those of the larger organization, Global Winds. The Northwind team, encouraged by Andrew's proactive leadership, decided that they could improve upon many of Global Wind's corporate goals as a result of the Lean Office they were implementing. For example, they believed that the global target of closing service problems in an average of 24 hours could be reduced to 4 hours - within the same day - by reducing waste in the process and tracking performance visibly. The key here was that the team 'bought-in' to taking on this aggressive, stretch goal. Andrew was pleased with the team for doing so, but knew meeting such a challenging target would take a strong, coordinated effort by everyone.

Another important feature of the Goal Card is that it ties in the importance of the Northwind Lean initiative to the overall strategy of the company. The team members were all quite proud of the overall contribution in learning and development that they were all making to the company. The Goal Card was physically posted in everyone's area and a link was provided to its location on the shared network drive.

Northwind Traders

Providing the finest international delicacies to the most discerning purveyors of fine foods

Message from the VP of Sales of Northwind Traders

We look forward to making the journey to Lean in the Northwind Sales Department. The Global Winds Board of Directors has chosen our team to be the first in the company to implement Lean practices in an office environment.

The methods of Lean, based on the Toyota Production System, have been proven many times to drastically eliminate waste and non value-added activities for many organizations in many types of activities, products, and services. The management team of Global Winds especially embraces the focus of Lean on the customer as the driver for all activities. As such, this approach promises to reinforce the strong, customer-oriented values we all share. We will use the resources freed up by the elimination of waste to increase our focus on growing the business.

I appreciate your enthusiastic support of these objectives and your energy and creativity in realizing the adaption of Lean to our organization.

Sincerely,

Andrew Cencini

Message from the CEO of Global Winds

Global Winds supplies fine grocers and food marketers across the United States with the best specialty food products. We help our clients to meet – and exceed— the needs and desires of their most discriminating customers. We do so by delivering the finest products on time, meeting well-understood specifications, with thorough and completely reliable service and customer relations. We seek to make the clients' job easy.

In order for every unit of Global Winds to deliver on these goals, we must be completely consistent, introducing no waste in our internal processes and work. Doing so will enable all of us to focus maximum time and energy to serving existing customers, winning new ones, and developing our own skills and capabilities. Thus our company will continue to grow, the true test for the long-term prosperity of any business.

Please join us in this ongoing journey to sustainable company-wide excellence.

Sincerely,

Charles King

Front of the Northwind's Goal Card

Global Winds
Strategic Goals

The following goals comprise the balanced scorecard for Global Winds:

Finance Goals

Operating Margin (%)	7.0
Annual Sales Growth (%)	12.0

Quality and Service

Closure of service problems (hrs)	24
On-time delivery (%)	95

Internal Processes

Implement Lean Methods (Div/yr)	3
Opportunity success rate (%)	15

Satisfaction

Sales Satisfaction (0-10)	8
Service Satisfaction (0-10)	8

Northwind Traders
Strategic Goals

The following goals are Northwinds' goals for the next fiscal year::

Finance Goals

Operating Margin (%)	8.0
Annual Sales Growth (%)	15.0

Quality and Service

Closure of service problems (hrs)	4
On-time delivery (%)	97

Internal Processes

Implement Lean Methods (months)	3
Opportunity success rate (%)	15

Satisfaction

Sales Satisfaction (0-10)	8
Service Satisfaction (0-10)	8

Team Commitment

We, the Northwind Sales team, accept as our stretch goal that each of us individually will achieve the departmental strategic goals. Additionally, we each pledge to participate, fully and faithfully, to the best of our abilities, to create, support, and implement the Lean initiatives in support of meeting our goals.

Signatures:

Andrew Cencini   *Steven Thorpe*

Nancy Freehafer   **Jan Kotas**

Mariya Sergienko   *Michael Neipper*

Robert Zare   *Ann Hellung-Larsen*

Laura Giussani

Back of the Northwind's Goal Card

Chapter 12

The Visual Office and Mistake Proofing

Continue to Improve

Chapter Overview

This chapter explains how to create a visual communication system which ensures work and service standards are in place so that work is completed on schedule, without errors. Visual aids notifying the appropriate people if something deviates from established work standards will also be presented.

Visual controls in the office will accomplish the following:

- Allow 5S to be standardized and sustained
- Ensure metrics are posted and continuous improvement efforts are directed toward negative trends
- Improve office productivity
- Reduce and eliminate errors
- Reduce stress

Why use visual controls?

Visual controls establish a visual communication system which ensures standards are met so work is completed on schedule and without errors. The Lean project team should ensure that visual controls are included as part of all continuous improvement activities.

Creating a visual office requires seven steps:

1. Form and train the visual office team.
2. Create an implementation plan.
3. Begin implementation.
4. Ensure 5S system implementation.
5. Standardize visual metrics.
6. Standardize visual displays.
7. Standardize visual controls.

1. Form and train the visual office team.

This may be a subset of the Lean Office project team. Lean Office project teams typically do not dedicate sufficient time to this vital activity. It will be the team's task to:

- Create the locations where visual displays and standards will be posted
- Establish visual metrics (VM), visual displays (VD), and visual controls (VC)
- Create standards for all visuals (location, updates, themes, etc.)
- Decide how to implement visual controls with computer-based displays and controls (i.e., hyperlinks, locked fields, drop-down selections, etc.)

2. Create an implementation plan.

The core team must designate specific areas and online locations to post the appropriate visuals (i.e., VM, VD, and/or VC) along with a time line for training and implementing. Use the Visual Office Worksheet for planning.

Visual Office Worksheet

Team Champion _____ Date _____

Department/Work Area _____

Evaluation Date	5S Completion Date	VM Completion Date	VD Completion Date	VC Completion Date

3. Begin implementation.

The team should use the information from (2) to create actual physical and digital displays. Displays can be turned into visual controls when and where appropriate.

4. Ensure 5S system implementation.

Groups, departments, units, etc. may be at various stages of the 5S implementation. Consider allocating time and creating a 5S organizational-wide, cross-functional team to assess and continue implementation of 5S, while promoting additional visual displays.

5. Standardize visual metrics.

Lean projects should have identified appropriate metrics from the Goal Card, Team Charter, or other performance measurements critical to the organization. The metrics should be standardized in terms of:

- Data collected that is easy to understand and interpret
- Relevancy to what is measured
- Simple means of data presentation in terms of charts and graphs

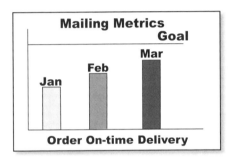

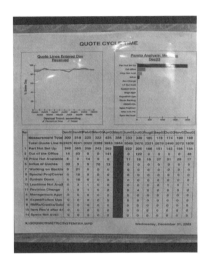

Visual metrics must be:

- Directly related to strategy
- Non-financial
- Location-specific
- Changing over time
- Easy to collect and post
- Provide timely feedback
- Useful for team/individual motivation

6. Standardize visual displays.

Visual displays communicate important information about the work in terms of safety, environment, or business-related activities. Signboards are often used as visual displays, supplemented by on-line communication methods.

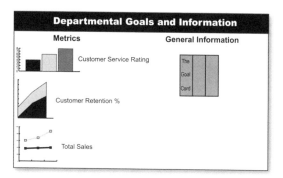

7. Standardize visual controls.

Standards must be created to integrate visual metrics, visual displays, and visual controls. The following illustration explains the levels of visual controls. At this step, there should be processes, tasks, checklists, and computer programs to ensure that what has been created in the visual control system is sustained.

Let us use an example of medications that need to be administered to a patient in a hospital. To eliminate errors, there are the 7 Rights and Triple Check standards that are commonly known throughout healthcare. The 7 Rights standard is:

1. Right patient
2. Right medications
3. Right dose
4. Right route
5. Right time
6. Right technique
7. Right documentation

Many times an 8th Right would include patient education.

The Triple Check standard is:

1. Check medication as you take it off the shelf
2. Check medication as you prepare it
3. Check medication as you replace it on the shelf

A visual display would be locating a placard listing the 7 Rights and Triple Check standards on the medication cart or on the cabinet where the medications are stored. A visual control can be a finger print or your ID card scanned on a reader prior to accessing the medications. The visual metric would be tracking medication errors (which probably in this case would not be wise to post in a common area).

The following is a list of the various visual tools and their general purpose.

Type	General Purpose
Storyboards	Share information about projects or improvements To educate and motivate
Signboards	Share vital information at point-of-use
Maps	Share actual processes, standard operating procedures, directions, etc.
Kanbans	Control the withdrawal of work (or supplies) in and out of supermarkets, work areas, etc. Can be used to regulate work in FIFO lanes
Checklists	Provide an operational tool that facilitates adherence to standards, procedures, etc.
Indicators, Color Codes	Show correct location, item types, amount, or direction of work flow
Alarms	Provide a strong, unavoidable sign or signal where there is an abnormality or action that needs to be taken (email alert, pager code, etc.)

Mistake Proofing

Poka-yoke is Japanese for mistake proofing. It is derived from "Poka" - inadvertent mistake and "yoke" - avoid. A Poka-yoke (or error-proofing) device is any mechanism that prevents a mistake from being made or ensures the mistake is made obvious at a glance. These devices (or processes) are used to prevent those circumstances that cause defects, or to inexpensively inspect each work unit that is produced, created, or modified to determine whether it is acceptable or defective. The ability to find mistakes at a glance is essential. The causes of defects lie in worker errors and defects are the result of those errors. These mistakes will not turn into defects if the worker errors are discovered and eliminated beforehand. Defects occur because errors are made; the two have a cause-and-effect relationship. However, errors will not turn into defects if feedback and action take place prior to the error stage. Many times visual controls will play a large role in reducing the opportunity for errors to occur, thereby ensuring no defects from the process.

To be a defect:

- The process produced something unacceptable that deviated from specifications or standards (an error occurred)
- The process did not meet customer (internal or external) specifications

To be an error:

- The process must have deviated from specifications or standards that may or may not have been identified by the customer
- All defects are created by errors, but not all errors result in defects

There are three levels of control that error proofing devices can achieve:

Level 1 - Indicators - providing information about the immediate environment, area, department or process. These are passive and people may or may not notice them or respond to them. A Level 1 visual control may be a sign displaying the customer requirements for the discount levels as a dialogue box once the customer name is entered into a field.

Level 2 - Signals - causing a visual or auditory alarm that should grab your attention and is a warning that a mistake or error is about to occur. People still may ignore these, but they are very aware that something may be wrong. A Level 2 visual control may be attempting to enter a customer discount level and a dialogue box appears "Are you sure of the discount being entered?"

Level 3 - Physical or Electronic Controls - limiting or preventing something from occurring due to its negative impact it will have on the process or area, often referred to as mistake proofing devices. A Level 3 visual control may be the system not allowing the discount to be entered and referring it to the manager.

Clearly Level 3 is most desirable, but not always possible or cost effective.

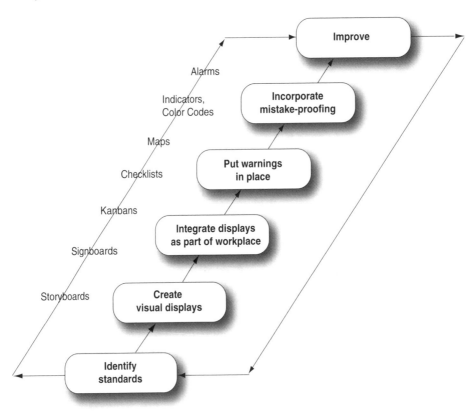

Continually strive to create new processes that will eliminate errors and the opportunity for errors to occur in all Lean projects. When solving any problem or applying any Lean tool, ensure visual controls and mistake proofing devices are considered.

Emulate the advancements in computers and their peripherals in terms of visual controls and mistake proofing devices. Today, nearly anyone and everyone can install a computer along with the numerous peripherals in the market without a mistake.

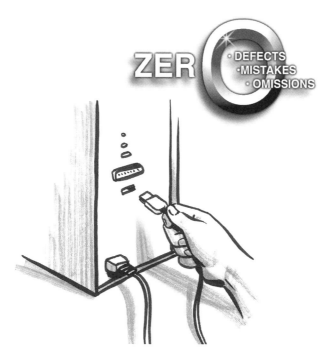

Chapter Summary

Establishing a visual communication system that includes mistake proofing in the office will separate an organization from having cursory Lean implementation efforts to realizing full, sustainable Lean implementation results. Visuals aids are an excellent tool to complement any Lean project or initiative. Consider when you travel and arrive at an airport you have never been to previously. It is fairly easy to find the luggage claim, car rental, and taxi stand areas without delay due to the visual displays and visual controls that are used in airport terminals. Consider your administrative processes to be like an airport terminal and create visual aids and mistake proofing devices for your processes so anyone can learn and complete tasks associated with your processes without delay or error.

Observations from the Lean Office

These observations may assist in understanding how to apply the concepts and tools contained in this chapter:

- One picture is worth a thousand words. That is what the visual office is about. If a picture, diagram, menu selection, link, etc. is exactly where you need it, when you need it to ensure a work or service standard is met, then it is well worth the time and effort.
- Visual displays and controls should be part of all Lean tool applications.
- Visuals displays should begin with the first Lean project team meeting by posting (physically and electronically) the Team Charter and Meeting Information Form.
- Visual controls are Just-In-Time information.
- Ensure visual controls are updated regularly as part of the Lean Office System.
- Incorporate mistake proofing devices in all process improvements to prevent errors from occurring.

Application Case Study

Many, if not most, office software applications today have built-in capabilities for displaying visual information to communicate the status of work. The Northwind team explored such capabilities first in the ACT! application and discovered that indeed ACT! included a module for Dashboards. Dashboards are single graphical panels designed to provide "at-a-glance" overviews of key activities, results, and opportunities.

ACT!, for example, has three built-in, standard Dashboards to capture the status of what is going on within the CRM system. However, these standard reports can be modified, or redesigned entirely. This is, in fact, what the Northwind team did and the result is shown in the following screen shot.

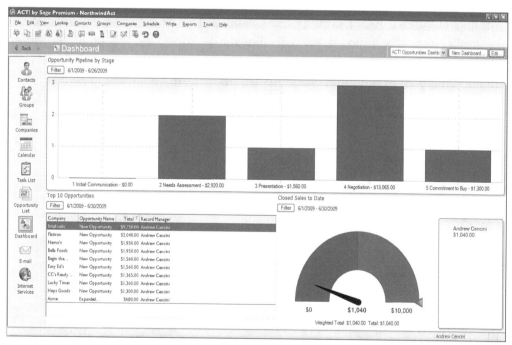

Visualizing Northwind's Performance with an ACT! Dashboard

The team chose to display three cells of information on the Dashboard panel. Other information can be added to the panel at any time but the team decided to focus on only three initially. The top cell shows in bar graph form the amount of potential business in the various stages of prospecting for a particular day. Each day the information will be automatically updated to show progress. (Typically Dashboards will be displaying color, however, the screen shots shown in this book are gray-scale only.)

The lower left cell shows the top 10 new opportunities in terms of sales potential. Finally, the lower right cell shows the closed sales for the month against the sales target for the month, in this case $10,000. It is straightforward to revise the target and to note any interim targets as well. In this example, the interim target of $5,000 is shown in dark gray.

Another feature of ACT! permits the Dashboard to be displayed upon opening the application. The following screen shot shows how to set this up under Preferences within ACT!. This feature is available in many database applications and supports the goal of having a visual office. In fact, this goal would be buttressed by having completely up-to-date information displayed every time a team member opens the application. How visible and how current is that?

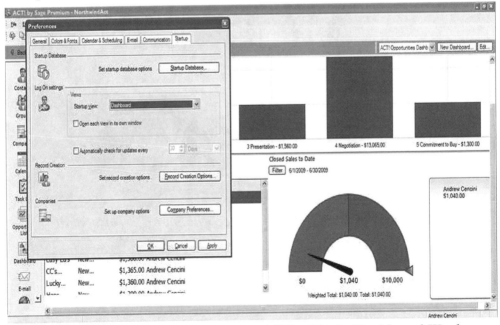

Setting Up the Preference to Open ACT! with the Dashboard Window

The very nature of computer applications today have built in many mistake-proofing features. One example, that most users take for granted, is a database form (as shown in the following screen shot within ACT!) which assures that the data going into a table is complete and in the correct format (number, text, date, etc.). Also, note the use of pull-down menus which mistake proof against typing errors and the potentially confusing use of synonyms or of alternate terminology so that filtering and sort functions end up being much more accurate.

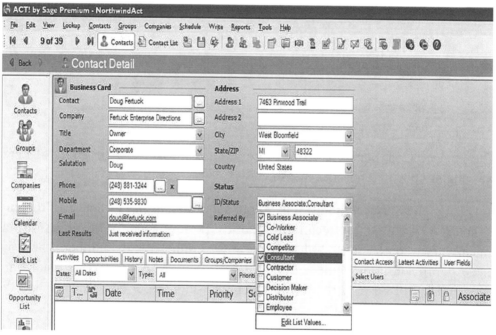

Using Database Forms for Mistake Proofing

Computer software, when designed and applied thoughtfully, provides valuable tools for making data visible, up-to-date, and error-free.

So after six months, how did Northwind's performance change as a result of the Lean Office initiatives? Recall from the Goal Card the set of annual objectives set for the team. After six months, the Northwind performance measurements (next page) shows the performance to those goals. The team directly attributed these changes to the Lean Office project.

	Annual Goals	6 Month Progress with Lean
Finance Goals		
Operating Margin (%)	8	8.5
Annualized Sales Growth (%)	15	18
Quality and Service		
Closure of Service problems (hrs)	4	6
On-Time delivery (%)	97	96
Internal Processes		
Implement Lean methods (months)	3	2.5
Opportunity Success Rate (%)	15	17
Satisfaction		
Sales satisfaction (0-10)	8	N/A
Service satisfaction (0-10)	8	N/A
Supplemental Goal		
New Sales per month	240	255

The Finance Goal performance, a more indirect measure of the effect of Lean, was slightly positive for both measures.

In Quality and Service, the team is falling short on Closure of Service Problems (6 hours vs. 4 hours), but recall the historical performance for this measure was much worse, approaching 24 hours as by the Global Winds number. The team made significant improvement, but further focus and additional continuous improvements will be required in the second six-month period. Andrew and the team planned to conduct a specific Kaizen Event on service calls.

In Internal Processes, the key set of goals addressed by Lean, the target of implementing Lean was met. Also, the Opportunity Success Rate was increased by 2 percentage points over the target of 15%. Focusing on the Prospecting Value Stream was paying off in greater effectiveness in developing new clients. Northwind only measures Customer Satisfaction once a year so no data was available yet on progress towards meeting those goals. However, as a supplementary measure, Andrew looked at how the team was doing with respect to meeting the sales goal of 240 new customers per month since this goal also relates to the Prospecting Value Stream. Again for this metric, the team exceeded the target.

Overall, the Lean initiative at Northwind Traders was moving forward in the areas most specifically affected by process improvements. Andrew and the team were pleased and proud, but not complacent. They had just begun!

APPENDIXES

The Lean Office Assessment

The Lean Office Assessment will provide a clear understanding of what needs to be improved or corrected relative to Lean practices. Conduct the Lean Office Assessment with an internal team of employees, the Lean Champion, and, if appropriate, an outside consultant.

The Lean Office Assessment involves three parts:

> Part 1. Scoring
> Part 2. Evaluating
> Part 3. Planning and Executing

Part 1. Scoring

In this part of the Assessment, the scoring areas are used to allocate points for each of the 10 Lean Office building blocks being assessed. The Scoring Sheet uses a 0-4 point range to allocate points for each guideline. The points are recorded in the appropriate box under the assessment guideline.

If a concept or tool does not have relevancy to an area being scored, then N/A (non-applicable) is written in the box.

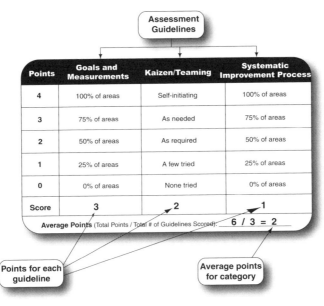

General guidelines are:

- Under Comments/Suggestions, define the parameters that are unique to your office arrangement so they are documented when conducting a follow-up assessment.
- As a group, be honest with the score, as you are probably just beginning Lean Office.
- Areas referenced in this assessment can be an individual department, a specific value stream, or the entire organization.

People completing the scoring sheets will determine the appropriate points for each guideline that best describes the Lean Office practice being assessed.

Utilize the next 10 pages to conduct the Lean Office Assessment.

Assessment Guidelines for 5S

Points	Sorting	Set-In-Order	Shine	Standardize	Sustain
4	100% of areas	100% of areas	100% of areas	100% of areas	100% of areas
3	75% of areas	75% of areas	75% of areas	75% of areas	75% of areas
2	50% of areas	50% of areas	50% of areas	50% of areas	50% of areas
1	25% of areas	25% of areas	25% of areas	25% of areas	25% of areas
0	0% of areas	0% of areas	0% of areas	0% of areas	0% of areas
Score					

Average Points (Total Points / Total # of Guidelines Scored): _____

World Class 4.0 Tips

Audits are peformed regularly.

Current audits are posted and are up-to-date.

Office is well-lit.

All cabinets, shelves, etc. are labeled; drawers are neat and organized.

Workers are proud to display their work areas.

5S Benefits

Allow everyone to be involved.

Provide the foundation for the Lean Office.

Eliminate waste.

Smooth work flow.

Reduce employee stress.

Improve office productivity.

Notes:

_____

_____

_____

_____

Assessment Guidelines for Continuous Flow

Points	Processes Linked Through Value Stream Analysis	Optimal Work Flow	Time in Queue
4	100% of areas	100% of areas	None
3	75% of areas	75% of areas	Minutes
2	50% of areas	50% of areas	Hours
1	25% of areas	25% of areas	Days
0	0% of areas	0% of areas	Weeks
Score			

Average Points (Total Points / Total # of Guidelines Scored): _____

World Class 4.0 Tips

Critical processes are linked through value (or process) stream analysis. ·

Work unit sizes to assist flow have been defined and are being used.

Time in queue is continually being reduced between processes to ensure Just-In-Time work is achieved.

Continuous Flow Benefits

Improve work flow.

Allow for leveling to be better utilized.

Reduce wastes of travel and motion.

Reduce errors.

Reduce employee stress.

Improve office productivity.

Notes:

_____

_____

_____

_____

Assessment Guidelines for Work Areas

Points	Well Defined Physical Area(s)	Defined Value Streams	Technology Utilized
4	100% of areas	100% of areas	100% of areas
3	75% of areas	75% of areas	75% of areas
2	50% of areas	50% of areas	50% of areas
1	25% of areas	25% of areas	25% of areas
0	0% of areas	0% of areas	0% of areas
Score			

Average Points (Total Points / Total # of Guidelines Scored): _____

World Class 4.0 Tips

Work areas are maximized for efficiency of people, space, and equipment.

Continuous improvements are achieved in the future states.

Technology is continually reviewed and utilized to its fullest.

Work areas allow for work to flow seamlessly.

Work Area Office Benefits

Continuous flow becomes a focus.

Reduction in travel and motion waste.

Improve quality.

Foster teamwork.

Improve office productivity.

Notes:

_____

_____

_____

_____

Assessment Guidelines for Visual Controls

Points	Signal Systems	Visual Displays	Clear Action Procedures	Up-to-Date Metrics
4	100% of areas	100% of areas	100% of areas	100% of areas
3	75% of areas	75% of areas	75% of areas	75% of areas
2	50% of areas	50% of areas	50% of areas	50% of areas
1	25% of areas	25% of areas	25% of areas	25% of areas
0	0% of areas	0% of areas	0% of areas	0% of areas
Score				

Average Points (Total Points / Total # of Guidelines Scored): _____

World Class 4.0 Tips

Utilization of lights, e-mail alerts, flags, etc. allow for immediate problem notification and correction.

Color coding, markings, labels, and signs are used for identifying conditions.

Clear action procedures are established and posted.

Metrics are posted and are up-to-date.

Visual Control Benefits

Reduction in internal errors.

Smoother work flow.

Just-In-Time information.

Reduce cross-training time.

Reduce process variation.

Improve office productivity.

Notes:

_____

_____

_____

_____

Assessment Guidelines for Standard Work

Points	Takt Time	Work Sequence Charts	Documented Work Procedures
4	100% of work	100% of areas	100% of areas
3	75% of work	75% of areas	75% of areas
2	50% of work	50% of areas	50% of areas
1	25% of work	25% of areas	25% of areas
0	0% of work	0% of areas	0% of areas
Score			

Average Points (Total Points / Total # of Guidelines Scored): _____

World Class 4.0 Tips

Takt time is used to determine resource allocation to meet office work loads.

Standard Work (or Sequence) Charts are used to ensure critical processes are completed without variation.

Work procedures are well-documented to ensure all processes are completed without variation.

Standard Work Benefits

Reduce internal DPPMs.

Excellent training aids.

Eliminate waste.

Contribute to leveling work.

Reduce employee stress.

Improve office productivity.

Notes:

_____

_____

_____

_____

Assessment Guidelines for Quality

Points	Internal DPPMs	Mistake Proofing	Formal Problem Solving	Internal Audits
4	0	100% of areas	100% of areas	100% of areas
3	<50	75% of areas	75% of areas	75% of areas
2	>50, but <250	50% of areas	50% of areas	50% of areas
1	>250, but <1000	25% of areas	25% of areas	25% of areas
0	>1000	0% of areas	0% of areas	0% of areas
Score				

Average Points (Total Points / Total # of Guidelines Scored): _____

World Class 4.0 Tips

Internal errors are being measured.

Mistake Proofing is understood as a viable process in preventing errors.

Preventive tools such as problem solving are a way of life.

Internal audits are peformed on a regular basis.

Quality Office Benefits

Create attention to work expectations.

Foster teamwork.

Solve problems permanently.

Reduce internal DPPMs.

Improve customer satisfaction.

Improve office productivity.

Notes:

_____

_____

_____

_____

Assessment Guidelines for Pull Systems

Points	Kanbans for Office Supplies	FIFO Lanes	In-Process Supermarkets
4	100% of office supplies	100% of required areas	100% of required areas
3	75% of office supplies	75% of required areas	75% of required areas
2	50% of office supplies	50% of required areas	50% of required areas
1	25% of office supplies	25% of required areas	25% of required areas
0	0% of office supplies	0% of required areas	0% of required areas
Score			

Average Points (Total Points / Total # of Guidelines Scored): _____

World Class 4.0 Tips

Office supplies have been kanbanned.

FIFO lanes are being utilized to improve process flow.

In-process supermarkets are being utilized to improve process flow.

Kanbans serve as a visual control for value stream work.

Pull System Benefits

Improve office work flow.

Reduce errors.

Upstream processes never over-produce work.

Reduce employee stress.

Improve office productivity.

Notes:

_____

_____

_____

_____

Assessment Guidelines for Leveling

Points	Work Load Balancing	Visual Work Board	Flexible Work Force
4	Scheduled by the hour	100% of areas	Fully implemented
3	Scheduled by the day	75% of areas	All critical processes
2	Scheduled by the week	50% of areas	Most critical processes
1	Scheduled by the month	25% of areas	Some processes
0	No schedule	0% of areas	No processes
Score			

Average Points (Total Points / Total # of Guidelines Scored): _____

World Class 4.0 Tips

Work loads have been distributed as appropriate to meet customer demand.

Visual work boards or a heijunka box are utilized to 'see' work progress.

Cross-trained employees are being utilized.

Work schedules are being incorporated into heijunka.

Leveling Benefits

Improve work flow.

Reduce need for overtime.

Identify problems early.

Create a sense of urgency.

Reduce employee stress.

Improve office productivity.

Notes:

_____

_____

_____

_____

Assessment Guidelines for Continuous Improvement

Points	Goals and Measurements	Kaizen/Teaming	Systematic Improvement Process
4	100% of areas	Self-initiating	100% of areas
3	75% of areas	As needed	75% of areas
2	50% of areas	As required	50% of areas
1	25% of areas	A few tried	25% of areas
0	0% of areas	None tried	0% of areas
Score			

Average Points (Total Points / Total # of Guidelines Scored): _____

World Class 4.0 Tips

Metrics have been established and are current.

Employees contribute new ideas to improve metrics.

Kaizen and teaming are being conducted at all levels.

The continuous improvement process has a process for improvement.

Improvement Benefits

Allow everyone to be involved.

Provide the foundation for the Lean Office.

Eliminate wastes of all types.

Reduce employee stress.

Improve office productivity.

Notes:

_____

_____

_____

_____

Assessment Guidelines for Training

Points	Formal Training Plan	Percent of Employees Trained to Plan	Training Results Verified
4	100% of employees	100% of employees	100% of employees
3	75% of employees	75% of employees	75% of employees
2	50% of employees	50% of employees	50% of employees
1	25% of employees	25% of employees	25% of employees
0	<25% of employees	<25% of employees	<25% of employees
Score			

Average Points (Total Points / Total # of Guidelines Scored): _____

World Class 4.0 Tips

Formal training plans exist and are linked to company goals.

Records indicate employees are trained to plan.

Training is linked to baseline performance metrics to ensure required skills are obtained.

Training Benefits

More knowledgeable worker.

Increase contributions to kaizen activities.

Employees feel more value to the organization.

Reduce employee stress.

Improve office productivity.

Notes:

_____

_____

_____

_____

Part 2. Evaluation

There are three steps to this part.

Step 1. Plot scores on the Lean Office Radar Chart. Draw a line connecting the point values for each Lean value on the chart for a visual representation of the organization's overall Lean Office profile.

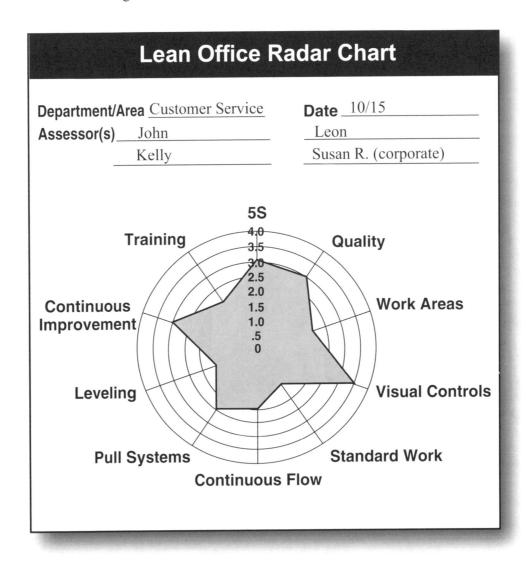

Lean Office Radar Chart

Department/Area Customer Service   **Date** 10/15

Assessor(s) John   Leon

Kelly   Susan R. (corporate)

Part 2. Evaluation - continued

Step 2. Complete a Lean Assessment Summary Form by transferring the Average Point Score on each Lean Guideline or from the Lean Office Radar Chart. This will serve as a benchmark for current and future assessments.

	Category	Previous Score	Current Score
Lean Assessment Summary Form			
1	5S	1.5	3.0
2	Quality	2	3.0
3	Work Areas	2.5	2.0
4	Visual Controls	2.5	3.5
5	Standard Work	2	1.5
6	Continuous Flow	1	2.0
7	Pull Systems	2	2.5
8	Leveling	.5	1.5
9	Continuous Improvement	1	3.0
10	Training	2	2.0
	Total Points	17	24
	Assessment Score (total points / 10)	**1.7**	**2.4**

Part 2. Evaluation - continued

Step 3. Find your place in the Lean Office Rating Scale.

Lean Office Rating Scale

3.6 - 4.0 **World-class status**
Results are being achieved at all levels.
Remember, competition is not stagnant, there is a
need to drive continuous improvement efforts.

2.6 - 3.5 **Results being felt at all levels**
The Lean Office is now becoming part of the
administrative culture. World-class
performance is within sight.

1.6 - 2.5 **Change is becoming visible**
There is a need to leverage momentum to
prevent sliding back to old habits.

0.6 - 1.5 **Beginning the Lean Office journey**
Accelerating a Lean focus will drive change.

0.0 - 0.5 **No Lean commitment**
Adoption and commitment are necessary to
remain competitive and stay in business!

Part 3. Planning and Executing

Now that you know how the organization compares to World Class Lean Office organizations, utilize the Lean Office Guide to Improve.

Lean Office Guide to Improve

3.6 - 4.0 World-class status
Continue to benchmark. Host Lean Office events. Speak and share results. Ensure audits are performed.

2.6 - 3.5 Results being felt at all levels
Continue to benchmark. Ensure reward and recognition are appropriate. Continue to focus on cross-training. Work on the visual office. Ensure standard work is a priority.

1.6 - 2.5 Change is becoming visible
Continue to benchmark. Attend seminars and workshops - preferably those that offer Lean Office tours. Read articles, obtain videos, and read books on how Lean can be further advanced into the organization.

0.6 - 1.5 Beginning the Lean Office journey
Benchmark immediately. Ensure teams go out and see other world-class office practices. Read Lean Office books and articles - in all industry types. 5S must be a major thrust. Ensure teams are chartered. Get employees involved.

0.0 - 0.5 No Lean commitment
Do something! Benchmark, read, and attend workshops. Initiate a plan to do 5S today! Create the business case for the Lean Office. Do something!

The Waste Audit

Conduct this audit with the team. At the end of this section of the Appendix there is a four page layout to further assist you in conducting a waste audit. Use these questions to stimulate other questions specific to your targeted area. This is a tool to use after you have created the current state value stream map. It will assist in creating a waste-free future state.

There are ten types of waste that are costly to an organization and are as follows:

1. Overproduction
2. Waiting Waste
3. Motion Waste
4. Transport Waste
5. Overprocessing Waste
6. Inventory Waste
7. Defect Waste
8. People's Skills
9. Office Politics
10. Unevenness

Many times an activity identified as wasteful can be categorized into more than one type of waste. Do not get hung up on that. The important point is to identify that a waste exists.

Anything that adds cost or time without adding value is waste. Eliminating wastes will accomplish the following:

- Reduce cost to the organization
- Reduce queue time between processes
- Improve office productivity
- Improve quality
- Make the organization more competitive
- Encourage teamwork and employee involvement.

The process of waste elimination can be applied to any process, task, activity, or value stream. The ten areas of waste will be explained with reference to the various Lean tools and practices that can be used in their identification and elimination.

1. The Waste of Overproduction

This waste is producing work or providing a service prior to it being required or requested. That is the greatest of all the wastes. If you overproduce some type of work or service, it encompasses many of the other wastes. For example, if you are preparing a quote for a customer without a request, and it is never requested, you most likely have waste in: excessive processing, transport, motion, etc., not to mention additional waste that you may have acquired information from.

Examples of overproduction wastes are:

- Producing reports no one reads or needs
- Making extra copies
- Printing, emailing, sending, or faxing the same document multiple times
- Entering repetitive information on work documents or forms

To eliminate this type of waste, use:

- Takt Time
- Data Collection Techniques
- Pitch
- Standard Work
- Leveling or Heijunka
- Predictable Output
- Continuous Flow
- Pull Systems
- Others as appropriate

List below the areas or processes that overproduce work or service. Also, list the Lean tools that could be used to reduce or eliminate this waste.

_____

_____

_____

_____

2. The Waste of Waiting (Time In Queue)

Waiting for anything – people, signatures, information, etc. - is waste. This waste of waiting is considered the "low hanging fruit." It is easy to identify and ripe for the taking. We often do not think of paper sitting in an In-basket as waste. However, when looking for an item, how many times do we mull through the In-basket to try and find it? How many times do you actually touch something before it is completed? It is the finish it, file it, or throw it away system that can help with eliminating this waste.

Examples of waiting wastes are:

- Too many signatures or approvals
- Dependency on others to complete tasks
- Delays in receiving information
- Computer program version problems
- Cross-departmental resource commitments

To eliminate this type of waste, use:

- Value Stream Mapping
- 5S
- Data Collection Techniques
- Lean Reporting and Communications
- Pitch
- Work Load Balancing
- Runners
- Office File System
- Others as appropriate

List below the areas or processes that have excessive wait times. Also, list the Lean tools that could be used to reduce or eliminate this waste.

_____

_____

_____

_____

3. The Waste of Motion

Any movement of people, paper, or electronic exchanges that does not add value is waste. This waste can be created by poor office layout or design, ineffective office equipment, supplies located afar, etc.

Examples of motion wastes are:

- Searching for computer files on your desktop
- Searching for work documents
- Reviewing manuals for information
- Hand-carrying paperwork to another department or process

To eliminate this type of waste, use:

- Standard Work
- 5S
- Office Layout
- Document Tagging
- Office File System
- Just-In-Time
- Kanbans for Office Supplies
- Pull Systems
- Others as appropriate

List below the areas or processes that have excessive motion. Also, list the Lean tools that could be used to reduce or eliminate this waste.

_____

_____

_____

_____

4. The Waste of Transport (or conveyance)

Transport is an important and ubiquitous element. It affects the delivery of any work within the office. It is the movement of work that does not add value.

Examples of transport wastes are:

- Delivering documents that are not required
- Excessive filing of work documents
- E-mail distribution lists that are not up-to-date

To eliminate this type of waste, use:

- Standard Work
- 5S
- Office Layout
- Document Tagging
- Work Load Balancing
- Runners
- Office File System
- Continuous Flow
- Kaizen Events
- Others as appropriate

List below the areas or processes that have excessive transport. Also, list the Lean tools that could be used to reduce or eliminate this waste.

_____

_____

_____

_____

5. The Waste of Overprocessing

Putting more work or effort into work required by the internal or external customer is waste. This excessive processing does not add value for the customer and the customer will not pay for it.

Examples of overprocessing wastes are:

- Duplicating reports or information
- Repetitive data entry
- Changing how information is conveyed between processes or departments
- Constantly revising documents

To eliminate this type of waste, use:

- Value Stream Mapping
- Standard Work
- Document Tagging
- Lean Reporting and Communications
- Work Load Balancing
- Kaizen Events
- Data Collection Techniques
- Visual Controls
- Others as appropriate

List below the areas or processes that have overprocessing. Also, list the Lean tools that could be used to reduce or eliminate this waste.

_____

_____

_____

_____

6. The Waste of Inventory

Stock, work piles, and excess supplies are waste. They all take up space and may become obsolete if customer requirements change. Time is considered inventory. Customers waiting for services may also be considered inventory.

Examples of inventory wastes are:

- Files awaiting signatures or approvals
- Files awaiting task completion by others
- Purchasing excessive office supplies
- Obsolete files
- Obsolete office equipment
- Patients waiting for services

To eliminate this type of waste, use:

- 5S
- Value Stream Mapping
- Standard Work
- Visual Controls
- Pull Systems
- Kanbans for Office Supplies
- Heijunka - Leveling
- Cycle Time
- Others as appropriate

List below the areas or processes that have excessive inventory. Also, list the Lean tools that could be used to reduce or eliminate this waste.

_____

_____

_____

_____

7. The Waste of Defects

This category of waste refers to all processing required to correct a defect. Defects (either internal or external) result in additional administrative processes that will add no value to the product or service. The idea is that it takes a shorter time to do it correctly the first time than it does to do it over to correct a problem or defect. Rework is waste and adds more cost, which reduces any profit to the bottom line.

Examples of defect wastes are:

- Data entry errors
- Pricing and quoting errors
- Forwarding partial documentation to the next process
- Lost files or records
- Incorrect information on a document

To eliminate this type of waste, use:

- Standard Work
- Predictable Output
- Visual Controls
- Mistake-Proofing
- Office File System
- Interruptions and Random Arrivals
- Others as appropriate

List below the areas or processes that produce defects or errors. Also, list the Lean tools that could be used to reduce or eliminate this waste.

_____

_____

_____

_____

8. The Waste of People's Skills

The under-utilization of people is a result of not placing people where they can and will use their knowledge, skills, and abilities to the fullest providing value-added work and services.

Examples of People's Skills wastes are:

- High absenteeism and turnover
- Project deadlines not being met
- Incomplete job skill assessment

To eliminate this type of waste, you would use:

- Standard Work
- Process Capture

List below the areas or processes that waste people's skills. Also, list the Lean tools that could be used to reduce or eliminate this waste.

_____

_____

_____

_____

9. The Waste of Office Politics

Additional work that is done (possibly also considered as overprocessing) solely to gain favor with management can be considered a ninth waste. This is a delicate subject, but must be addressed, as it has proven to be a real issue within organizations.

Examples of Office Politics wastes are:

- Excessive reporting
- Politically motivated tasks and meetings

To eliminate this type of waste, use:

- Standard Work
- Work Load Balancing

List below the areas or processes that waste resources due to office politics. Also, list the Lean tools that could be used to reduce or eliminate this waste.

_____

_____

_____

_____

10. The Waste of Unevenness

Lack of a consistent flow of inputs/information/scheduled work from upstream processes causes any of the other types of waste previously mentioned.

Examples of Unevenness wastes are:

- Scheduling large reports month-end only
- Holding information unnecessarily before passing it on

To eliminate this type of waste, use:

- Value Stream Mapping
- Work Load Balancing

List below the areas or processes that process work unevenly. Also, list the Lean tools that could be used to reduce or eliminate this waste.

_____

_____

_____

_____

This was a quick review of the wastes and suggested Lean Office tools that can be used for their elimination. Consider the following questions:

1. How can I start to communicate how to eliminate these wastes throughout the organization?
2. What are some low-hanging fruit?
3. What can be done immediately to improve customer satisfaction?

Use the next four pages of this Appendix to further organize the application of Lean tools and concepts in support of the identification and elimination of waste.

Waste Category	Definition	Administrative Examples
Overproduction	This waste is producing work or providing a service prior to it being required or requested. This is the greatest of all the wastes. In that, if you overproduce some type of work or service, it encompasses many of the other wastes.	Inadequate patient work-up leading to unnecessary tests Duplicate files Producing reports no one reads or needs Making extra copies Printing, emailing, sending, or faxing the same document
Waiting (Time in Queue)	Waiting for anything – people, signatures, information, etc. - is waste. This waste of waiting is considered the "low hanging fruit." It is easy to identify and ripe for the taking. We often don't think of paper sitting in an In-basket as waste. However, when looking for an item, how many times do we mull through the In-basket to try and find it? How many times do you actually touch something before it is completed? It's the finish it, file it, or throw it away system that can help with eliminating this waste.	Delay in receiving discharge orders Delay in room assignments Excessive signatures or approvals Dependency on others to complete tasks Delays in receiving information Computer program version problems Cross-departmental resource commitments
Motion	Any movement of people, paper, or electronic exchanges that does not add value is waste. This waste can be created by poor office layout or design, ineffective office equipment, supplies located afar, etc.	Searching for patient records or meds Searching for charts Searching for computer files on your desktop Searching for work documents (files) Reviewing manuals for information Hand-carrying paperwork to another department or process
Transport	Transport is an important and ubiquitous element. It affects the delivery of any work within the office. It is the movement of work that does not add value.	Delivering documents that are not required Excessive filing of work documents Email distribution lists that are not up-to-date
Office Politics	Additional work that is done (possibly considered as overprocessing) solely to gain favor with management.	Creating excessive management reports Peforming tasks that are politically motivated

To Detect This Waste Ask	Notes for Your Target Area
Is this test being performed a repeat of recent results already obtained? Is this form a duplicate of some other form? Can the information on this form be used in other areas? Is someone using all the information that is being provided?	
Are there delays in the delivery of information? Are there issues with punctuality with internal, as well as external, customers? Are there certain times where delays are more prevelant? Is there a bottleneck in the process due to excessive review? Have delays always been a problem or are they a recent development?	
Can walking be reduced by repositioning equipment and/or supplies? Is the information to do the work easily accessible? Are new and current employees properly trained in the process? Are prodedures in place for all critical processes? Are there certain areas that impede work flow?	
Is the information or work that is being transformed being hand delivered to other processes? Is work being delivered to the right place at the right time? Has work been consolidated where appropriate?	
Is the information or work being performed part of my job duties? Are the resources being used wisely?	

Waste Category	Definition	Administrative Examples
Overprocessing	Putting more work or effort into the work required by internal or external customers is waste. Excessive processing does not add value for the customer, and the customer will not pay for it. This is one of the most difficult administrative wastes to uncover.	Duplicative reports or information Repetitive data entry Incorrect information being shared Unnecessary testing Duplicative documentation Lack of accurate project planning
Inventory	Work piles, excessive supplies, and excessive signature requirements are waste. They all take up space or require someone's time. If a document is waiting for additional information (i.e., signature, etc.) and there is a change, then the time the document has been waiting is waste. There are basically two types of inventory waste related to administrative areas: 1) office supplies, and 2) time.	Files/charts awaiting signatures or approvals Work awaiting task completion by others Obsolete files Obsolete equipment Insufficient training of back-ups Purchasing excessive supplies
Defects (Mistakes)	Defect waste refers to all processing required in creating a defect and the additional work required to correct a defect. And defects (either internal or external) result in additional administrative processing that will add no value to the product or service. It takes less time to do work correctly the first time than the time it would take to do it over. Rework is waste and adds more cost to any product or service. This waste can also reduce profits significantly.	Data entry errors Wrong billing codes Pricing errors Forwarding incomplete documentation Lost files or records Med dispensing errors Incorrect information on document Not appropriate staffing to service customer
People's Time	The underutilization of people is a result of not placing people where they can (and will) use their knowledge, skills, and abilities to the fullest. Use company policies and procedures to effectively place people where they will most benefit the organization.	Project deadlines not being met Work loads not evenly balanced due to lack of cross-training High absenteeism and turnover Incomplete job skill assessment prior to hiring
Unevenness	Lack of a consistent flow of inputs/information/scheduled work from upstream processes.	Not having information ahead of time to meet deadlines Not leveling work adequately Poor office standards No good communications with other departments

To Detect This Waste Ask	Notes for Your Target Area
Has this paperwork been done before? Is this a repeat of some earlier work? Has someone confirmed that this is exactly what the customer requested? Is there more information obtained than what is required? Are there redundant phone calls or e-mails to obtain information?	
Are there supply boxes sitting on the floor? Are you using the hall for storage? Are there expired medications in the area? Are internal or external customers waiting for information or a service to be provided? Is everyone working to their full capacity?	
Are there well-documented standard processes? Does equipment have a maintenance schedule? Are there issues with the customer/patient keeping a scheduled appointment? Are there effective cross-training programs? Do employees have the proper amount of time?	
Are employees effectively cross-trained? Are employees encourgaged to suggest improvements? Are employees empowered to implement improvements? Are new employees trained to best practice?	
Are all employees working to capacity? Are departments working together to improve the overall flow of work?	

Six Sigma

Six Sigma is a sophisticated problem solving approach for improving business performance. Six Sigma is "management driven by data." It is based upon improving processes by controlling and understanding variation, thus improving predictability of business processes. It is a disciplined, data-driven, decision-making method.

In its purest form, Six Sigma is a term used to describe a measure of quality control that is near perfection. The Six Sigma Process uses data and rigorous statistical analysis to identify "defects" in a process, service, or product, reduce variability, and achieve as close to zero defects as possible.

Less than Six Sigma is not good enough because we would have to accept the following:

- 16,000 pieces of mail lost by the U.S.P.S. every hour
- Two unsafe plane landings per day at O'Hare International Airport in Chicago, Illinois
- 32,000 missed heartbeats per person per year
- 20,000 incorrect drug prescriptions per year in the U.S.
- 22,000 checks deducted from the wrong bank accounts every hour in the U.S.
- 50 newborn babies dropped at birth per day in the U.S.

The Six Sigma process usually is facilitated by a Black Belt trained staff member. Achieving Black Belt certification signifies that the individual has successfully completed an improvement activity with a defined cost savings.

Six Sigma provides the organization with the following:

- Improved internal and external customer satisfaction
- Improved productivity of employees
- Improved problem solving skills
- Reduced costs
- Reduced number of errors or mistakes
- Standard continuous improvement methodology
- Fact-based decision making process

Six Sigma can be effective when used as part of a business improvement strategy. When combined with the philosophy and methods of Lean, it becomes a powerful method for continuous improvement.

Six Sigma is a reference to the goal of reducing defects or mistakes to zero. Sigma is the Greek letter mathematicians use to represent the "standard deviation of a population." The standard deviation of a population represents the variability there is within a group of items, i.e., the population.

Six Sigma is a measure of variation that achieves 3.4 defects per million opportunities, or 99.99966 percent acceptable. It is represented by the following bell curve (also known as normal distribution). The higher the sigma value, the better.

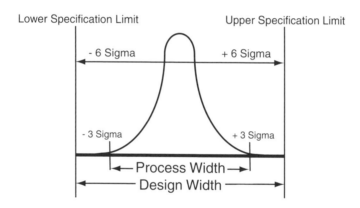

Six Sigma uses a five-step problem solving tool called **D-M-A-I-C**:

1. **D**efine
2. **M**easure
3. **A**nalyze
4. **I**mprove
5. **C**ontrol

1. Define

Define the customers, their requirements, the team charter, and the key processes that may affect the customer. The following tools can be utilized:

- Team Charter
- Cause and Effect Diagram
- Process Mapping
- Voice of the Customer (VOC)

2. Measure

Identify the key measures and the data collection plan for the process in question. Execute the plan for data collection. The following tools can be utilized:

- Document Tagging
- Data Collection and Check Sheet

3. Analyze

Analyze the data collected, as well as the process, to determine the root causes for why the process is not performing as desired. The following tools can be utilized:

- Histogram
- Scatter Diagram
- Design of Experiments (DOE)
- Pareto
- Control or Run Chart

4. Improve

Generate and determine potential solutions and plot them on a small scale to determine if they positively improve process performance. The following tools can be utilized:

- Process Mapping or Flowcharting
- Paynter Chart

5. Control

Develop, document, and implement a plan to ensure performance improvement remains at the desired level. The following tools can be utilized:

- Control or Run Charts
- Paynter Chart
- Standard Work

The following is an example of how to calculate the Six Sigma capability for one of your processes:

Six Sigma Calculation Worksheet

Process Name Order Entry   **Date** 2/16

No.	Action	Equations	Your Calculations
1	Name the process.		Order Entry
2	The number of units produced by the process.		1,283
3	The number of units that were error-free.		1,138
4	Compute the yield for the process.	= (Step 3) / (Step 2)	.887
5	Compute the defect rate based on Step 4.	= 1 - (Step 4)	.113
6	Determine the number of potential things that could create a defect (note: use N = 10 as a conservative number of potential defects).	= N number of Critical-To-Quality characteristics (CTQs)	10
7	Compute the defect rate per CTQ characteristic.	= (Step 5) / (Step 6)	.0113
8	Compute the Defects Per Million Opportunities (DPMO).	= (Step 7) x 1,000,000	11,300
9	Convert the DPMO (Step 8) into a Sigma value, using a Six Sigma Conversion Chart (google: six sigma conversion table).	Includes a 1.5 sigma shift for all listed values of Z	3.8
10	Draw conclusions.		Opportunity for improvement

Preview of *The Lean Desktop and Networking Pocket Guide XL*

(Appendix D examples are excerpts from the book *The Lean Desktop and Networking Pocket Guide XL*)

Pivot Tables (MS Excel)

This is one of Excel's most powerful functions/features. It is used when you have a large number of raw data points (i.e., from only a few lines to +60,000 lines of data) and you wish to summarize and display the data in table format. The Pivot Table function enables you to pick the key data points that will be displayed on the ROW axis, the COLUMN axis, and then those selections will be displayed in the DATA field area. The PAGE field operates like the ROW and COLUMN fields but provides a third dimension for your data. It allows for you to add another sorting qualifier for the data set. You will be able to display 60,000+ lines of data in a summarized table format within a few seconds (i.e., for further analysis and stratification to help identify a critical process or a value stream). Pivot Tables are designed to avoid data errors by automating the table generation process and improving productivity by completing the table generation activity in seconds instead of minutes. The Lean concept that this relates to is:

- Jidoka or Mistake proofing – reducing the probability of error due to the higher level of automation and building better data collection controls through the use of automated functions
- Visual control – generating meaningful data to support decision-making, highlighting exceptions, notifications, or deviations, and thus enabling timely corrective actions
- Workflow – streamlining and speeding up the table generation process, releasing resources, and reducing bottlenecks

The Pivot Table can be used to automatically extract, organize, and summarize your data. You can use this report to analyze the data, make comparisons, detect patterns and relationships, and discover trends.

For example, let us say there is a large amount of data that you extracted from your business system and you need to create a report quickly and easily. The first step is knowing "what" data you want to see and understand.

The following example is data extracted from an accounting software system that shows three business days for a Small-to-Medium Enterprise (SME). You may wish to see:

- Sales by Department
- Sales by Customer

- Sales by Day
- Sales by Product etc.

Any of these measurements will require a unique set of field settings in the Pivot Table. For the purposes of this example, we will measure Sales by Day.

	A	B	C	D	E	F	G	H
1	Delivery Doc No.	Sales Dept	Cust No	Invoice Value	Invoice Date	Product No	Qty	Cust Order
2	80856944	EU01	101324	2,000.00	5/01/2009	10671000	2	625112
3	80857699	AU01	117493	410.00	5/01/2009	3961205	2	627125
4	80857749	DU01	110698	1,230.00	5/01/2009	1067205	6	625744
5	80857591	AU01	10230	3,000.00	6/01/2009	3099005	4	626945
6	80857894	AU01	101250	2,500.00	6/01/2009	1897205	1	625975
7	80857900	EU01	10234	340.00	6/01/2009	1663020	1	627271
8	80857901	AU01	10234	450.00	6/01/2009	1177015	1	627271
9	80857949	AU01	105670	560.00	6/01/2009	1959450	72	627297
10	80857965	DU01	119823	2,000.00	6/01/2009	2456020	1	627326
11	80858017	AU01	117379	450.00	6/01/2009	1957020	1	627343
12	80858018	AU01	117379	5,600.00	6/01/2009	2436020	4	627343
13	80858030	AU01	10234	3,400.00	6/01/2009	1347020	1	625196
14	80858058	EU01	101638	1,200.00	6/01/2009	1668020	33	627395
15	80855519	AU01	114744	3,400.00	7/01/2009	1579205	1	625631
16	80857487	DU01	115976	2,300.00	7/01/2009	1959450	24	626992
17	80857895	AU01	119690	1,200.00	7/01/2009	2137001	12	627249
18	80857896	DU01	115398	6,700.00	7/01/2009	2557205	1	626175
19	80857908	DU01	119690	3,800.00	7/01/2009	2798005	4	627249
20	80857909	AU01	119695	2,340.00	7/01/2009	2169020	3	627249
21	80857910	EU01	119690	4,535.00	7/01/2009	1959450	24	627249
22	80857920	EU01	10250	1,275.00	7/01/2009	2493005	8	550471
23	80857921	AU01	105426	3,200.00	7/01/2009	2421005	8	559601
24	80857922	DU01	117694	1,670.00	7/01/2009	2436020	4	565079
25	80857923	AU01	10250	320.00	7/01/2009	2436010	1	563992
26	80857924	AU01	10072	200.00	7/01/2009	2135005	4	564757
27	80857925	AU01	113360	500.00	7/01/2009	2421020	1	565339
28	80857926	EU01	115973	350.00	7/01/2009	2125020	3	559075
29	80857927	AU01	113333	125.00	7/01/2009	2131005	4	559075
30	80857928	AU01	112891	350.00	7/01/2009	2436205	1	564827

1. Select **Data** in the Excel tool bar menu, then click **PivotTable and PivotChart Report....**

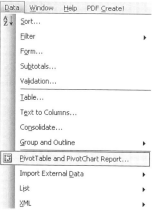

3. The Pivot Table function will ask for a data range as shown below. Highlight and select the entire sheet from cell A1 to H30. Then click **Next**.

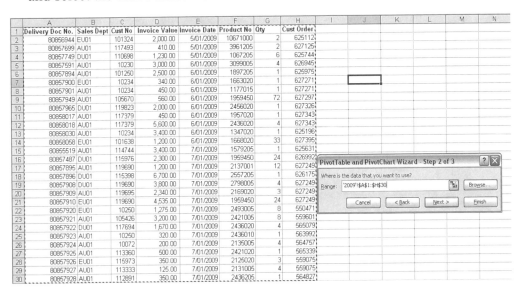

4. Click **Layout**.

5. This is the critical point in the Pivot Table function where you select "what" data you wish to display in the final results of the Pivot Table. If you do not like the results, you can always go back and modify the layout of your Pivot Table and then refresh the results.

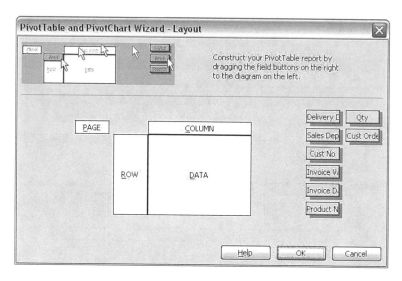

6. Since we are looking for "Sales by Day," you will need to display the table as shown below. To do this, you need to "drag and drop" the data points into the table on the left. In this example, we are dragging "Invoice Date" into the ROW section and "Invoice Value" into the DATA section of the table as shown below. Then click **OK**.

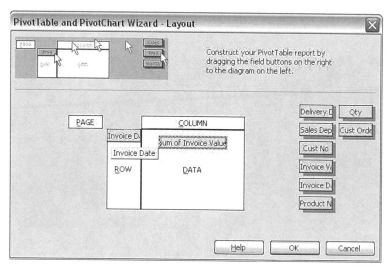

7. Select **New worksheet**, then your Pivot Table will appear in a "new" sheet. The Pivot Table shown below has displayed the data extracted in a succinct, easy-to-read format, where numerous sales figures have been summarized into Total Sales by Day.

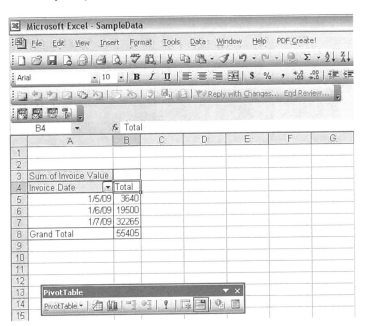

8. You may often find that your initial layout did not produce the desired result. For example, analyzing the three consecutive business days for the month may not reveal useful/meaningful information. So, step back through the Pivot Table screens and refresh the field settings to display Total Sales in the first week of each month. It is common to step back-and-forth through the same Pivot Table several times until you get a meaningful result. In this case, you may find that the Sales in the first week of each month are 25% lower than the same time last year, but this would not have been as easy to identify, if you did not change the field settings from "consecutive business day" to "week." So, if the output is not as expected, you can always go back into the field settings of the Pivot Table and make modifications. To go backwards, just place your mouse anywhere over the Pivot Table itself, right-click your mouse and select **PivotTable Wizard** as shown below.

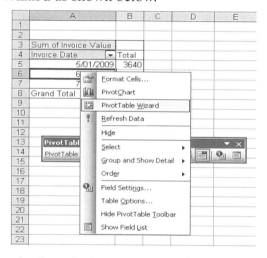

This will take you back to the Layout page, where you can make modifications to the Table Layout, and then click **Finish** to display your new results.

The Pivot Table function is not just useful for organizing and displaying data. It also plays an important role when gathering data for a value stream mapping initiative, to aggregate data from document tagging initiatives, and/or to analyze value stream maps that may have a number of complex business measurements. The Pivot Table function can consolidate and aggregate these business measurements to give a meaningful insight into the problem/issue at hand by identifying an area of focus for improvement (i.e., a value stream).

Note: Pivot Tables can also be generated in MS Access. However, MS Access is more challenging to utilize than MS Excel and the functions are trickier.

Value Stream Mapping (MS Visio)

A value stream map is very useful if it is used within a systematic approach to Lean implementation. Do not use this tool strictly for management, allow as many workers as possible to assist in creating a value stream map. Share the maps by posting them on the Intranet and placing a hardcopy in the appropriate area.

If there are numerous branches (Yes - No type decisions in the processes identified), then consider a type of process map (i.e., deployment, macro, mini, spaghetti diagram, swim lane, etc.). Keep in mind that a value stream map is the 10,000 foot view and provides the basic plan for improvement (i.e., Lean Project).

Whether to create a value stream map in Excel or Visio will be determined by several factors. These factors are driven by the limited drawing capabilities of Excel, and the considerable and advanced drawing capabilities of Visio.

Factors to consider for when to use Excel:

- A simple value stream map with limited (5-10) number of process boxes
- A single function value stream (within the same department)
- A minimal number of data sets (e.g., cycle times, wait times, First Time Right (FTR), quality measures, etc.)
- A limited volume/throughput of work (i.e., documents, orders, applications, etc.) throughout the value stream
- A repeatable process
- A required step graph that will sum up total cycle and queue times from process boxes (using Excel formulas)

Pro's when using Excel:

- Easy to create simple value stream maps
- Accessible/available software package on nearly all PCs
- Less computer knowledge required to use than Visio
- Easy to "group" your autoshapes together to move them around the page
- Easy to use Excel's add/subtract/sum features to calculate process metrics

Con's when using Excel:

- Limited number of unique autoshapes for use
- Difficult to rescale your map once created (i.e., hard to adjust the size of the whole page)
- Generally not viewed as a sophisticated "drawing" tool and has limited capabilities
- No easy feature to use when you need to grab, move, and/or adjust the drawing
- Hard to insert objects and images from Visio into Excel
- Hard to write text onto and/or into all autoshapes

Factors to consider for when to use Visio:

- A complex value stream map with 10+ process boxes
- Complex, cross-functional and cross-boundary (with suppliers/customers) processes
- Complex data sets (e.g. cycle times, wait times, First Time Right (FTR) or quality measures)
- A high volume throughput of work (i.e., documents, orders, applications, high $ value, etc.)
- Numerous process owners with multiple lines of reporting
- Processes with a high degree of individual discretion

Pro's when using Visio:

- Easy to create simple value stream maps
- Very easy to rescale your map once created and add more complexity to it
- A large range of unique autoshapes provided for almost "any" drawing requirements
- Easy to "group" autoshapes together to move them around the page
- Sophisticated "drawing" tool with many drawing capabilities
- Easy to use "click, select" feature to grab, move, and/or adjust all or parts of the drawing
- Easy to insert objects and images from Excel into Visio
- Easy to write text onto and/or into all autoshapes

Con's when using Visio:

- Less accessible/available software package
- More computer knowledge required to use than Excel
- Not available on all office PC's and other users may not be able to open your Visio .dwg (unless you save it as a PDF)

1. Open Visio. Select **Flowchart | Cross Functional Flowchart**. This will enable you to create a single page for your value stream map. Select **Create**.

2. If your version of Visio does not display the screen shown above, then just go to **File | New | Flowchart | Cross Functional Flowchart** as shown below.

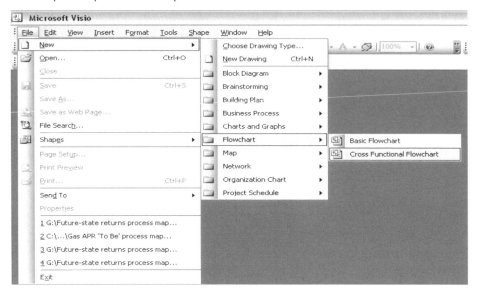

3. Select **Horizontal** orientation, and for Number of bands: enter **1**. Click **OK**.

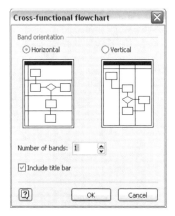

4. Note that your screen should look similar to the one shown below.

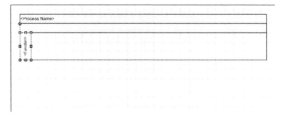

5. Increase the size of the value stream map appropriately. Move your mouse, click and drag the button identified by the dialogue box as shown below.

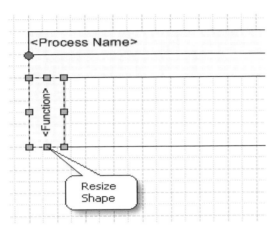

6. Note on the left side of your screen, you will see three different tool bars: (i) Arrow Shapes, (ii) Basic Flowchart Shapes, (iii) Cross Functional Flowchart Shapes. Click on **Basic Flowchart Shapes**, which will display a large range of standard shapes to create an effective value stream map.

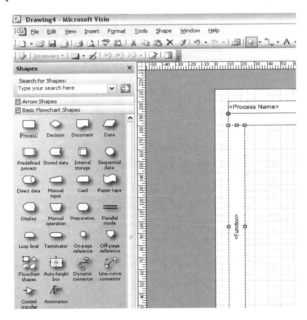

7. Drag and drop the "process" icon into your blank value stream map. Repeat this step for each of your processes defined by the value stream. The value stream map should look something like the one shown below.

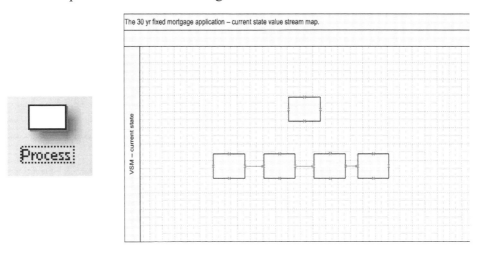

8. Double-click inside each of the boxes and write a description of the process. You can also double-click inside the horizontal area to add further details (if appropriate).

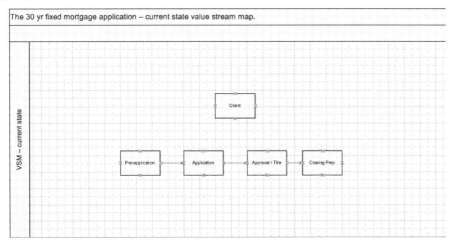

9. Connect the value stream boxes. Select the following "connector tool" on the tool bar as shown below.

10. Move the mouse over the first RED point (denoted by "+" sign within a small box) on the process box, you should be able to "drag and drop" your connector tool from the first RED point (shown as small box with an x in it) to the second RED point, as shown below.

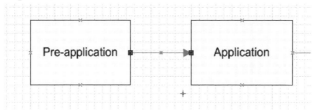

11. Connect all the boxes as shown below.

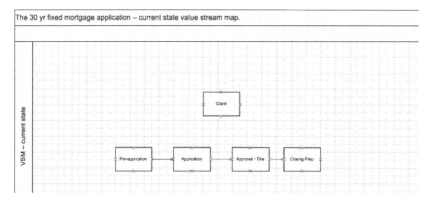

12. Drag and drop the "process" icon into your blank value stream map. These will represent the various attributes of the process. Repeat this step several times as shown below until you have data (attribute) sets under each value stream process.

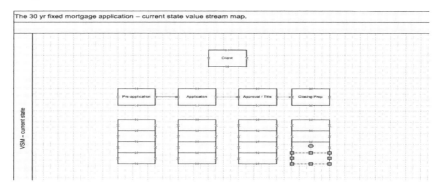

13. Drag and drop other icons that suit your requirements (such as the WAIT icon shown below). Double-click in any box or icon, and enter text, then just click back out of the icon. You can then start to populate the value stream map with icons as shown below.

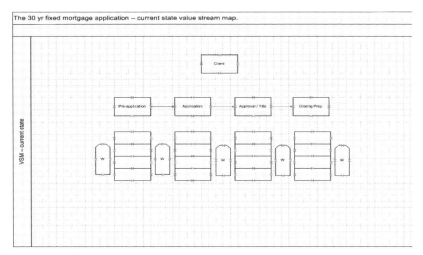

14. Double-click into the data boxes and start entering the detailed events that take place within each value stream box.

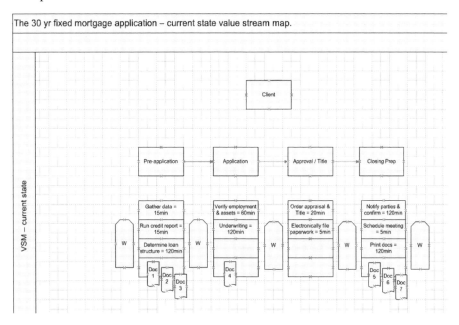

The following example will step you through learning how to create a step graph using the basic drawing capabilities of Visio.

1. Note on the left side of your screen, you will see three different tool bars: (i) Arrow Shapes, (ii) Basic Flowchart Shapes, (iii) Cross Functional Flowchart Shapes. Click on **Basic Flowchart Shapes**, which will display a large range of standard shapes to create the value stream map which was done in Step 6.

2. Drag and drop the Dynamic Connector icon into your blank value stream map as shown below.

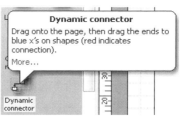

3. Repeat Step 2 several times. Start connecting them to create the step graph. Your value stream map should look something like the one shown below.

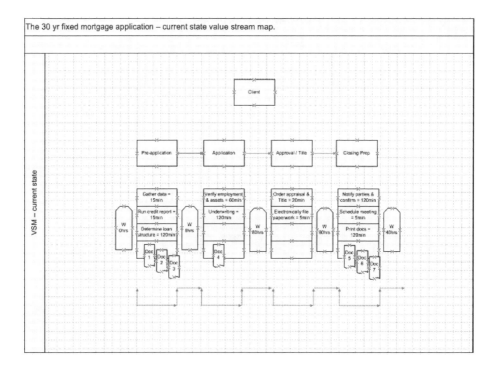

4. Double-click on any step graph and manually type in the relevant time values, which are just a sum of the individual (i.e., cycle) time values shown in the data (attribute) boxes as shown below.

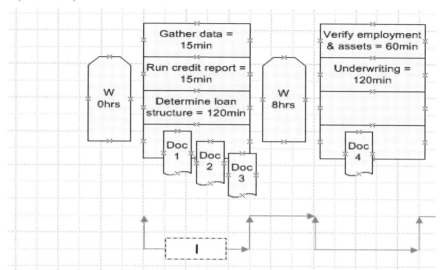

5. Note that the value stream map should be similar to the one shown below.

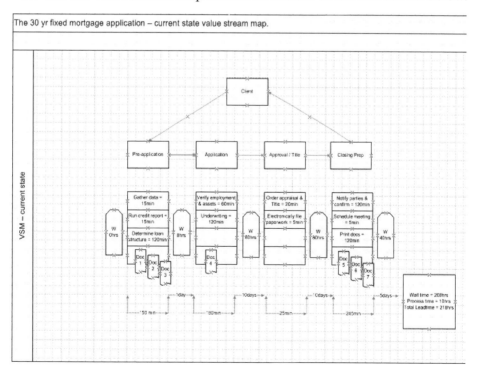

Employee Balance Chart (MS Excel)

The following example will serve as a guide for learning how to create an Employee Balance Chart (see page 252) in Excel. It may be of value to enter the data that is shown in the following screen shot and then follow the steps.

1. Create a blank worksheet similar to the one below.

	A	B	C	D	E	F	G	H	I
1				CURRENT STATE WORK BALANCE CHART					
2	Work Element	CSR#1	CSR#2	CSR#3	PROC#1	PROC#2	PROC#3	PLANNING#1	PLANNING#2
3	Open program and log-in	2	2	2	2	2	2	2	2
4	Check urgent emails	10	10	15	12	6	8	22	18
5	Check accuracy of data	5	6	6	10	8	20	2	2
6	Check inventory levels	3	3	3	3	3	3	3	3
7	Submit order	2	2	2	0	0	0	0	0
8	Allocate materials	0	0	0	5	8	8	0	0
9	Confirm supplier delivery	0	0	0	0	0	0	12	15
10	Check outstanding orders	3	4	3	8	8	6	12	12
11	Create new email distribution for order	0	0	0	6	6	6	0	0
12	File attachment with order	3	2	3	0	0	0	0	0
13	Enter info into Excel spreadsheet	0	0	0	0	0	0	12	15
14	Extract finance part and send to manager							8	10
15	Meetings	30	30	30	45	45	45	60	60
16									
17	Total	58	59	64	91	86	98	133	137

2. Make a copy of this sheet and name the tab 'Your Future Data.'

3. Create another new sheet named 'Your Charts.'

4. Choose **Insert** from the main menu and select **Chart**.

5. Select **Stacked column with a 3-D visual effect**.

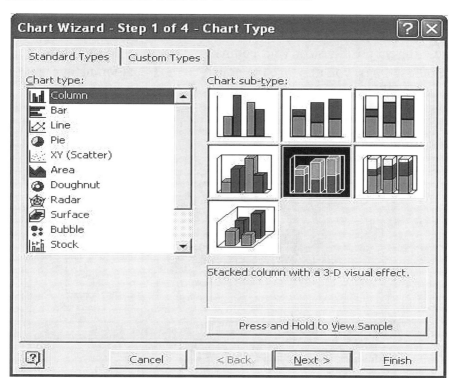

6. Click **Next** and you will be given the option to select your data range. Click back to the 'Your Current Data' sheet and highlight cells B3 - B15, which shows how many Work Elements you have, and across to I3-I15, which shows the number of users or positions you have that correspond to the Work Elements. Select Series in: **Rows**. Next, click the Series tab. Here we will set the X Axis Labels and the names of the departmental positions with the Series Labels and the Work Elements.

7. Each 'Series' listed represents one of the Work Elements. Click **Series1**, then click the box next to Name:. Return to 'Your Current Data' sheet and click the cell containing the first Work Element, then hit <**Enter**>. Select **Back** and repeat this for each Series listed until all of your series are assigned to a Work Element. Note that the Work Elements will populate the Legend, typically to the right of the graph. Select **Add** to increase the number of Series or Work Elements, if needed.

8. Once completed, click down to the Category (X) axis labels: then click back to the 'Your Current Data' sheet. Select the cells containing the titles of your departmental positions and then click **Next** and this will label the X-Axis with the different positions for your company. However, depending on your Axis default settings, you may need to adjust the text positioning at Step 3 of 4 of the Chart Wizard.

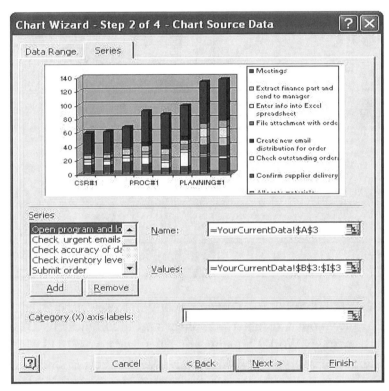

9. Label the Chart title: **Current State Data**, Category (X) axis: **Positions**, and Value (Z) axis: **Time** as shown on the top of the next page.

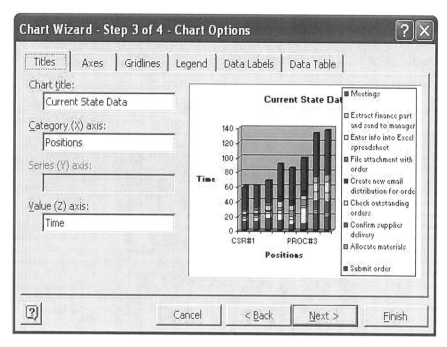

10. Select **Next**.

11. Select **As object in:** and then **Finish**.

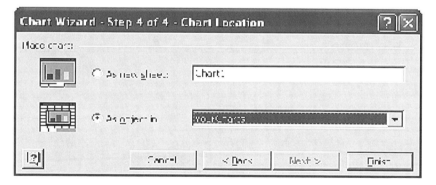

12. The chart will require modifications to the default attributes. Double-click on the X-Axis chart to bring up the format menu. Click on the Scale tab and set the Number of categories between tick-mark labels: to **1**. Then, under the Alignment tab, select Orientation to **-90** Degrees by either entering the -90 or grabbing the Text line in the window and moving it downward -90 degrees. Select **OK**.

Note: If the Z axis is not correct due to your defaults settings, double-click on it and select the appropriate attributes.

13. Double-click on the Legend. Change the font size to **8** and resize the chart appropriately to ensure all the Legend information is included. The chart should appear as shown below.

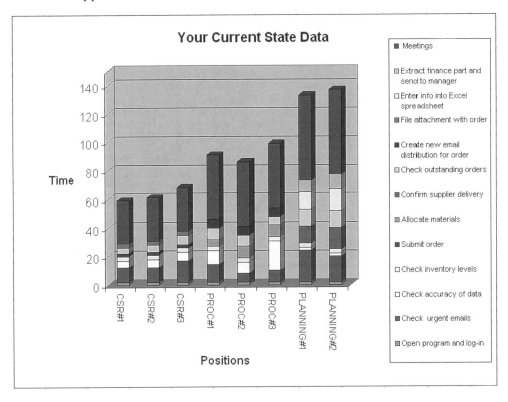

14. To add a line on the chart representing takt time, select **Insert | Picture | Autoshapes**. Under Autoshapes, select the Line tool and place a line on the chart so it aligns with the 60 minute mark, which was the takt time for this example, on the Z Axis. You can resize the line so that it covers the entire chart area as well as change the color and line weight.

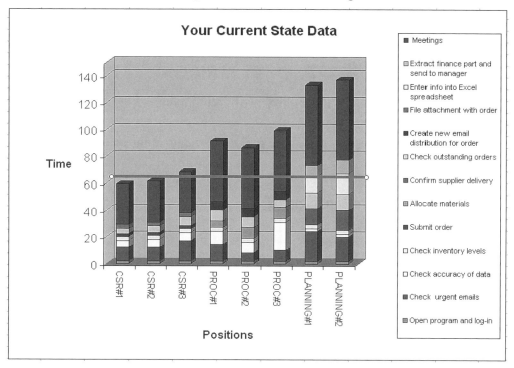

15. Repeat the above steps for creating a sheet titled Your Future Data. You will use Your Current Data to begin with and at a later date, compare the results with a separate set of data that will be input into the Your Future Data sheet. Insert the appropriate future state chart in Your Charts and compare the two.

Note: This example demonstrates that cross-training in certain functions or re-allocating Work Elements would better balance the work loads given the takt time of 60 minutes. This may not always be practical, but using a chart such as this, will open up discussions for improvements.

Glossary of Lean Office Terms

5S - A process to ensure work areas are systematically kept clean and organized, to ensure employee safety, and to provide the foundation on which to build a Lean Office.

Active State - The horizontal position of a file folder indicating work needs to be completed.

Activity - The single act or multiple acts of taking a course of action.

Assessment - An instrument used to analyze a department or area relative to a particular topic.

Benchmarking - A structured approach to identify and adapt world-class practices to an organization.

Brainstorming - The process of capturing people's ideas and organizing those thoughts around common themes.

Catchball - The back and forth communication between levels of an organization to ensure team alignment.

Cause and Effect Diagram - A visual representation which clearly displays the various factors affecting a process.

Continuous Flow - A process's characteristics which replenish a single work unit or service activity that has been requested or 'pulled' from a downstream process. Continuous flow is synonymous with Just-In-Time (JIT), which ensures both internal and external customers receive the work unit or service when it is needed and in the exact amounts.

Check Sheet - The visual representation of the number of times an activity, event, or process occurred over a specified time period.

Control Chart - The visual representation of tracking progress over time.

Control Point - A physical element of work within a process that has clearly set limits.

Cycle Time -The time elapsed from the beginning of a work process request until it is completed.

Customer Demand - The quantity of product or service required by the customer. Also referred to as takt time.

Data - Factual information used as a basis for analysis.

Document Tagging - The physical attachment of a form to a process work unit to document dates and times.

First-In-First-Out (FIFO) - The work-control method to ensure the oldest work upstream (first-in) is the first to be processed downstream (first-out).

Fishbone Diagram - See Cause and Effect Diagram.

Flow - The movement of material or information.

Frequency Chart - The visual representation of the number of times an activity, event, or process occurred over a specified time period.

Goal Card - A document displaying the strategic mission of the organization, along with departmental, team, and/or individual goals.

Group Cycle Time - The rate of completing a group task or objective. It is the total individual cycle times added together for a project.

Heijunka (same as Leveling) - The balancing of work amongst the employees during a period of time both by volume and variety.

Heijunka Box - A physical device to hold the work units arranged by value streams. This is similar to a group of mailboxes.

Histogram - A visual representation displaying the spread and shape of data distribution.

Individual Cycle Time - The rate of completion of an individual task or single operation of work.

In-Process Supermarket - The control of work units in and out of an area residing between two processes to improve work flow.

Interruption - The stopping of a process without notice.

Leveling (same as Heijunka) - See Heijunka.

Just-In-Time (JIT) - Synonymous with continuous flow. It is the provision that the process or customer is supplied with the exact product or service, in the right amount, at the right time.

Kaizen - 'Kai' means to "take apart" and 'zen' means to "make good". Kaizen is synonymous with continuous improvement.

Kaizen Event - Conducted by a focused group of individuals dedicated to applying Lean tools to a specific area within a certain time period.

Kanban - A card or visual indicator that serves as a means of communicating to an upstream process (or group) precisely what is required at the specified time.

Lean Office - The administrative area working systematically to identify and eliminate all waste.

Metric - Specific data that compares after measurements before and after improvement initiatives.

Mistake Proofing - It is derived from "Poka" - inadvertent mistake and "yoke" - avoid. A Poka-yoke device is any mechanism that prevents a mistake from being made or ensures the mistake is made obvious at a glance.

Office File System - The arrangement of administrative work such that it is organized and processed more efficiently.

Office Layout - A self-contained, well-occupied space that improves the flow of work and data transactions.

Pareto Chart - The visual representation, in a bar chart form, listing issues in descending order of importance.

Passive State - The vertical position of a file folder indicating work has been completed.

Pitch - The adjusted takt time to move work units throughout the value stream.

Predictable Output - The assurance that a work unit or service will be exactly what is expected.

Problem Solving - A team working together, following a structured process, to remedy a situation that caused a deviation from a norm.

Process - A sequence of tasks (or activities) to deliver a product or service.

Process Folder - The specific information and detailed flow for a particular process.

Process Mapping - Visual representation of a sequence of operations (tasks) consisting of people, work duties, and transactions that occur for the design and delivery of a product or service.

Process Master Document - The listing of all processes within a department or value stream.

Pull - A system in which nothing is produced by the upstream (supplier process) until the downstream (customer process) signals the need for it. This enables work to flow without detailed schedules.

Push - A system in which work is pushed along regardless of need or request.

Queue Time - The amount of time a work unit or service request must wait until it is released.

Random Arrival - The interruption of a process by another process or person.

Red Tag - A label used in the 5S process to identify items that are not needed or are placed in the wrong area.

Resistance - The opposition to an idea or concept.

Root Cause - The origin or source of the problem.

Runner - A designated function for a person to maintain value stream pitch integrity.

Scatter and Concentration Plots - The visual representation of data to study the possible relationship between one variable and another.

Set-In-Order - The second activity in the 5S system. This ensures items are stored in the correct location.

Shine - The third activity in the 5S system. This involves cleaning everything thoroughly and ensuring cleaning is part of the audit process.

Six Sigma - A sophisticated problem solving approach for improving business performance.

Sort - The first activity in the 5S system. This involves the disposal of items in the target area that have not been used for a period of time or are not expected to be used.

Simplified Folder System - A process to ensure work is organized, processed correctly, and becomes a basis for improvement activities.

Standardize - The fourth activity in the 5S system. This involves creating documents/rules to ensure the first 3S's will be made visual and done regularly.

Standard Work - A process to gather relevant information to document the best practices for producing a work unit or providing a service. It is the basis for all continuous improvement activities.

Standard Work Combination Table - A visual representation displaying the flow of work through all the steps required to complete a process.

Standard Work Chart - A visual representation displaying the sequence, process layout, and work units for a process.

Status Report - The document detailing the team's progress to date, as well as issues and plans to keep on track.

Storyboard - A graphically-rich, visual representation of a Lean or problem solving project that displays critical information.

Supermarket - The system to store a certain level of in-process work or service capacity to be pulled by the downstream customer when there is a difference in process cycle times.

Sustain - The fifth activity in the 5S system. This involves the process to monitor and ensure adherence to the first 4S's, often a regular audit.

System Folder - The "keeper" of all pertinent information about the processes within a department or value stream.

Takt Time - The pace of customer demand. Takt time determines how fast a process must run to meet customer demand.

Task - A single event within a process.

Team Charter - A document detailing the team's mission to ensure strategic alignment.

Total Cycle Time - The rate of completion of a process or group of tasks that have a common element. It is calculated by adding up the individual cycle times for that process or value stream.

Value-Added Time Reporting Log - A document tracking the process cycle times.

Value Stream - A sequence of processes connected by a common customer, product, or service request.

Value Stream Mapping - A visual representation of the processes (work units and information required) involved in meeting customer demand.

Visual Control - A visual indicator used to ensure a process produces what is expected. A visual control will support a standard.

Visual Metric - A display of measurements.

Visual Office - An ability to convey all relevant information about a product or service by the means of signs, posters, or anything that appeals to the eye.

Waste - Anything that adds cost or time without adding value. The seven most common wastes are: 1) Overproducing, 2) Waiting, 3) Transport, 4) Overprocessing, 5) Inventory, 6) Motion, 7) Defects, 8) People Utilization 9) Office Politics, and 10) Unevenness.

Work Load Balancing - The distribution of work units across the value stream to meet takt time or pitch.

Work Unit - A specific, measurable amount of work that can be segmented or treated as a whole. Examples of work units are: a customer order, a report, an e-mail request, or a bank deposit.

Index